Early praise for
iPad and iPhone Kung Fu

iPad and iPhone Kung Fu is a handy and fun reference for those new to iOS, as well as those who have a lot of experience. The tips contained in this book can help users open up a new level of usefulness for their Apple devices.

➤ **Jon Kurz**
   President, Dycet Research Group

This is a really great book. In fact, I'm recommending it to my dad! I have used an iPhone since the 3G version and am surprised I had so many things to learn!

➤ **Jeff Holland**
   Web developer, University of Wisconsin—Eau Claire

iOS devices are awesome and amazingly intuitive, but I was surprised to find out how much I didn't know. This book has tips and hints that take "It just works" to a whole different level.

➤ **Tony Bradley**
   Principal analyst at Bradley Strategy Group

Within minutes of picking up this book, I found several tips that helped me move around the interface more easily, enter text more quickly and accurately, and enjoy my iPad more. Whether you just started using an iPad or have had one since the early days, this book offers something for you.

➤ **Ian Dees**
   Author of *Cucumber Recipes*

iPad and iPhone Kung Fu

Tips, Tricks, Hints, and Hacks for iOS 7

Keir Thomas

The Pragmatic Bookshelf

Dallas, Texas • Raleigh, North Carolina

Pragmatic Bookshelf

Many of the designations used by manufacturers and sellers to distinguish their products are claimed as trademarks. Where those designations appear in this book, and The Pragmatic Programmers, LLC was aware of a trademark claim, the designations have been printed in initial capital letters or in all capitals. The Pragmatic Starter Kit, The Pragmatic Programmer, Pragmatic Programming, Pragmatic Bookshelf, PragProg and the linking *g* device are trademarks of The Pragmatic Programmers, LLC.

Every precaution was taken in the preparation of this book. However, the publisher assumes no responsibility for errors or omissions, or for damages that may result from the use of information (including program listings) contained herein.

Our Pragmatic courses, workshops, and other products can help you and your team create better software and have more fun. For more information, as well as the latest Pragmatic titles, please visit us at *http://pragprog.com*.

The team that produced this book includes:

Jacquelyn Carter (editor)
Potomac Indexing, LLC (indexer)
Candace Cunningham (copyeditor)
David J Kelly (typesetter)
Janet Furlow (producer)
Ellie Callahan (support)

For international rights, please contact *rights@pragprog.com*.

Printed in the United States of America.
ISBN-13: 978-1-93778-572-7
Printed on acid-free paper.
Book version: P1.0—February 2014

3 9547 00395 4604

Contents

Contents by Topic

Tip 87.	Play the drums better in GarageBand	110
Tip 93.	Take long and tall shots using Panorama mode	116
Tip 94.	Take photos like you would with a point-and-shoot camera	117
Tip 97.	Undo photo edits—even after you've saved them	119
Tip 108.	Share and print "moments" photo albums	127
Tip 119.	Take photos without touching your iPad or iPhone	134
Tip 121.	See larger thumbnail previews when browsing photos	135
Tip 125.	Jump to the beginning or end of an iMovie project	138
Tip 128.	Deal with photo-stream warnings when importing images	141
Tip 135.	Move the browser pane in iPhoto	144
Tip 158.	Beam items using iPhoto	158
Tip 165.	Quickly adjust color and brightness in iPhoto	163
Tip 170.	Hide photos in iPhoto	166
Tip 177.	Access photo-stream pics on a Windows PC	171
Tip 179.	Save website images for viewing later	172
Tip 181.	See the full video frame when recording	172
Tip 191.	Zoom in further to pictures	177
Tip 192.	Remove a photo filter	178
Tip 194.	Crop a photo for printing	179
Tip 196.	Export high-res edited images in iPhoto	181
Tip 198.	Get pictures off your device without iCloud	182
Tip 205.	Zoom when recording video or taking photos	188
Tip 206.	Bounce to activate the lock-screen camera	189
Tip 225.	View larger thumbnails in iPhoto	200
Tip 249.	Scroll and zoom when using brushes in iPhoto	215
Tip 252.	Cue back and forth in iMovie without hassle	217
Tip 266.	Interview people using your phone	226
Tip 271.	Mass-delete photos	231
Tip 272.	Change iMovie's theme without re-editing	232
Tip 290.	Rotate and crop photos in iPhoto	247
Tip 292.	Upload GarageBand songs to iCloud	248
Tip 294.	Apply multiple effects in iPhoto	249
Tip 304.	Add more detail to iMovie's timeline	259
Tip 313.	Cut an iMovie clip quickly and easily	266
Tip 317.	Record more-fluid HD video	267

Entertainment

System and Security

Calls, Messages, and Communication

Acknowledgments

Many thanks to those who reviewed *iPad and iPhone Kung Fu* prior to publication: Tony Bradley, Ian Dees, Kevin Gisi, Jeff Holland, Jon Kurz, Mike Riley, and Loren Sands-Ramshaw. Their comments, corrections, and suggestions were invaluable.

Thanks to Jacquelyn Carter for expertly guiding me through my fourth book with Pragmatic Bookshelf, and, of course, thanks to all those switched-on individuals at Pragmatic who run perhaps the most extraordinary and amazing publishing outfit I've had the privilege of working with (there's no need to send me another polo shirt, guys; I wear the one I have with pride!).

Finally, apologies to my partner, who had to put up with me saying strange things to Siri all day and often much of the night.

Preface

Welcome to *iPad and iPhone Kung Fu*, the only title you need to get the very best from iOS 7—the latest major release of Apple's mobile operating system.

What This book Is

iPad and iPhone Kung Fu squeezes out every possible tip, trick, hint, and hack there is—and then squeezes some more to reveal a substantial number of secrets.

No other book has the same drive to help you boost productivity, save time, and simply do things the best way possible when using an Apple handheld device running iOS 7—all while having fun, of course.

Each of the 300+ tips in this book meets one or more of the following criteria:

- It is genuinely useful for newcomers and old hands alike.

- It will substantially improve the way you use your iPad, iPhone, or iPod Touch.

- It shows the amazing things that can be done with an iPad, iPhone, or iPod Touch.

Many of the tips are blockbusters, but not all of them are. Some point out very subtle tricks. But even these will change the way you work and play.

Who This Book Is For

The tips in this book are good for users of any of the following Apple handhelds:

- iPad Air
- iPad Mini (both Retina and non-Retina)
- iPad (both Retina and non-Retina)
- iPhone 5s, 5c, and 5
- iPhone 4 and 4s
- iPod Touch (fifth generation)

Importantly, for the sake of convenience throughout the book we refer simply to the iPad or iPhone. When seeing "iPad" you should read "iPad Air, iPad, and iPad Mini"; when seeing "iPhone" you should read "iPhone and iPod Touch."

How to Read This Book

In a nutshell, *iPad and iPhone Kung Fu* is a big book of tips. As such, I don't recommend any particular way of reading it. You don't need to be using your iPad, iPhone, or iPod Touch while you read. The whole point of *iPad and iPhone Kung Fu* is that you can jump in anywhere. Start at the beginning, or start in the middle. You could even start at the end and work your way to the front. Just start reading. If you find a tip you like, then try it!

The tips were written for the version 7 release of iOS, Apple's operating system for portable devices. That isn't to say many won't work on previous releases of iOS. However, we have tested the tips only against iOS 7, and some terminology changed in this release. If you do intend to use the book with an older release, some common sense will go a long way.

Sharing

If you'd like to share some of the tips from this book on your blog, then feel free. It's unlikely my publisher will be too happy if you take liberties, but sharing a couple of tips you've found useful can only be a good thing. If you do, it would be great if you could mention the book and provide a link to the book's official web page—see below.

Online Resources

You can find this book's official web page at http://pragprog.com/book/ktios/ipad-and-iphone-kung-fu. There you can report any errata in the book as well as make suggestions for future editions. You can also get involved in a discussion with other readers in the book's official forum and ask me questions. We'd love to see you there!

Keir Thomas
February 2014

CHAPTER 1

A Crash Course in iOS 7

iOS is the name of the operating system at the heart of the iPad and iPhone, and this chapter presents a concise beginner's guide.

Note that any references to onscreen buttons or icons in this book assume the iPad or iPhone is being held in portrait mode rather than landscape mode unless specified otherwise.

First-Time Setup

After removing your iPad or iPhone from the box for the first time, you should connect it to a power source via the USB cable, then switch it on by pressing and holding the Lock/Sleep button at the top of the device until the screen becomes active. Booting will then commence and take a minute or two, during which time you'll see the Apple logo.

Once it's booted you'll be prompted to step through several configuration options. You'll need to be within range of Internet-enabled Wi-Fi for these (except for iPhones and 3G/4G iPads, which can use their cellular data connection). Alternatively, you can connect to a Mac or Windows PC using a USB cable, as prompted during the setup steps.

After you've confirmed your location and region, the setup wizard will walk you through some options, as follows:

- Wi-Fi: The first option is to choose the Wi-Fi base station to connect to. You'll need to enter its password, as shown in Figure 1, *Setting up Wi-Fi on an iPad during initial setup*, on page 2—just tap your Wi-Fi base station's entry within the list. As mentioned earlier, setup can't continue unless you're online in some fashion.

- Location Services: You're invited to enable Location Services. All iPhones and iPads come with global positioning system (GPS) capabilities (see

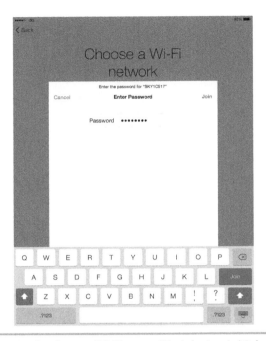

Figure 1—Setting up Wi-Fi on an iPad during initial setup

Location Services, on page 5). Lots of apps use Location Services, not to mention Apple's own Maps app, so enabling it is a good idea.

- Restoring from backup: You're offered the choice of setting up the iPad or iPhone afresh, or restoring from a backup. If you've previously owned an iPad or iPhone, you can restore from a backup that was stored in iCloud, or on the hard disk of your computer via iTunes (which will require a USB connection). Restoring a backup is possible even if the backup was made on an older device and/or an older version of iOS.

- Apple ID: You're prompted to enter your Apple ID, if you have one, or to create one. (See *Apple ID*, on page 13, for more details about what an Apple ID is.) You can skip creating or inputting an Apple ID here, although you'll be prompted as necessary when using the device, such as when you attempt to make App Store purchases.

- Terms and conditions: Be sure to read the full terms and conditions for using iOS.

- iCloud: iCloud is Apple's technology that lets you seamlessly share and sync data and settings across all your devices and computers—see *iCloud*, on page 26. Here you can choose whether to use it on this device.

- Find My iPhone/iPad: If your iPhone or iPad is lost or stolen, Find My iPhone/iPad lets you lock it, locate it, or remotely wipe its data, as discussed in *Security*, on page 30. Enabling it is a very good idea.

- iMessage and FaceTime: As explained in *Calls and Messaging*, on page 16, iMessage lets other iPhone, iPad, and Mac users communicate with you via short text messages (with file attachments), while FaceTime lets users communicate with you via video and audio calls sent over the Internet. Here you can choose which cell-phone number and email addresses you wish to be contacted via.

- Touch ID: If you're using an iPhone 5s you'll be invited to set up Touch ID fingerprint recognition, which will be used in the future to unlock the device (see *Touch ID*, on page 8). Setup involves tapping the Home button several times from various angles and approaches with your chosen finger(s), as prompted, until a print is recorded and stored.

- Creating a passcode: Although users of the iPhone 5s can rely upon fingerprint detection to unlock a device, they'll still need to enter a passcode, as will users of all other iPhones and iPads. A passcode is a four-digit PIN used to unlock non–Touch ID devices, and in certain other situations where important settings might be changed. Here you'll be invited to create that PIN. Note that once the phone is up and running it's possible to create longer passcodes—see *Security*, on page 30.

- Siri: If you're using an iPhone 4s or later, or an iPad third generation or later, you'll be prompted to set up Siri, as shown in Figure 2, *Setting up Siri on an iPad*, on page 4. Siri is Apple's digital assistant, and you can activate it once you've set up the iPhone or iPad by pressing and holding the Home button. Because Siri sends your speech and personal details to Apple, there are some potential privacy issues.[1]

- Diagnostics: Apple improves its products based on reports from real-life users, and you can opt in to help Apple. Reports are sent automatically, virtually anonymously, and in the background.

Switching On and Off

iPads and iPhones are designed to spend all their time switched on, although when not being used they will go into sleep mode to conserve power. Depending on what services are activated on the phone, an iPad or iPhone can last up to two weeks during sleep mode.

---

1. http://www.apple.com/apples-commitment-to-customer-privacy/

Figure 2—Setting up Siri on an iPad

An iPad or iPhone will automatically enter sleep mode after not being used for a moment (unless you've changed this setting), although you can manually put a device to sleep in the following ways:

- By pressing the Lock/Sleep button on top of the unit

- By placing the Smart Cover over the front of the device, in the case of an iPad or iPad Mini (or the cover of a Smart Case)

You can wake a device from sleep by pressing the Home button or the Lock/Sleep button, or by lifting the Smart Cover (or the cover of a Smart Case) for an iPad or iPad Mini. Usually a device will then need to be unlocked by providing a passcode, although on an iPhone 5s both waking and unlocking are achieved by simply pressing the Home button.

Location Services

All iPads and iPhones come with Location Services, by which the device can be pinpointed on the globe with varying degrees of accuracy. Apps make use of this to provide mapping services, for example, or to track the device's location over a period of time (useful for apps that track your running or walking). Social apps like Facebook use the information to automatically add your location to any postings you make, and the Find My iPhone/iPad service uses the information to locate the device if it's stolen.

All iPhones and 3G/4G iPads capable of running iOS 7 come with global positioning system (GPS) hardware that, provided a clear signal is available, can accurately locate the device to within a few feet of its position. Additionally, a slightly less accurate system called the Wi-Fi Positioning System (WPS) is used to augment the GPS signal. WPS uses the location of the Wi-Fi base station to which you're connected to discover your general location. This is possible because Apple maintains a database of the physical locations of most Wi-Fi base stations in the world—from those in cafés and offices to those in homes. It does this using a fleet of cars that drive across the country logging the information. Strange but true!

Non–3G/4G iPads and iPod Touch devices lack actual GPS hardware, so they use WPS exclusively to discover their location. This means their accuracy can be limited to simply placing you within a building or on a particular street, for example. If you're not connected to a Wi-Fi base station, then the accuracy will be severely compromised and it can take several minutes to get a fix.

Location Services brings with it privacy concerns because it lets Apple and apps log places you visit.[a] For example, iOS 7 is designed to learn where you live and where you work, so it can automatically display transit times within Notification Center. You can control Location Services settings by opening the Settings app, tapping the Privacy heading, then selecting the Location Services option.

Bear in mind that, unlike with dedicated GPS devices, iOS 7 doesn't store nationwide street-level map data on the iPad or iPhone. Instead, it's looked up online when necessary. This means the Maps app is very likely to be useless if the Internet signal is lost—street-level maps for your local area might be viewable because the data is usually stored on your device for quick access but you won't be able to search for destinations, or view detailed maps for locations even a relatively short distance away. However, some third-party mapping apps do store map data on the device, and this is usually made clear within an app's description in the App Store.

a.   https://www.eff.org/issues/location-privacy

Additionally, an iPad or iPhone will automatically wake to show incoming calls, messages, and notifications, although you can use a feature called Do Not Disturb within the Settings app (see *The Settings App*, on page 37) to stop the iPad or iPhone from alerting you in this way during particular periods, such as when you're sleeping.

Because sleep mode is so effective at conserving battery life, there's no need to completely power down devices when you're not using them. However, should you legitimately need to turn off an iPad or iPhone, you can do so by pressing and holding the Lock/Sleep button for a few seconds until Slide to Power Off appears at the top of the screen. Sliding your finger across this will turn off the device. However, even when entirely powered down, an iPad or iPhone will still use a trickle of power and will therefore deplete its battery over time.

Setting Up Non-Apple Accounts

Although Apple sets up or creates your iCloud account automatically during setup, you can connect to your Google, Yahoo!, AOL, and Outlook.com (Microsoft Live) accounts with similar ease once the device is up and running.

Setup

Open the Settings app, then tap the Mail, Contacts, Calendars heading and tap the Add Account button. From there, all you need do for setup is select your desired provider and enter your username and password. You'll then be able to choose which services to sync with your phone by tapping the switch alongside each (see Figure 3, *Setting up a Yahoo! account on an iPhone 5*, on page 7). The services you can sync with are as follows:

- Gmail: Email, contacts, calendars, and notes
- Yahoo!: Email, contacts, calendars, reminders, and notes
- AOL: Email and notes
- Outlook.com: Email, contacts, calendars, and reminders

You'll send and receive email in a way that means the messages are still stored on the server so they can be accessed by other computers and devices.

You may have noticed that instant messaging and video calling were not listed there. Other than iMessage, which is part of iCloud, iOS 7 doesn't let you add any chat accounts to the Messaging app or the FaceTime app. The only way to access messaging or video chat from other providers is to download dedicated apps via the App Store; most providers have supplied an app (including RIM, which provides a Blackberry Messaging app).

In addition to services from major providers, you can configure an account to access an Exchange server run by a business. You will need to consult your technical-services department to find out the server address and the domain name. You'll be able to sync with email, contacts, and calendars stored on the server.

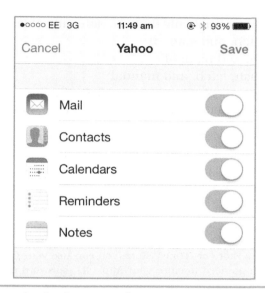

Figure 3—Setting up a Yahoo! account on an iPhone 5

You can also manually add email accounts, provided you know the SMTP and IMAP/POP3 server addresses. Additionally, you can add LDAP and CardDAV accounts to sync contacts, and CalDAV accounts for calendar sharing. In each case you'll need to know the server address and login details.

Clicking on a Calendar link file sent to you by email will also offer the opportunity to subscribe to a calendar. Such files typically have the extension .ics.

Push vs. Fetch

Once you've configured a third-party account, be sure to tap the Fetch New Data heading in the Mail, Contacts, Calendars section of the Settings app. Here you can set in what way the accounts are synced, and how frequently. Alongside a setting for configuring manual checking, there are two choices for the manner in which data is automatically retrieved: push and fetch. Push is the better choice because it uses less battery power and updates are near instantaneous—you'll be notified of email almost as soon as it arrives in your inbox, for example. Unfortunately, not all providers offer push services, so instead data must be *fetched* from the server periodically. You can alter the frequency of attempts to fetch data under the Fetch heading, but beware that fetching too frequently can cause battery life to be depleted quickly.

Here's how third-party accounts break down with regard to support for push and fetch:

- Gmail: Fetch and manual only (but see note after this list)
- Yahoo!: Push, fetch, and manual
- AOL: Push, fetch, and manual
- Outlook.com: Push, fetch, and manual
- Manually configured Exchange accounts: Push, fetch, and manual
- Manually configured POP3/IMAP accounts: Fetch and manual

Note that Gmail accessed as part of a paid-for Google Apps for Business account offers push support.[2] Consult your domain administrator for details.

Touch ID

The iPhone 5s is the first phone to make fingerprint recognition reliable enough for everyday use. Once it's been set up, simply touching a finger against the Home button's sensor will unlock the device within a second or two. Additionally, when purchasing apps through the App Store or iTunes Store, you can use your fingerprint as proof of your identity, with no need to enter your Apple ID password as you do on other Apple devices.

Touch ID is not foolproof. It requires a dry, relatively clean finger, although just wiping the fingertip on a tissue or garment should be enough to provide a usable scanning surface.

It might sound odd, but at no time does Touch ID record a photographic representation of your fingerprint. Instead, thousands of tiny sensors map the ridges and pits of your skin, and a mathematical algorithm creates an encrypted representation called a *hash*. This data is stored in a specially protected area of the main system-on-a-chip that forms the heart of every Apple device. In other words, it is literally impossible for a hacker to get an image of your fingerprint—it doesn't exist.

Like all fingerprint ID systems, Touch ID is difficult to bypass, but not impossible. Hackers have a variety of methods of manufacturing fake fingerprints. Some do so using resins and glues, requiring just a high-resolution photograph of a fingerprint left on a glass surface. However, the expertise and effort involved in creating such a fake, as well as the difficulty of sourcing a fingerprint sample of sufficiently high quality, mean that bypassing Touch ID is unlikely to be an everyday occurrence.

You can disable Touch ID under the General heading of the Settings app, in which case your device will revert to using passcodes for authorization and you'll be required to enter your Apple ID password when making purchases.

Status Bar

Running along the top of the iPad and iPhone screen is a status bar that shows the type of connection the device is using or the modes to which it's

---

2.   https://www.google.com/enterprise/apps/business/

been set. The icons are identical on the iPad and iPhone. The following figure shows an annotated example.

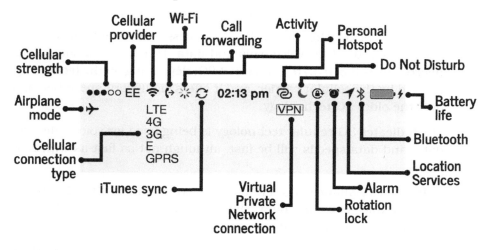

Figure 4—The iOS 7 status-bar icons

See the following list for details of what each icon indicates (*The Settings App*, on page 37 provides details of the technologies mentioned):

- Airplane mode: This status-bar symbol replaces the cellular information and indicates the iPad or iPhone is in airplane mode, in which cellular, Wi-Fi, and Bluetooth hardware inside the device are deactivated. See *Control Center*, on page 34.

- Cellular strength: Indicates the strength of the cellular signal, ranging from one dot for a virtually nonexistent signal to five full dots for a strong signal. If there is no signal, "No service" will be shown.

- Cellular provider: This is the name of the cellular provider.

- Wi-Fi: Indicates the device is connected to a Wi-Fi base station. The three bars indicate the strength of the signal, ranging between one bar (weak) and three bars (strong).

- Cellular connection: If you're not connected to Wi-Fi or if it's deactivated, the type of cellular connection will be displayed. This helps you evaluate likely data speeds. There are several different types of cellular connection types, as follows, and which one your phone connects to depends on the contract you have with your cellular provider as well as what's available in your locality:

- LTE: Indicates cellular communications are using Long-Term Evolution (LTE) speeds, which at present offer the fastest possible cellular data speeds. Use of LTE can be configured in the Settings app.

- 4G: Indicates 4G (High-Speed Packet Access; HSPA) cellular technology is being used for voice calls and data. HSPA is also sometimes referred to as 3.5G, 3.75G, or even 3.9G, depending on the technology utilized by the cellular carrier, and it offers significant speed benefits over the older 3G technology.

- 3G: Indicates 3G cellular technology is being used for voice calls and data, and data speeds will be fast, although not as fast as with LTE or 4G.

- E: Indicates Enhanced Data Rates for GSM Evolution (EDGE) is being used for voice calls and data. Data-transfer rates will likely be slow over cellular if EDGE is in use.

- GPRS: Indicates GPRS or 1xRTT (CDMA) technology is being used for voice calls and data. Data-transfer rates will likely be very slow over cellular if these technologies are being used—to the point of being unusable, especially if the cellular signal is weak. On some networks a circle symbol may be displayed instead.

• Call forwarding: This indicates that your iPhone is set to forward calls to another number. Note that this reflects only what's been toggled in the Settings app, and not any call-forwarding setting configured independently using your cellular carrier.

• Activity: This rotating pinwheel pattern appears whenever the device is fetching data or, in some cases, working on a background task.

• iTunes sync: Indicates that the device is currently syncing with iTunes on a Mac or Windows PC.

• Personal Hotspot: Indicates the iPad or iPhone is connected to a Personal Hotspot provided by another iPad or iPhone. If the device itself is providing a Personal Hotspot for another computer or device, the icon will appear and the status bar will turn blue. An additional status bar will appear beneath, showing the number of devices connected.

• VPN: Indicates a virtual private network (VPN) connection is in use, by which secure connections can be made to Internet computers for the purposes of data transfer and logging into office networks.

• Do Not Disturb: Indicates Do Not Disturb mode is in use.

- Rotation lock: Indicates that the screen orientation has been locked to landscape or portrait mode.

- Alarm: Indicates that an alarm is set in the Clock app.

- Location Services (GPS): Indicates an app is using Location Services to discover the geographical location of the device.

- Bluetooth: When light-colored, indicates Bluetooth is activated; when dark, the iPad or iPhone is currently connected to a Bluetooth device, such as a headset or a keyboard.

- Battery: Gives a graphical representation of the battery strength. A lightning bolt appearing alongside indicates the battery is being charged.

Charging Your iPad or iPhone

To charge your iPad or iPhone, use the included USB cable and attach it either to a charger outlet or the USB connection of a computer. Beware that charging via a computer may take a long time, particularly in the case of an iPad. Additionally, it's unlikely either an iPhone or iPad will charge at all when connected to an unpowered USB hub (that is, a hub that lacks a power supply of its own).

If using third-party chargers, remember that to charge in a reasonable amount of time an iPad requires a USB charger outputting at least 10 watts (that is, 5 volts at greater than 2 amps). This is usually more than the output of chargers designed for phones or other handheld devices, such as music players.

Apps

Everything you might want to do with an iPad or iPhone is done via an app, whether that's making a phone call, sending a message, or performing sophisticated tasks like working out a route using the Maps app.

Home Screen

Apps are represented by icons on the home screens (see Figure 5, *The home screen of an iPad just after first booting*, on page 12). You can move between home screens by swiping a finger left or right. Several important everyday apps are located on the Dock, at the bottom of the screen, which doesn't change even when you scroll through the home screens.

Figure 5—The home screen of an iPad just after first booting

All iPads and iPhones come with a complement of built-in apps, and you can download more to the device using the App Store app. Download and installation happen automatically once you opt to purchase an app, at which point you'll need to provide your Apple ID password (or Touch ID authentication) to verify your identity. Although some apps are free, Apple still considers downloading them to be a purchase, and you'll still need to enter your password (or provide Touch ID authentication).

Updates for apps are also provided via the App Store. A number set against the App Store's home-screen icon indicates how many updates are available and you can view the list by opening the App Store and tapping the Updates icon at the bottom.

You can also view and buy apps via the App Store with iTunes on a Mac or Windows PC (click iTunes Store at the top right, then App Store on the top-middle tab bar). Apps will be copied to your iPad or iPhone the next time you sync via USB or Wi-Fi. Alternatively, you can activate automatic downloads under the iTunes & App Store heading of the Settings app on the iPad or iPhone, which will automatically download and install apps regardless of where or how you buy them. This will take place in the background, even if the device is in sleep mode.

Apple ID

Your Apple ID is your identity card in the Apple universe. It's significantly more than a request to register your personal details, as with other manufacturers. An Apple ID provides three things in particular:

- Identification: Your Apple ID tells Apple who you are, especially online, although often in real life too. You'll need an Apple ID to book an appointment with a Genius at an Apple Store, for example, and to track subsequent repairs. Your purchase history and a list of devices you own are stored against your Apple ID, and this can help Apple Store staff identify loyal customers, who sometimes receive preferential treatment.

- iCloud: An Apple ID brings with it iCloud access (see *iCloud*, on page 26), although you only gain full iCloud access after one or more of your devices or Mac computers has signed in using the Apple ID—something that usually happens during the first-time setup. However, this means you can't create an Apple ID on a Windows PC without owning an Apple device, for example, then log into the iCloud website.[a]

- iTunes and App Store: In addition to providing name and address details, creating an Apple ID usually requires registering a payment card, which lets you use your Apple ID to log into the iTunes and App Stores to make purchases. Using a registered payment card is the only way to make App Store/iTunes Store purchases other than using an iTunes gift card.[b]

Although Apple doesn't recommend it, it's possible to use two separate Apple IDs—one for payments, and one for iCloud use. Simply enter the iCloud address into the iCloud component of the Settings app (see *The Settings App*, on page 37), and enter the payment Apple ID when prompted in the iTunes and App Store apps. Notably, Apple offers no facility to merge two or more Apple IDs, so it's best in most circumstances to use a single Apple ID.

It's also possible to create an Apple ID without registering a payment card, which can be useful for iPads or iPhones owned by children. An Apple support document explains the steps,[c] which you can take (using the App Store or using iTunes on a Mac or Windows PC) once an iPad or iPhone is up and running. Apple IDs that don't have a payment card registered can be used to download and install free apps.

---

a. https://icloud.com
b. https://www.apple.com/itunes/gifts/
c. http://support.apple.com/kb/ht2534

Uninstalling Apps and Rearranging Apps and Folders

To remove an app from an iOS device, begin by tapping and holding its icon until all the home-screen icons begin to wobble. Then tap the X at the top left of the icon to uninstall the app and its data from your device (it will remain installed on other iOS devices you own). Note that built-in apps provided as part of iOS cannot be uninstalled.

Uninstalling an app doesn't mean you no longer own it. You can reinstall an app at a later date by finding its entry in the Purchased list within the App Store (click the Purchased icon on an iPad, or the Updates icon on an iPhone) and tapping the cloud icon.

While the icons are wobbling you can also rearrange their order on your home screen by tapping and dragging them, and create folders by hovering one icon over another. Folders are deleted by removing all the icons inside them; to remove the icons in a folder you can either uninstall the apps or move them to a new location on the home screen.

You can also rearrange the icons on the Dock when the device is in this mode, and in the case of the iPad add icons to the Dock to join the four that are there by default. Up to six icons can be kept in the iPad's Dock, and up to four on the iPhone's.

Click the Home button when you've finished.

Multitasking and Switching Apps

You can view which apps are open by double-clicking the Home button, which will show the multitasking screen. Figure 6, *Opening the multitasking apps list on an iPhone*, on page 15 shows an example taken from an iPad. You can switch to an app by tapping its icon or window preview.

Swipe left or right to see other running apps—there are likely quite a few, and you can switch to any by tapping its icon or the window preview above it. You can quit apps by flicking the preview of the app window toward the top of the screen. Note that, unlike applications on a Mac or Windows PC, there's usually no need to manually quit apps in iOS. Whenever you return to the home screen or a new app is launched, all other apps are moved to the background so that they consume negligible system sources. In theory, you could open every app installed on an iOS device without any impact on overall system performance.

However, iOS includes limited multitasking support; some apps can continue certain functions when you switch away from them. Some apps can continue

Figure 6—Opening the multitasking apps list on an iPhone

to receive data, for example, so that they're up to date the instant you switch back to them. The Clock app will continue any stopwatch or countdown that you've started, and music will continue to play when you switch away from the Music app. However, most apps will simply pause when you switch away from them—quite literally in the case of the Video app or games, where switching away effectively presses the pause button.

App Rules

Rules govern how apps can be bought and used.

Purchasing

A key feature of Apple's App Store system is that an app purchase includes a license to install it on all iOS devices that you own and that are logged in with the same Apple ID (in a home environment; corporate and academic users managing a range of iOS devices require individual licenses).[3]

Purchase the popular Angry Birds game, for example, and you can install it on any iPhones, iPads, or iPod Touches that you own and on which you're logged into the App Store with your Apple ID. This rule applies to music and movies you purchase via iTunes, too.

---

3.   See http://www.apple.com/business/vpp/ and https://www.apple.com/education/ipad/volume-purchase-program/.

Versions

Often apps will work in different ways depending on whether they're installed on an iPad or an iPhone. The increased screen size allows Pages on the iPad to show several toolbars that are not shown on the smaller iPhone screen, for example. However, some developers create separate apps for the iPhone and iPad, and sell them separately.

When it comes to app cross-compatibility, the following rules apply:

- iPhone apps: Some apps are specifically designed for an iPhone, without any thought to their being used on an iPad. In this case, the app can still be used on an iPad, although it will appear in an iPhone-sized window in the middle of the screen. Additionally, the onscreen keyboard will be that of an iPhone rather than an iPad. Tapping the 2x button will magnify the app so it almost fills the screen by simply blowing up the original pixels, although often this can make things look blocky. iPhone games work best in this mode; other apps look and feel a little odd, and it's often better to see if an iPad-specific version is available.

- iPad apps: Apps designed specifically for an iPad cannot be used on an iPhone because they're designed for a much larger screen size, so they simply won't fit on the iPhone's screen.

Once you've purchased and installed a cross-compatible app on one device, you can install it on another by opening the App Store app on that device and tapping the Purchased icon (tap Updates > Purchased on the iPhone). If automatic downloads are enabled in the Settings app, as discussed earlier, installation will take place automatically in the background.

Built-in Apps

Here's a brief listing of the built-in apps, along with their key features:

Calls and Messaging

A modern Internet device would be lost without the core functionality of calls and messaging, and iOS includes several very powerful apps that meet this need:

- Phone (iPhone only): Make calls and access voicemail, and view a list of calls received, made, and missed via the Recents icon. You can access your contacts list to make calls, or use an onscreen keypad to dial numbers. The keypad can also be used for interactive services requiring dual-tone multifrequency tones, such as automated phone services. Once a call is in progress, tapping the Hide button will offer the options to switch to speakerphone, add another call, and mute the microphone for privacy.

- Messages: View or send iMessages to other iPad, iPhone, and Mac users, and send SMS/MMS messages to other cell-phone users (iPhone only; iPads equipped with cellular data cannot send SMS/MMS). Just select an existing conversation to send a message, or tap the New Message icon and then type the contact details in the To: field, and the message below. Messages will always default to iMessage if the recipient also uses iMessage (see Tip 15, *Know when iMessage is being used*, on page 64). SMS/MMS messages are sent via the cellular network, as with any cell phone, while iMessages are sent via the Internet and can include image and video file attachments—just tap the camera icon to the left of the message area to choose.

- FaceTime: Make video and voice calls with other iPad, iPhone, and Mac users running OS X (Mavericks or later and iOS 7 or later are required for voice calls). Note that you can make FaceTime calls to only people in your contacts list, so when contacting somebody for the first time you may need to add or update an entry for that person within the Contacts app. FaceTime calls can be made to cell-phone numbers, Apple IDs, or email addresses, depending on which details the individuals you're calling has registered with FaceTime on their devices (via the FaceTime heading within the Settings app). FaceTime calls take place over the Internet, so they won't incur call charges with your provider (although they might incur data charges, of course).

Entertainment and Creativity

iOS includes several tools that let you enjoy stuff created by others and put your own creativity into practice.

- Camera: Take pictures and record HD movies using either the camera on the back of the iPad or iPhone, or the FaceTime camera on the front (to switch between cameras tap the icon at the top right of the screen). Pictures can be taken at full resolution or in square format for use in social-media apps, and you can switch between modes by swiping left and right in the main picture area (or up and down on an iPad held in portrait mode). Images can also have filters applied to them on the iPhone 4s and later devices (tap the overlapping-circles icon), although these effects can also be applied later to photos using the Photos app on any iPhone or iPad—see the next list item.

AirPlay

AirPlay is Apple's technology that lets users of iPads, iPhones, and Mac computers stream video and audio over the network to a TV or projector connected to an Apple TV or other compatible device. Additionally, audio output can be streamed to an AirPort Express Wi-Fi router, which includes audio outputs for connecting to audio equipment with line inputs, or an optical audio input. The entire screen of an iPad or iPhone can also be mirrored via AirPlay, which can be useful when watching movies or playing games, or when giving business presentations from apps like Keynote.

AirPlay is extremely easy to use. Whenever a device capable of receiving and playing back AirPlay streams is active and on the same network as your iPad or iPhone, you can open Control Center and select to use it for video or audio. Alternatively, when using the Video app on your iPad or iPhone you'll see the AirPlay icon appear at the right of the playback controls. Tapping it will let you switch to using the device. Some third-party apps, like YouTube, also support AirPlay in this way.

Don't forget to switch back afterward if you want playback to happen only on the iPad or iPhone—you can do this by again opening Control Center or tapping the AirPlay icon and selecting the device name from the list.

Note that because of copyright limitations it's impossible to play certain purchased or rented TV shows and movies over AirPlay. However, you can simply download the purchased material directly to an Apple TV.

• Photos: View albums of images you've taken, those you've shared, or those that have been shared with you. To see an overview of photos or videos stored on the device, click the Albums icon at the bottom, then select from the list. All photos and videos you create are saved to the camera roll. To specifically view and create photo streams (see Figure 7, *Viewing images via the Photos app on an iPad*, on page 19 and *Photo Stream*, on page 20), tap the Shared button.

To view your photos sorted by the date and time they were taken, or the location at which they were captured, tap the Photos icon. This will arrange the photos into *Years*, which collates photos by the year they were taken, or *Collections*, which are arranged by date and location. You can also create your own custom albums by switching to the Albums view and tapping the plus (+) icon. Once a photo has been opened for viewing, clicking the Edit button will let you tweak the photo to repair poor exposure, fix red-eye, apply photo filters, and crop. To create slideshows, open any image in an album you wish to turn into a slideshow, then tap the Slideshow button on an iPad, or the share button (a square with an upward-pointing arrow) then Slideshow on an iPhone. Perhaps counter-intuitively, the Photos app is also where you can view movies recorded

Figure 7—Viewing images via the Photos app on an iPad

with your device (movies are identified by a movie-camera icon at the bottom left of their thumbnails).

- Music: Better known as the "iPod" part of an iPhone or iPad, this app lets you access your music library—including tracks purchased from iTunes or synced from a computer—and listen into iTunes Radio channels (tap the Radio icon at the bottom left). To view all the music on the device, tap the Artists, Songs, or Albums button. Music you've purchased but that isn't on the device is also listed, and tapping the cloud icon alongside each entry will download it. You can access and create playlists, including Genius playlists, which are automatically constructed based on your favorite music (tracks you play often and rate highly), coupled with Apple's knowledge of what tracks work best together. Note that music will continue playing if you switch away from the app.

- Videos: Play video or music video files, whether you've purchased them via iTunes or downloaded them from a third party and synced them from a Mac or Windows PC via iTunes (in which case they'll appear when you tap the Home Videos button). However, any videos you've recorded yourself via the Camera app are accessible only via the Photos app. Any movies you've previously purchased but that aren't on the device will also be listed within each category, and clicking the cloud icon at the top right will download them. To play a video over AirPlay (see *AirPlay*, on page 18), start the movie playing, then tap the AirPlay icon to the right of the playback controls and choose the AirPlay device from the list.

Photo Stream

Photo Stream is Apple's technology that uses iCloud to share pictures across multiple devices and computers, with the option to manually share videos too. All iCloud users have a personal photo stream to which images are automatically uploaded after being taken. These are then automatically downloaded by any other iOS devices they own, and suitably configured Macs and Windows PCs. (PCs need the iCloud Control Panel installed,[a] and Macs need to have either iPhoto or Aperture installed.[b,c]) Photo Stream means that, no matter where you take a photo, or with what Apple device, you can always access the pictures. However, there's an important limitation—photos exist within iCloud for only 30 days. Once they've been downloaded to a device, they will remain until they're manually deleted.

You can also opt to create shared photo streams. You can add both pictures and videos to a shared photo stream, and each picture or video can have comments added by anybody with access. Each can be "Liked" in a similar way to images on Facebook.

To add a photo or video to an existing shared photo stream or create a new one, open the photo or video for viewing in the Photos app and then tap the share button at the bottom left of the screen. Then tap the iCloud option in the list. Select the existing photo stream you want to use alongside the Stream heading, or tap the stream name alongside the heading to view the option of creating a new shared photo stream, at which point you'll be prompted to provide the email address(es) of the other person(s) (entries will be automatically suggested when you type, based on your contacts list). You'll be notified when those you invite have joined (see *Notifications*, on page 46).

Other people can share photo streams with you, of course, in which case you'll receive an email message and should click the button therein to confirm you wish to join.

---

a. https://www.apple.com/icloud/setup/pc.html
b. http://www.apple.com/mac/iphoto/
c. http://www.apple.com/aperture/

- iTunes Store: Purchase music, audiobooks, music videos, and ringtones, or view Genius suggestions generated from Apple's recommendations based on what you've bought in the past. You can also rent or purchase movies and TV shows. You can view or download any previous purchases you've made by tapping the Purchased button on an iPad, or More > Purchased on an iPhone.

- Newsstand: Browse and read magazines, newspapers, or other periodicals. Note that searching for new titles takes place within the App Store app, and clicking the Store icon in Newsstand will take you there. Tapping Install alongside a Newsstand title in the App Store will add it to Newsstand without charge, and subsequently the purchasing of individual issues or multiple-issue subscriptions will take place within the Newsstand app. Unlike traditional ebooks, each Newsstand title is actually a simple app, accessed via Newsstand, and often offers unique features. A household-lifestyle magazine may have a searchable recipe database, for example.

- Game Center: View achievements and high scores in games you've installed, along with high scores from other Game Center players (see the figure here). Challenge others in games that support turn-based play. The games must utilize Game Center (not all do) and your friend must also have an iOS device. To challenge a friend you'll first need to "friend" that person within Game Center by tapping Friends > Add. An email message will then be sent to your potential new friend.

Figure 8—Game Center lets you challenge other iOS users.

Internet and Email

Browsing the Web and receiving email are core functions of any Internet-equipped device, and iOS comes close to offering a desktop-like experience, even on the smaller screen of the iPhone:

- Safari: Browse the Web, including creating bookmarks that sync over iCloud with other iOS devices and the Safari browser on a Mac, or a Windows PC with the iCloud Control Panel installed.[4] Browser tabs are shown beneath the toolbar on an iPad (see Figure 9, *Safari running on an iPad*, on page 22), and tapping the X at the right of each will close that tab, as with a desktop web browser.

  To switch between browser tabs on an iPhone, tap the bookmarks icon (overlapping squares) at the bottom right of the screen and swipe the tab preview left to discard that tab. Private browsing mode, by which browsing data isn't stored, can be activated on an iPhone by opening the list of tabs as described previously and tapping the Private button at the bottom left. To access private browsing on an iPad, tap the plus (+) icon at the top right to create a new tab and then tap the Private button at the bottom

---

4. https://www.apple.com/icloud/setup/pc.html

Figure 9—Safari running on an iPad

left. You can also view what browser tabs are open on other Apple devices or Mac computers you own by clicking the cloud toolbar icon on an iPad, or opening the tab listing on an iPhone and scrolling to the bottom of the tab previews.

• Mail: Send and receive email using the @icloud.com or @me.com addresses that come as part of iCloud, or via other email providers (see *Setting Up Non-Apple Accounts*, on page 6). To view the list of account mailboxes, swipe from the left on the message list, or tap the back button (labeled Mailboxes in this case). If you have multiple accounts configured, scroll to the Accounts heading below the main mailboxes listing and tap each account to view the individual mailboxes for each provider (that is, Sent, Spam, and so on). If you have only one account configured then only one inbox will be shown at the top of the mailbox listing. In addition, you can create a VIP mailbox, which filters important messages by who sent them and notifies you accordingly. To set up a VIP mailbox, return to the mailbox listing as described previously, then tap the Edit link at the top right and put a check alongside the VIP heading. Click Done, then tap the new VIP mailbox heading, and choose any contacts you wish to add. In order to add someone there must be an entry for that person in your contacts list.

System

When it comes to administering the system, the following two apps are all you need (however, see also *Control Center*, on page 34):

• Settings: Configure hardware and software settings on your device. You can also administer your iCloud account. For more details see *The Settings App*, on page 37.

• App Store: Browse and purchase new apps, along with Newsstand titles. To "purchase" a free app, simply tap its icon in the app listing so its detail window appears, then tap Free > Install. To purchase a pay title, tap the icon in the app listing to view the app's details, then tap the button listing the price, then tap the Buy button. In either case you will need to provide your Apple ID password, or tap the Touch ID sensor in the case of an iPhone 5s. In addition to purchasing apps, you can review apps you've purchased; find them in the store, tap the Reviews tab, then tap Write a Review.

Information and Office

iOS includes several personal-information-management tools that are equally adept for home use and office use:

• Calendar: Create and view appointments, complete with alert reminders. Click the plus (+) icon at the top left to create a new event, and swipe left or right to move between days, weeks, and months, depending on the view (hold an iPhone in landscape mode to switch to five-day-week view). Calendar events sync automatically over iCloud with other iOS devices and Macs, and with Windows PCs that have the iCloud Control Panel installed.[5]

• Clock: View the time in cities around the world, set alarms, time events using a stopwatch, and set timers to count down. Figure 10, *The Clock app showing worldwide time on an iPhone* shows an example taken from an iPhone.

Figure 10—The Clock app showing worldwide time on an iPhone

---

5.   https://www.apple.com/icloud/setup/pc.html

- Maps: View a map of your local area in both traditional map and satellite views. Traffic information and construction work can be seen too—tap the (i) button at the bottom right to select what view mode you wish to use. Tap the direction arrow at the bottom left to switch instantly to your current location, and create routes for getting to a location—whether by driving or walking—by searching for the destination, then tapping the right-facing arrow of the pop-out window that appears over the destination. You can also create bookmarks of favorite locations by tapping and holding to drop a virtual pin on the map. Some geographic locations are covered by 3D maps, which let you "fly around" buildings and roads. In such a case, switch to satellite view, and an icon depicting high-rise buildings will appear at the bottom of the screen. Tapping it will let you switch in and out of 3D mode.

- Notes: Create simple text documents that sync via iCloud with your other iOS devices or Mac computers.

- Reminders: Create to-do-style reminders that can have alarms attached to them and be "geofenced," which is to say a notification for the reminder will appear when you enter or leave a particular area (tap a reminder to switch it to edit mode, then tap the (i) symbol alongside a reminder to set notification options).

- Weather (iPhone only): Shows the weather where you are and in other areas that you add (tap the menu icon at the bottom right, then the plus icon—+—at the bottom). The data is provided by Yahoo!

- Contacts: View entries within your address book, and create new ones or edit existing entries (to edit an entry on the iPhone select it for viewing, then tap the Edit button). Your contacts list syncs automatically over iCloud with other iOS devices and Macs, and PCs that have the iCloud Control Panel installed.[6]

- Calculator (iPhone only): Do math on a facsimile of a standard calculator.

- Compass (iPhone only): Orient yourself with a facsimile of a compass.

- Voice Memos (iPhone only): Record voice memos of any length (limited only by free memory space), and then trim them to remove unneeded portions. You can also share recordings with other users. Once a voice memo has been recorded, you can access it in the list within the Voice Memos interface.

---

6. https://www.apple.com/icloud/setup/pc.html

- Passbook (iPhone only): View or present any stored tickets, coupons, loyalty cards, passes, and so on that you've purchased via Passbook-compatible vendors and organizations. Add new passes by "scanning" a barcode using the camera.

- Stocks (iPhone only): View information and news about publicly traded organizations, with the data provided by Yahoo! To add a new stock, tap the menu icon, then the plus (+) icon at the top left, then enter its ticker code.

Other Apple Apps

In addition to the default apps, you might consider installing several Apple apps. All are available in the App Store and most are free for those who purchased an iOS device after September 1, 2013. For users of older devices, some of the titles can be purchased (the US price is indicated in parentheses in the following lists).

Entertainment and Creativity

Apple has managed to cram astonishing creative and learning potential into a small space with the following apps, most of which have desktop equivalents for Mac computers:

- GarageBand ($4.99): Create music complete with realistic instrument sounds, audio effects, and the ability to record vocals. The figure here shows an example taken from an iPad. Those who downloaded GarageBand free with a new iPad or iPhone can download additional instruments and sounds via in-app payments.

Figure 11—Creating music with GarageBand on an iPad

iCloud

iCloud automatically and invisibly stores data (including the following) and syncs settings with any other iPhones, iPads, Mac computers, and PCs that you might own (PCs must be running the iCloud Control Panel).[a]

- @icloud.com and @me.com email, including VIP mailboxes
- Your contacts list
- Calendar events
- Entries and lists added to the Reminders app
- Safari bookmarks, reading list, and currently open tabs on all devices
- Items created by the Notes app
- Passbook tickets, passes, and vouchers
- Usernames and passwords used on websites (also know as the *Keychain*)
- Photos and videos you take and choose to share via photo stream (see *Photo Stream*, on page 20)
- Documents and data created by iCloud-compatible apps, including the iWork and iLife apps[b,c]
- Device backups (see *The Settings App*, on page 37)
- Songs in your iTunes library via iTunes Match[d]
- iBook notes, bookmarks, and highlighting

Additionally, the Find My iPhone/iPad service (see *Security*, on page 30) is part of iCloud, as is Back to My Mac, which allows Mac users to remotely access files on computers in their homes or workplaces.

5GB of storage is provided free of charge, although photo streams are not included in this limitation.

Using iCloud is optional, but even if you have only one Apple device it's still a good idea to sign up because you can access many iCloud services via the iCloud website, using any computer and browser combination.

You can deactivate individual features of iCloud. For example, to deactivate the iCloud sharing of your Safari data, open the Settings app, tap the iCloud heading, then deactivate the switch alongside Safari within the list.

---

a. https://www.apple.com/icloud/setup/pc.html
b. https://www.apple.com/creativity-apps/ios/
c. https://www.apple.com/creativity-apps/ios/
d. https://www.apple.com/itunes/itunes-match/

- iPhoto ($4.99): Edit photos you've taken with your iOS device and apply effects.

- iMovie ($4.99): Cut together video clips you've taken with your device into a complete movie or trailer. Projects can include title sequences and sound effects, and can be shared via iMovie Theater with other iOS devices and Macs running iMovie.

- iBooks: Purchase, read, and annotate ebooks.

- Podcasts: Browse, subscribe to, and listen to podcasts.

- iTunes U: Download free teaching materials from worldwide educational establishments and organizations.

- iTunes Festival: Watch recorded performances from the yearly iTunes Festival, or tune in live while the festival runs in September each year.

- Trailers: Watch movie trailers in high definition (1080p), and check nearby theaters for showtimes. You can even purchase tickets!

Office

Apple offers three iOS apps as part of its broader iWork range, which also includes desktop-equivalent applications for the Mac computer and online apps accessible via the iCloud website. All iWork apps automatically sync their files via iCloud with other iOS devices and Mac computers running desktop versions of the same app.

- Pages ($9.99): Create text-based documents ranging from simple to complex, with desktop-publishing features available too—see Figure 12, *Editing a document within Pages on an iPad*, on page 28 for an example of Pages on an iPad.

- Numbers ($9.99): Create spreadsheets in this simple-to-use application, with a focus on layout and graphing.

- Keynote ($9.99): Create and give presentations using animations and multimedia.

- Keynote Remote ($0.99): Remotely control a Mac, iPad, or iPhone giving a Keynote presentation—via Wi-Fi when controlling a Mac or Bluetooth when controlling another iPad or iPhone.

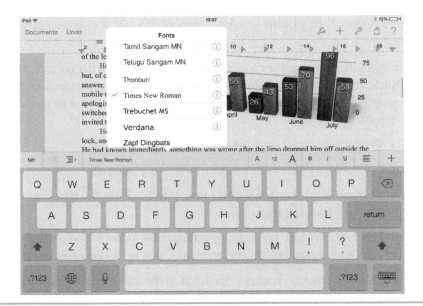

Figure 12—Editing a document within Pages on an iPad

Developer

App and content creators working with iOS will find the following apps useful:

- WWDC: Keep abreast of news and presentations during and after Apple's yearly Worldwide Developers Conference.

- iAd Gallery: View some of the most effective advertising used on Apple's iAd advertising network.

- iTunes Connect Mobile: Allows app developers and iBook creators to view sales and catalog data.

System and Security

Apple offers a handful of apps for controlling other hardware, along with an additional vital security tool:

- Find My iPhone/iPad: Locate lost or stolen Apple hardware that's registered with the Find My iPhone/iPad service (see *Security*, on page 30).

- Remote: Remotely control any network-connected Apple TV, Mac, or Windows PC running iTunes.

- AirPort Utility: Remotely configure Apple's AirPort Wi-Fi router.

Miscellaneous

Apps that refuse to fall into other categories include the following:

- Find My Friends: Discover the locations of your friends who are also running the Find My Friends app on their iOS devices.

- Apple Store: View and purchase Apple products directly from your device, using the payment card registered with your Apple ID.

Gestures

In addition to tapping and dragging, you can use a number of *gestures* to quickly do things like switch between apps. Gestures involve dragging one or more fingers across the screen in various ways.

iPad and iPhone

The iPad and iPhone share the following gestures:

- Back and forward: Swipe a finger from the left edge of the screen to the right in apps including Settings, the App Store, and Safari to move back to the previous screen or website—the equivalent of tapping the back button in Safari or the previous-page button at the top left in apps such as the App Store. Swipe from the right of the screen to move forward in certain apps—the equivalent of tapping the forward button. Additionally, in some iPad apps, including Mail, swiping in from the left side of the screen will reveal additional menus and options.

- Double-tap to zoom: Double-tap in apps such as Safari or Photos to zoom in on the current area. Double-tap again to zoom back out.

- Pinch to zoom: Where thumbnails are displayed in apps such as Photos, you can hold a thumb and finger together over the thumbnail and slowly move them apart to enlarge the thumbnail to full size. Performing the gesture on an album's thumbnail will open the album for viewing. Additionally, when viewing a photo full size the same gesture can be used to zoom in and out (to zoom out, bring the thumb and finger closer together again).

- Rotate: In some apps you can rotate an image by holding one finger on the surface and rotating another around it. Most frequently, the thumb and index finger are used to do this because it's most convenient.

iPad Only

The bigger screen of the iPad allows additional gestures, as follows. These can be optionally deactivated by opening Settings, tapping the General heading, and deactivating the switch alongside Multitasking Gestures:

- Return to home screen: To quickly switch out of an app and return to the home screen, space apart four fingers and a thumb on the screen and then contract in a pinching motion.

- Activate the multitasking screen: Rather than double-clicking the Home button to access the multitasking feature of iOS, you can swipe up anywhere on the screen with four fingers. Swipe down again to cancel. Be careful not to start this gesture near the bottom of the screen, however, because this could activate Control Center (see *Control Center*, on page 34).

- Switch between apps: To switch between currently open apps, place four fingers anywhere on the screen in a roughly horizontal fashion, and swipe right or left. As with the multitasking screen, apps are arranged in the sequence in which they were last used or activated.

Security

Three additional setup tasks immeasurably enhance the security of your iOS device:

- Setting a strong lock-screen passcode, in the case of non–iPhone 5s devices

- Enabling the Find My iPhone/iPad service if you didn't during initial setup

- Deactivating lock-screen access to Siri, Control Center, and Notification Center

These settings can be changed as follows.

Lock-Screen Passcode

Because four-digit PINs can be surprisingly easy for attackers to guess, you can instead create a longer password or passphrase, involving numbers, letters, or symbols (see Figure 13, *Using a longer passcode*, on page 31).

To do so, open the Settings app then tap the General heading, then Passcode Lock. Enter your existing passcode when prompted, then tap the switch alongside Simple Passcode so that it's deactivated, and follow the instructions that appear. You can create single-word passcodes or even type an entire

Figure 13—Using a longer passcode

phrase involving spaces, such as your favorite quotation (although bear in mind that longer sentences might be annoying to type each time you wake your device from sleep).

In the same Settings options list you can also set the iOS device to erase its data after 10 failed passcode attempts—tap the switch alongside Erase Data. This is potentially dangerous if you have young children in the house, or if anybody else uses your device and might struggle to remember the code. However, if nobody but you uses your iPhone or iPad, then it's certainly worth considering.

Find My iPhone/iPad

The second vital security measure is to register the device with iCloud's Find My iPhone/iPad system, if you didn't during the initial setup steps. Despite the name of this service, iPod Touches and even Mac computers can be registered in addition to iPads and iPhones.

To register a device, open the Settings app, then tap the iCloud heading and tap the switch alongside the Find My iPhone/iPad heading so it's activated.

Find My iPhone/iPad offers three very useful features when a phone is lost or stolen. These features are accessible via the iCloud website from any computer or smartphone, or the Find My iPhone (sic) app running on another iOS device:

- You can view a map showing the device's location. Note that the location reported isn't guaranteed to be accurate, and that the location can be spoofed using various apps and online services.[7]

- You can make the lost or stolen iOS device emit a sound, even if the volume is set to mute. This can help locate it if you've lost it in your home or workplace.

- You can set the device to Lost mode which will cause a message to pop up on the screen to tell anybody who has the phone to call you to arrange return (see the figure here). The device will also lock and require the usual PIN/passcode before it can be used again.

- If the device is irretrievable, you can issue a remote wipe order that will wipe all the data off of it. Once a remote wipe has taken place it will be impossible to set up the device from scratch without inputting your Apple ID and password. This is designed to make stolen devices useless to thieves.

Figure 14—An iPhone showing a "Lost mode" message via Find My iPhone

All of those enhancements assume the device is able to get online and hasn't simply been switched off by a thief. They also assume the battery hasn't run out of power. However, if the device is offline, all the aforementioned requests will be queued to take place as soon as the device comes back online again.

Deactivate Lock-Screen Feature Access

Although being able to access Control Center, Notification Center, and Siri from the lock screen is convenient, those all represent potential security issues if a device is stolen or lost. Apple works hard to limit what phone features and personal data can be accessed when the phone is in Lock mode but, upon the release of iOS 7, it was possible to use Siri to deactivate the

---

7. See http://modmyi.com/info/fakemyi.php and www.locationholic.com.

Find My iPad/iPhone service without entering a passcode/using Touch ID to unlock the device. This has since been fixed.

To disable Control Center access from the lock screen, open the Settings app and tap Control Center, then deactivate the switch alongside Access on Lock Screen.

To disable Notification Center access from the lock screen, open the Settings app, then tap the Notification Center heading. Deactivate the switches alongside Notifications View and Today View under the Access on Lock Screen heading.

To disable Siri access when the device is locked, open the Settings app, then tap General > Passcode Lock, and type your passcode when prompted. Deactivate the switch alongside Siri under the Allow Access When Locked heading.

You might also choose to enable two-step authentication for your Apple account, as described in Tip 25, *Enable two-step verification for extra security*, on page 70.

iTunes

iTunes is Apple's application for Macs and PCs that lets users play and manage their audio and video collections, as well as purchase new titles through the iTunes Store.

Coupling your iPad or iPhone to iTunes on a Mac or Windows PC was a necessity just a few years ago in order to initially set up the device and sync music and video purchases, but nowadays using iTunes is not mandatory. Put simply, iOS devices are designed to be fully independent.

From an iPad or iPhone perspective, the primary use of iTunes today is to let you sync to your device any existing music or video files you might own (including tracks ripped from CD/DVD, or downloaded via non-Apple websites or services). You can also sync any playlists you create using iTunes, and iTunes offers access to the iTunes and iOS App Stores, circumventing the need to use the apps on your device.

iTunes can connect to your device via a USB cable or over Wi-Fi. The former is the more reliable and quicker of the two methods.

Perhaps iTunes's most useful feature is its ability to create backups of your iOS device, which can offer a safeguard against problems when upgrading to a new release of iOS (it's also possible to back up to iCloud—open the Settings app, then tap iCloud > Storage & Backup).

The only time iTunes is absolutely required is when the device becomes locked after too many incorrect PIN/passcode attempts.

Spotlight Search

iOS's search tool is called Spotlight, and it lets you search by name for apps, music, videos, voice memos, audiobooks, and podcasts. Additionally, it lets you search for keywords within the content of your emails, notes, contacts, reminders, calendar events, and messages.

To access Spotlight, drag down in the app-icon area of the home screen. This will reveal a search field hidden at the top of the screen.

Can't find the app icon for Pages on your home screens? If you have hundreds of apps installed it can be genuinely difficult. Just bring down the Spotlight search field and type "pages." The results will appear immediately underneath the search field. Want to find any email messages that mention Chianti? Just bring down the Spotlight search field and type the word.

It's handy to know that the search field within many apps is hidden in the same way—just above the default screen area—and you can reveal it by dragging down a small amount in the main screen area. Try doing so in the Notes app's main listing, for example.

System Configuration

Settings within iOS can be configured using Control Center and the Settings app.

Control Center

We can swipe up from the bottom of the screen to reveal Control Center, which offers a way to activate and deactivate key hardware features as well as useful everyday apps (see Figure 15, *Control Center on an iPhone*, on page 35).

- Airplane mode: This deactivates all communication hardware within the device (that is, cellular, Wi-Fi, and Bluetooth). As the name suggests, this mode is designed for air travel, although it's also useful for saving power when the battery is running low and you don't mind being unable to receive calls and messages or access the Internet (if you're playing games on a long journey, for example).

- Wi-Fi: If you're using solely cellular data you can deactivate Wi-Fi by tapping this button. However, don't forget to activate it again when in range of your home or office network!

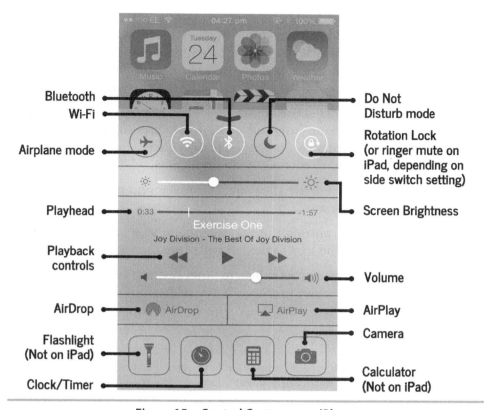

Figure 15—Control Center on an iPhone

- Bluetooth: You can switch Bluetooth on or off with this switch. If you don't use Bluetooth, then leaving it permanently switched off is a good idea because that will save battery life. Bluetooth devices you might use with your iOS device include earpieces and headsets, speakers, keyboards, and "eyes-free" dashboard modes within vehicles.

- Do Not Disturb: Although Do Not Disturb is designed to work according to the schedule you establish in the Settings app (see *The Settings App*, on page 37), you can force it to activate immediately by tapping this button. Tap again to deactivate it.

- Rotation lock: Tapping this button locks the iPhone's display to a portrait orientation, and the iPad's display to whichever orientation it is currently being held in (that is, if held in landscape then tapping the button will lock the display to landscape). Some apps are able to override the rotation lock—many games work only in landscape mode, for example.

- Ringer mute (iPad only): This mutes the ringer on an iPad, which is to say that audible notifications from apps like Messages are silenced (although notifications will still appear onscreen). Note that this does not mute the main volume, so it will not mute music or video playback, for example. On the iPhone the side switch performs an identical function.

- Brightness: Moving this slider adjusts the screen brightness, although if the device is set to auto-brightness within the Settings app then the brightness may immediately autoadjust to match ambient conditions (that is, it will be decreased or increased automatically).

- Playback controls: These are the same controls found in the Music app, and work in the same way.

- Volume: This slider controls the playback volume of audio, video, and games. Dragging all the way to the left will mute the volume.

- AirDrop: All iOS users can send files to other users via AirDrop—see the following sidebar. However, to receive a file via AirDrop you must activate AirDrop here.

AirDrop

AirDrop lets users instantly transfer files or links to other iPad or iPhone users and works via a combination of Bluetooth and Wi-Fi. Although there's a similar technology in Mac OS X, AirDrop in iOS lets you transfer files only to other AirDrop-compatible iOS devices (the iPhone 5, 5s, and 5c; iPad Air and iPad fourth generation; iPad Mini (standard and Retina); and iPod Touch fifth generation).

For AirDrop to work the recipient must enable it in Control Center (see *Control Center*, on page 34). The recipient will be able to choose whether to receive AirDrop files from only contacts, or from absolutely anyone. Choosing the latter option, of course, means that anybody in the same area could attempt to send a file or link to you—even somebody in another room or on a different floor of the building. The potential range is up to 30 meters.

The person sending the file should open the item she wants to share, then tap the share button and select the AirDrop option. The recipient will appear in a list of nearby AirDrop-activated devices, and tapping his entry in the list will initiate the transfer. Note that you may be prompted to activate Bluetooth if it isn't already activated—you can do this via Control Center.

A dialog box that pops up on the recipient's device will show a preview of the file. The recipient will be asked if he wants to accept it. If he does, the file transfer will complete within seconds.

- AirPlay: Here you can choose a device to which your iPhone can output audio and/or video, or on which the iPad or iPhone screen can be mirrored. See *AirPlay*, on page 18. If no AirPlay devices are nearby (that is, there are none on the same network), then this option will not appear.

- Flashlight (iPhone only): This is a small applet found only in Control Center; it activates the camera flash as a flashlight. Tapping again will deactivate it.

- Clock: This is a shortcut to the standard Clock app, as described in *Information and Office*, on page 23.

- Calculator (iPhone only): This provides a shortcut to the Calculator app, as discussed in *Information and Office*, on page 23.

- Camera: This is a shortcut to the Camera app, as described in *Entertainment and Creativity*, on page 17.

The Settings App

The Settings app provides access to all configurable hardware and software settings within iOS. See the following figure for an example.

Figure 16—The Settings app on an iPad

The settings options are listed as a series of headings down the left side of the screen on an iPad, or down the center of the screen on an iPhone. Additionally, some apps add their own configuration options to the Settings app and these appear below the main headings.

The options within the Settings apps are as follows:

- Airplane mode: As with Control Center, this switch deactivates cellular, Wi-Fi, and Bluetooth functionality in order to abide by airline requests during take-off and landing.

- Wi-Fi: Here you can choose the Wi-Fi base station to connect to, and disconnect if you're already connected. By tapping the (i) symbol alongside each you can view and adjust technical details about the connection and choose to "forget" particular networks, which will prevent your device from connecting automatically when the Wi-Fi base station comes within range.

- Bluetooth: You can switch Bluetooth on or off with this switch and choose which devices to pair with. As with the Wi-Fi heading, tapping the (i) icon will offer an option to let you "forget" the device so it won't connect automatically whenever the device is in range.

- Cellular (iPhone and 3G/4G iPad): Here you can adjust various aspects relating to the cellular connection, including whether to use cellular data, LTE connections, and data roaming. If your cellular contract allows Personal Hotspot (see the next list item), you can also enable that here, and you can enable and disable the ability of individual apps to use cellular data.

- Personal Hotspot (iPhone and 3G/4G iPad): If your cellular contract allows the feature, you can activate iOS's Personal Hotspot feature (otherwise known as data tethering) here. See Figure 17, *Configuring Personal Hotspot on an iPad*, on page 39 for an example from an iPad. Personal Hotspot allows you to connect other computers or devices to your iPad or iPhone via Wi-Fi, USB, and Bluetooth so they can share the cellular data connection.

- Carrier (iPhone and 3G/4G iPad): Shows details of your cellular carrier and lets you choose a carrier manually, if necessary.

- Notification Center: Sets various aspects of Notification Center, including what apps are allowed to appear within it, and whether you want to receive AMBER and Emergency Government Alerts (USA only).[8]

---

8. See https://www.fcc.gov/guides/wireless-emergency-alerts-wea and http://www.amberalert.gov

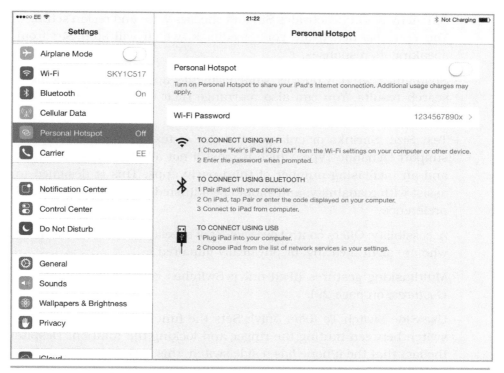

Figure 17—Configuring Personal Hotspot on an iPad

- Control Center: Sets whether Control Center is accessible from an unlocked device and whether it's accessible while an app is in use (that is, whether it should be accessible only when the user is accessing the home or lock screen).

- Do Not Disturb: Lets you turn off notifications and calls according to a schedule (overnight, for example) or manually (by activating the switch alongside the Manual heading). You can also create exceptions, and allow through calls that are repeated within a three-minute time frame (useful if somebody is urgently trying to contact you).

- General: An umbrella category containing the following subsettings:

  - About: Shows technical details about your device, such as the amount of free storage space and the version numbers of various system components.

  - Software Update: Checks for updates to iOS and, if there are any, starts the download and updating procedure.

- Siri: Activates or deactivates Siri and chooses voice and region settings. You can also deactivate voice feedback, which will stop Siri from speaking its responses.

- Spotlight Search: Controls what elements appear within Spotlight search results. You can also rearrange their order by dragging the handles at the right of each line.

- Text Size: Shrinks or enlarges the size of text in applications that support Dynamic Type, which is most if not all of Apple's own apps and an increasing number of third-party apps. This is designed to assist with readability, and should be adjusted according to personal preference.

- Accessibility: Offers control over a host of specialized features for those who are sight, hearing, or physically impaired.

- Multitasking gestures (iPad only): Switches gestures on or off (see *Gestures*, on page 29).

- Use Side Switch To (iPad only): Sets the function of the iPad's side switch between muting the ringer and locking the rotation. Despite the fact that the iPhone has a side switch, this option is not available on iPhones.

- Usage: Lets you view how much storage space is free and what apps are using the storage space. You can also view how much iCloud storage space is used within your account, and delete iCloud data and backups. Additionally, you can set a switch to control whether the remaining battery charge is displayed as a percentage at the top of the screen, and view the amount of time the device has been active since the last charge.

- Background App Refresh: Controls whether compatible apps or Newsstand titles are able to go online for new content or use Location Services when the device is in sleep mode.

- Auto-Lock: Controls how quickly the device enters sleep mode after a period of inactivity.

- Passcode Lock: Sets various aspects of the Passcode security system, including setting a nonsimple passcode (see *Security*, on page 30). Tapping the Require Passcode heading sets how quickly the device requires you to enter a PIN/passcode after it enters sleep mode—setting one minute, for example, means that should you wake your device less than a minute after it went into sleep mode, you won't be prompted for your PIN/passcode.

– Restrictions: Switches features of iOS on and off, usually to deactivate them when somebody else, such as a child, is using your device. You can also set parental-control content filtering (including for Siri results) and control which apps are able to access features of your device such as Location Services and the microphone.

– Lock/Unlock (iPad only): Lets you set whether an iPad is locked or unlocked by use of a Smart Cover or the cover of a Smart Case.

– Date & Time: Lets you set the date and time manually if you wish (by default it's set using Internet time servers). You can also adjust the time-zone setting, although this is automatically detected according to the location of your Wi-Fi base station. You can set the iPad or iPhone to display 24-hour time here, too.

– Keyboard: Sets various aspects of text entry on your device, such as whether words are capitalized automatically when they start sentences or new lines, and whether perceived typos are autocorrected. You can also choose additional international keyboard layouts and create shortcuts, which are words or abbreviations that when typed are automatically expanded into longer words or sentences (for example, you might type "omw" and it will automatically be expanded to "On my way!").

– International: Sets various country-specific features such as interface language and which currency symbol and calendar (Gregorian, Japanese, or Buddhist) is used by default.

– iTunes Wi-Fi Sync: Automatically back up and sync to iTunes on a Mac or Windows PC over Wi-Fi. You need to set this up initially while the iPad or iPhone is connected to the computer via a USB cable (open iTunes on the computer, select the device from the list at the top right, click the Summary tab, and select the Wi-Fi choice in the Options list). Note that syncing over Wi-Fi can happen only if the Mac or Windows PC is powered up and is on the same network as the iPad or iPhone to be synced, and the iPad or iPhone is connected to a power source.

– VPN: Configure a virtual private network tunneling connection, usually to an office network. L2TP, PPTP, and IPSec technologies are supported.

- Profile: Lets you view any Wi-Fi profiles you've added that facilitate automatic signing in on public networks, including networks supporting 802.1X.

- Reset: Lets you reset all settings on your device or erase all content. You can also reset individual network settings, the keyboard dictionary, the home-screen layout, and location and privacy settings.

• Sounds: Configure ringtones and vibration alerts for various system apps, including incoming calls and texts, along with the ringer and alert volume. You can also configure what sound effects are used for other events, such as tweeting or Calendar alerts.

• Wallpaper & Brightness: As the name suggests, this lets you select what wallpaper you want to use on the lock screen and home screen. You can also set the screen brightness and activate auto-brightness, which will adjust the screen's brightness based on ambient light levels and thereby save battery power.

• Privacy: Switch on or off various features of iOS that present potential privacy issues, such as Location Services, and control which apps can access those services. You can also control which apps are able to access your Facebook and Twitter accounts, if they've been set up on the device, and control advertising tracking (see Tip 116, *Stop advertisers from tracking you*, on page 131).

• iCloud: Control which iCloud account you're signed into, and switch on and off various iCloud services, such as Safari bookmark syncing and Find My iPhone/iPad. See Figure 18, *Setting iCloud options on an iPad*, on page 43 for an example. You can also view details of your iCloud account and upgrade if required, or even delete the entire account.

• Mail, Contacts, Calendars: Add non-iCloud email, messaging, and calendar accounts to iOS, as described in *Setting Up Non-Apple Accounts*, on page 6. You can also configure settings for the Mail, Contacts, and Calendar apps, such as how messages are listed and with what amount of detail.

• Notes: Configure the default account that the Notes app uses.

• Reminders: Configure whether all reminders generated on the device are synced, or just those that are new. Select the default list to which Siri adds new reminders.

• Messages: Switch iMessage on or off and configure which email addresses and phone numbers are used to identify you when sending and receiving

Figure 18—Setting iCloud options on an iPad

iMessages. Activate the function to send iMessages as SMS should iMessage not be available (if you're unable to get a strong enough network connection, for example). Additionally, you can choose to block individuals so you won't receive phone calls, messages, or FaceTime calls from them.

- FaceTime: Choose the Apple ID that you wish to use to make FaceTime calls, and indicate via which addresses/cell-phone numbers you wish to be contacted.

- Maps: Configure aspects of the Maps app, such as the volume of spoken directions and whether metric or imperial measurements are used.

- Safari: Configure Safari, such as the search engine it uses and whether pop-ups should be blocked. You can also clear the browser cache, cookies, and history here.

- iTunes & App Store: Controls aspects of the iTunes Store and App Store apps, including whether purchases and updates are automatically downloaded. You can also set whether cellular data is used to download new apps or updates and for iTunes Match,[9] a subscription service that allows you to access your music collection from all your devices via iCloud.

---

9. http://www.apple.com/itunes/itunes-match

- Music: Controls aspects of the Music app such as audio equalization and iTunes Match activation. You can also configure Home Sharing, which lets you share the device's music library over the network with other iOS devices (including an Apple TV) and computers running iTunes.

- Videos: Configure aspects of video playback via the Videos app, including whether to activate Home Sharing for the video library on the device, as mentioned previously.

- Photos & Camera: Controls functions of the Camera and Photos apps, such as whether to use photo stream and high dynamic range (HDR; see the following sidebar) when taking photos. Here you can also set the default slideshow settings.

High-Dynamic-Range Photography

HDR attempts to provide perfectly exposed photographs within the Camera app by taking several separate shots in quick succession and then automatically combining the best bits of each into one. Every source picture used for the HDR composite is exposed at a different light level, allowing the device to convey detail that with a single shot might be over- or underexposed.

You can activate HDR on an iPad or iPhone by tapping the HDR link before taking a picture. Note that the flash cannot be used at the same time as HDR, although one benefit of HDR is that it's better at low-light photography.

Unless you change the setting under the Photos & Camera heading in the Settings app, taking photographs with HDR will result in two identical snaps—one shot that uses HDR, and one standard shot that doesn't. This happens because HDR isn't guaranteed to produce acceptable results every time.

Because of the way it takes several shots in quick succession, using HDR to shoot fast-moving action may result in blurred images, and you must remember to keep the camera still for a moment before and after you tap the button to take the picture.

- iBooks: Controls the layout of ebooks when using the iBooks app, and functions related to purchasing of ebooks.

- Podcasts (if installed): Lets you control overall subscription settings for podcasts, such as how frequently they're refreshed.

- iTunes U (if installed): Lets you choose whether to sync details via iCloud.

- Game Center: Set the Apple ID that's used to sign into Game Center, how game invitations are handled, and whether friend recommendations are made from your contacts list and your list of Facebook friends.

- Twitter: Configure one or more Twitter accounts to use when sharing content (see *Sharing with Others*, on page 47).

- Facebook: Configure a Facebook account to use when sharing content (see *Sharing with Others*, on page 47), and set which third-party apps are able to use the account for various purposes, such as identifying you, posting on your behalf, or accessing areas of your Facebook account.

- Flickr: Configure a Flickr account for photo sharing (see *Sharing with Others*, on page 47).

- Vimeo: Configure a Vimeo account for video sharing (see *Sharing with Others*, on page 47).

Beneath the default headings within the Settings app are configuration options for apps you've installed. Some offer significant options to modify how the app works, whereas others may simply present a software version number. You might be surprised by the options you find.

Cutting, Copying, and Pasting

There are various ways to select text and images, as follows.

Selecting and Copying Text

There are three methods to select words, sentences, and paragraphs for copying or cutting. Which of them you use depends on personal preference, as well as which app you're using at the time:

- Tapping and holding: If you tap and hold a word or letter, it will be highlighted when you lift your finger. Subsequently dragging the handles to the left or right of the word will then let you change the selection area, with a magnifying glass showing a close-up view, as in the figure here. If you're zoomed out from the text within apps such as Safari, tapping and holding may select the entire paragraph rather than a single word, depending on the web-page layout.

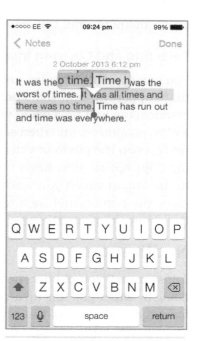

Figure 19—Selecting text in the Notes app on an iPhone

- Double-tapping: In apps in which the text is editable, you can double-tap the word. However, don't lift your finger on the second tap. Instead, drag it to define the selection area. Beware, though: in some apps a double-tap is interpreted as a request to zoom in, so this method does not work universally.

- Tapping a word: When the onscreen keyboard is visible, moving the cursor to the word in question and then tapping it will show a pop-up menu in which you can tap Select to highlight the word, and then drag the handles at either end of the word to select more. Alternatively, tap Select All to select all the text within the note or document.

Whichever method you choose, once you've made your selection a pop-out menu will appear offering the ability to cut or copy the text (you can also tap the Delete button on the onscreen keyboard to delete the text). To paste the text into a new location once it's been cut or copied, switch to the app or new location in the document in which you want to paste, then double-tap the screen when the keyboard is visible. A pop-up menu will appear, on which you can tap the Paste entry. Alternatively you can tap once and hold, then wait a moment until the menu appears.

Selecting and Copying Images

You can copy both photos and videos and then paste them into applications that support multimedia, such as the Messages or Mail app. To copy a photo or video, tap and hold when viewing the photo (or tap and hold its thumbnail within an album), and then select Copy from the menu that appears. Alternatively, open the photo or video for viewing, then tap the share button and tap the Copy option. Whichever copying method you use, you should then switch to the app in which you want to paste the item, tap once in a blank spot to place the cursor, and then tap again until a pop-up menu appears offering the chance to paste the item.

Notifications

Apps can tell you of important events or remind you when something needs doing by either popping up an alert box onscreen or folding down a notification message at the top of the screen. You can dismiss a dialog box by clicking the relevant button within it, and notifications will disappear by themselves after a few seconds (although you can help them on their way by flicking them up into the top of the screen).

Notification Center collates all notifications; you can open it by swiping down from the top of the screen.

You'll see three tabs in Notification Center: Today, All, and Missed. Today is limited to showing a summary of the day's events and the immediately upcoming weather. At the bottom you'll also see a nonspecific summary of any events taking place tomorrow (such as "There is one event scheduled for 9am").

The All tab shows notifications from all other apps, regardless of whether they occurred when you were using the phone or when the phone was in sleep mode. Tapping any entry in the list will open the app for further investigation.

The Missed tab filters the notification list for any events that took place when the device was in sleep mode.

You can modify Notification Center using the Settings app (see *The Settings App*, on page 37), and dismiss it by dragging the handle at the bottom back up to the top of the screen.

Some apps display numbered notifications against their app icons on the home screen. The Mail app will show how many unread messages there are, for example, and the Phone app will show the number of missed calls and voicemail messages. Usually opening the app will clear these notifications, although in the case of the Phone app you may have to view the Recents list by tapping its icon at the bottom of the screen, and listen to (and possibly delete, depending on your cellular operator) any voicemail messages.

Sharing with Others

A key feature of iOS is the share button in various applications—see Figure 20, *The share button (bottom left) within an iPhone's Photos app share button*, on page 48 for an example from the Photos app on an iPhone, where the button is located at the bottom left. Depending on the app, once tapped this offers a way of sharing everything from emails to photos by various means, and performing tasks such as printing.

Depending on which app you're sharing from, the options might include any of the following:

- AirDrop: Shares with other iOS 7 users who are nearby—see *AirDrop*, on page 36.

- Message: Shares via an iMessage or SMS/MMS message using the Messages app. Tapping the button will switch you to the Messages app, with the file attached.

- Mail: Creates a new message within the Mail app, with the shared item attached or displayed within the body of the email.

- iCloud: Shares with others via a shared photo stream. See *Photo Stream*, on page 20.

- Twitter: Shares via any Twitter accounts you have set up on the system, with the chance to add a message. You can add Twitter accounts via the Settings app.

- Facebook: Shares on your Facebook wall, with the chance to add a message (assuming you have an account set up within the Settings app). Unless you specify otherwise, images are added to an album called iOS Photos.

- Flickr: Shares photos and videos via the Flickr account set up on the system.[10]

Figure 20—The share button (bottom left) within an iPhone's Photos app

- Vimeo: Shares video files via the Vimeo video-sharing site,[11] assuming an account has been added in the Settings app.

- Bookmark (Safari and Mail only): Adds a web-browser bookmark.

- Add to Reading List (Safari only): Adds items to your reading list; these items are similar to regular browser bookmarks, except a copy of the page is stored on the device so you can read it even if there isn't an Internet connection.

- Add to Home Screen (Safari and Mail only): Adds a website as an app, complete with an icon on the home screen. Once tapped the "app" will open the site in a new Safari tab.

- Copy: Copies the item to the clipboard for pasting elsewhere.

---

10. www.flickr.com
11. https://vimeo.com/

- Slideshow: Displays the current image plus any others in the album in a slideshow.

- AirPlay: Sends the picture or video to an AirPlay device on the network.

- Assign to Contact: Opens the Contacts app so the selected picture can be used as the image for one of your contacts.

- Use as Wallpaper: Sets the image as the lock-screen or home-screen wallpaper (or both).

- Print: Prints to an AirPrint-compatible printer on the network (see the following sidebar).

In addition to these choices, non-US users may find other options, depending on their country settings—Chinese users will see Sina and Tencent Weibo options, for example.

Usability Tips and Tricks

Three basic but not-quite-obvious tricks can be used within most apps, as follows:

- Deleting items: In apps that have lists, you can often remove an entry by swiping left across it, which will reveal a Delete, Trash, or Archive button that you can then tap.

- Fetching new content: With some apps that regularly download new data, such as the Mail app, tapping and dragging down on a list will force the app to see if there's anything new available (assuming the list is already scrolled to the top, of course).

- Tap and hold: Tapping and holding an item onscreen will often reveal a pop-up menu showing additional options.

Jailbreaking

No book discussing iOS would be complete without at least a brief mention of *jailbreaking*, although it's not recommended for most users and comes with a substantial number of caveats.

Jailbreaking is the process of gaining root powers on a device—to become an administrator so that new software can be installed without Apple's authorization. It's achieved using software that exploits a bug in iOS or the iPad or iPhone hardware.

AirPrint

AirPrint is Apple's solution for printing from iOS devices. Put simply, if a printer is AirPrint compatible then an iOS device will automatically detect it when you tap Share > Print (in the Mail app you must tap the reply/forward button to see the Print option). Note that although AirPrint uses Wi-Fi, not all Wi-Fi–capable printers support AirPrint. Look for the AirPrint badge on the printer's box or in the manual.

Although the quality of the output through AirPrint is virtually identical to that of a desktop computer, AirPrint is intentionally simple to use. Unlike when printing from a desktop computer, you won't see a configuration panel where you can set the resolution or scaling. When printing via AirPrint the only option is how many copies you'd like.

See also Tip 81, *Print to any printer connected to a Mac or Windows PC*, on page 105.

Why would anybody do this? Apple keeps very tight control over which apps are listed in the App Store, and what they can do. This limits the options open to app developers and to users who desire more control over their devices. Apps are "sandboxed," for example, which means they're limited to running in their own space within the operating system and their interaction with other apps or the operating system is limited. Similarly, apps cannot modify how system components work, or even supply an alternative technology that would compete with a built-in system tool (although they can "wrap" underlying iOS technology to create a new app, which is why there are alternative web browsers in the app store).

Security and Legalities

The tight control is there for a reason: it's extremely effective at preventing malware from appearing in iOS, and it helps maintain a consistent user experience. It means iOS is significantly more secure than the world of Android apps and the Wild West nature of Android's Google Play,[12] where there's significant malware and piracy.

Some people crave more control over their iOS devices, however, or would like the ability to install apps that Apple doesn't approve of. Some people want to use alternative carriers. The solution in each case is jailbreaking.

Perhaps surprisingly, the US Copyright Office has deemed jailbreaking legal for iPhones, although not yet for iPads. In any case, Apple says that jailbreaking voids warranties, and outside the United States laws differ considerably.

---

12. See, for example, http://www.techrepublic.com/blog/google-in-the-enterprise/malware-in-the-google-play-store-enemy-inside-the-gates/.

Because jailbreaking exploits bugs, Apple plays a cat-and-mouse game with developers, patching security holes in software and hardware with new releases of iOS and within new devices, only to find that new holes have been spotted and exploited.

How to Jailbreak

There are two types of jailbreaking technology: tethered and untethered.

A tethered jailbreak requires the device to be booted each time via jailbreaking software on a Mac or Windows PC so that the jailbreak patch can be applied. In other words, the jailbreak will be lost if you restart your phone away from a computer. For various reasons, tethered jailbreaks are technologically easier to accomplish.

An untethered jailbreak means that the software in the device is permanently patched and you can restart the device whenever needed without losing the jailbreak.

In both cases, updating iOS will very likely repair the system component exploited by the jailbreak, which is why many who jailbreak don't upgrade as soon as an update is made available, but instead wait to see if the jailbreak is also updated.

However a jailbreak is achieved, the goal is to install an additional app store, and this is usually Cydia,[13] which we see in the figure here. Cydia allows the installation of apps and tweaks not authorized by Apple, although it works in a similar way to the official App Store—some apps are free and can be installed by tapping a button, and others have a price and can be purchased with a payment card.

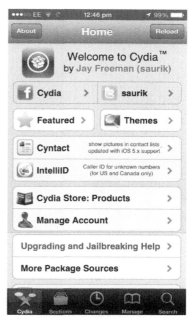

Figure 21—Cydia running on a jailbroken iPhone

---

13. http://cydia.saurik.com/

CHAPTER 2

The Tips

Welcome to the heart of *iPad and iPhone Kung Fu*—the tips! Start anywhere you like—at the beginning, in the middle, or at the end!

Note that references to iWork encompass the Pages word processor, Numbers spreadsheet, and Keynote presentation software. See *Office*, on page 27, for more details. Similarly, references to iLife refer to iMovie, iPhoto, and GarageBand.

Any references to onscreen buttons or icons assume the iPad or iPhone is held in portrait orientation rather than landscape orientation, unless specified otherwise.

Tip 1

Take photos in burst mode

If you're photographing sports or fast-moving action, then getting that perfect shot can feel like a matter of chance—can you tap the button at the perfect moment, or will you be a little late and end up with blur or an empty frame? Luckily, the iPad and iPhone let you cheat. By pressing and holding the button in the Camera app, you'll keep taking photos in burst mode until you lift your finger again.

Burst mode works differently depending on whether you have an iPhone 5s or another iOS device:

- iPhone 5s: On an iPhone 5s around 10 pictures will be taken every second and you'll see an onscreen counter showing how many shots you've taken. Once you've finished shooting you can tap the Choose Favorites button at the bottom to choose those you'd like to transfer to your camera roll as discrete pictures. Those you don't favorite won't get deleted. In the Photos app the burst-mode photos will appear as just one thumbnail that, when tapped, will again show a listing of all the photos, from which you can select one or more entries to be transferred to the camera roll.

- Other devices: On non–iPhone 5s devices, burst mode will take two or three pictures every second, which will be transferred to your camera roll just like any other photos you take. You can then manually delete those you don't want to keep.

Tip 2

Instantly clear lock-screen notifications

It can be embarrassing when your lock screen fills with a list of notifications, especially if your iPhone is mounted in a car holder, for example, where your passengers can easily view it. A quick way to instantly clear away all notifications on the lock screen—without the need to unlock the phone—is to drag down the notification center and then drag it back up.

The notifications will still be listed in Notification Center in case you wish to view them later, but the lock screen will now show nothing more than the time and date.

Tip 3

Let people FaceTime-call a specific iPad, iPhone, or Mac

FaceTime works by letting you register cell-phone numbers and email addresses by which people can contact you.

For example, anybody wishing to call me via FaceTime can do so by specifying my cell-phone number, my iCloud email address, or my personal email address. When they call, I'm notified of the call on my iPad, iPhone, and Mac computer simultaneously, and it's up to me which I use to take the call.

However, by selectively assigning just one email address or cell-phone number to a particular device, you can make it so that the caller can choose to FaceTime-call *just* your iPhone or your iPad or your Mac computer. In other words, the call won't ring out on all your devices. Here's how to set it up:

1. Choose the first of your Apple devices, then open the Settings app and tap the FaceTime heading.

2. Under the heading that reads You Can Be Reached by FaceTime At, remove the checks alongside all the entries except the cell-phone number or email address you wish to use for that particular device. Alternatively, you can tap the Add Another Email entry to add a new email address by which you want to be contacted for that device. Note that you will need to reply to a confirmation message at that email address to authorize its use.

3. Under the Caller ID heading, ensure the same address or cell-phone number as earlier is selected.

4. Repeat this step on the other Apple devices or Macs, assigning each a unique email address for use with FaceTime. Note that an iPhone must use its cell-phone number as identification, and it can't be deselected within the list.

5. Ask anybody who wants to FaceTime-call a specific one of your devices to create a new contact for you in their Contacts app. For example, I might ask family members to create a new contact called Keir Thomas iPad, with the only entry being the email address I've assigned for FaceTime calls on my iPad (typed within the FaceTime field of the contact card). This step should be repeated, so people add a new contact for any other Apple devices or Macs, in which the only entry will be the email address or cell-phone number registered with FaceTime on that device. Following this, those family members can FaceTime-call me by switching to the FaceTime app, opening the contacts list, then tapping the new entry they created for my iPad, Mac, or iPhone. FaceTime will "ring" only on the device they select to call.

Tip 4

Preview driving directions in Maps

One big drawback when asking the Maps app to plan a route for you is that you can't preview the required turns and maneuvers, other than by looking at the bird's-eye overview presented before you tap the Start button or seeing a list of turns by tapping the menu button at the bottom of the screen (you may need to tap the screen to make the toolbar visible). However, sometimes it's useful to step through the journey, as if you're driving or walking it, so that you can see what to expect on the map itself.

In fact, Maps can provide exactly this step-by-step preview via a little-known navigation mode, as the figure here shows. Here's how it's done:

1. Search for your destination in the usual way, or select it from the Recents list. This will set a pin on the spot. Unfortunately, choosing a destination from the bookmarks list sets a slightly different kind of pin incompatible with what we need, so instead you should make a note of the bookmark's zip/postal code and search for it.

2. Tap the right-facing arrow in the pin's pop-up menu. On the screen that appears, select Directions to Here.

3. On the next screen *don't use the default Current Location setting* in the Start field. Instead, tap the X to clear the field, then type the zip/postal code of your current location, although you could also specify a full address.

Figure 22—Previewing driving directions in the Maps app

4. Tap the Route button, and then the Start button to begin the navigation.

You can swipe left and right to move through the instructions at the top of the screen to see not only the instructions but also the junction or maneuver in question. When you're ready to drive the route, tap the current-location button at the bottom left, and a blue dot will indicate your position.

There are some big differences between using Maps this way and using it in the standard routing mode. There aren't any spoken directions, for example. Additionally, the route won't recalculate should you take a wrong turn, nor will the map zoom in and out to provide a view that matches your speed. Essentially, it's like following an old-fashioned route drawn on a paper map, except that your position on the map is indicated.

Tip 5

See recently closed browser tabs

Have you ever closed a tab within Safari and then regretted it? On the iPad (although not the iPhone) you can tap and hold the new-tab button at the top right of the screen (the icon is a plus symbol, +) to see a list of recently closed tabs. Selecting one will open it again. Additionally, the browsing history for that tab will be restored and you can go back to pages you were viewing before you closed the tab.

Tip 6

Easily select paragraphs, sentences, and lines

Selecting text for copying or cutting within iPad and iPhone apps is never easy, but can be straightforward if all you want to do is select a discrete line, sentence, or paragraph while editing text. Just tap the line, sentence, or paragraph with two fingers. This can be a difficult technique to get right, particularly when selecting single lines—the two fingers must be side-by-side and perhaps even pinched together. However, once mastered it's a technique that can save a lot of time and effort.

If after selecting text in this way you then drag apart the two fingers, the selection will expand line by line to encompass your selection area (although not in apps like Pages, where that gesture is used to zoom in and out of the document).

Tip 7

Use emoji—full-color emoticons

Emoji are Japanese emoticons that are full-color images and, although they're part of the Unicode specification for displaying text, it was the first iPhone that brought them to public notice. Since then they've spread beyond the iPhone to other smartphones and desktop PCs, although there's a lack of cross-platform compatibility—it's unlikely an Android user will receive emoji messages you send, for example, although other iPhone and iPad users will receive them fine.

Adding an Emoji Keyboard

To activate emoji on your phone or iPad, open the Settings app and tap the General heading, and then the Keyboard entry within the list. On the screen that follows this, tap Keyboards > Add New Keyboard. Scroll down the list and then tap Emoji.

Using Emoji

To use emoji in messages, emails, or wherever you type text, tap the small globe icon to the left of the Space key on the onscreen keyboard. This will switch the entire keyboard area to emoji and you can type any one by tapping it—see the following figure. Along the bottom are the emoji categories.

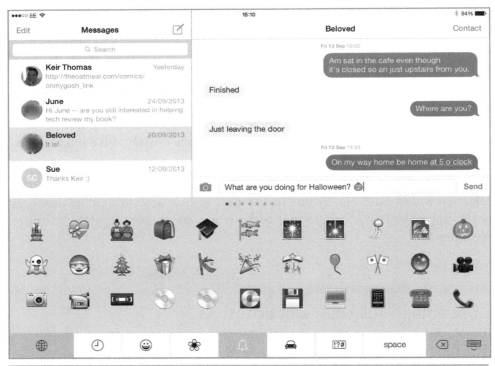

Figure 23—Using emoji in an iMessage

To return to the standard English keyboard, tap the globe icon at the bottom left once again. You can mix emoji into text messages, emails, or documents.

Emoji can be used anywhere—even when naming a folder on the home screen, for example.

Believe it or not, each emoji has a name. To hear what each emoji is, read Tip 118, *Have iBooks read to you*, on page 132, to learn how to activate the iPad/iPhone speech tool, and then select any emoji you've typed and select Speak. The name of the emoji will then be spoken.

Deactivating the Emoji Keyboard

To deactivate the emoji keyboard, repeat the preceding steps to add a new keyboard until the Add New Keyboard entry is visible, then swipe left on the Emoji entry in the list of existing keyboards until Delete appears at the right. Tap it to delete the emoji keyboard.

Tip 8

Automatically end web and email addresses

Users of iPads and iPhones that ran older versions of iOS might be wondering where the ".com" button went to when they upgraded to iOS 7. Well, it's still there! It's just hidden. If you type the first part of an address in Safari's URL field, or the address field of a new email, then tap and hold the period button (to the right of the Space key), a pop-out menu of address endings will appear—.com, .edu, .org, and so on). Just slide your finger over to the one you want and then lift to autocomplete the rest of the address. For example, to address an email to john@example.com, I would type john@example and then tap and hold the period key until the pop-out menu appeared. Then I'd slide my finger over to the .com entry before lifting my finger to have the address autocompleted.

Tip 9

Stop being told twice about new messages

Out of the box, iPhones will notify you twice about an SMS/MMS or iMessage when the device is in sleep mode. Clearly somebody at Apple thought this was a good idea, but it's downright confusing—did you receive a new message just now, or are you just being told about the message from two minutes ago?

Luckily, this feature is easy to turn off. Open the Settings app and tap the Notification Center heading, then tap the Messages entry in the list. Scroll down to the Repeat Alerts heading, and then tap it and select Never from the list that appears.

Tip 10

Record the screen of an iPad or iPhone

Unfortunately, the way iPads and iPhones work means that although taking screenshots is easy (see Tip 40, *Take a snapshot of the screen*, on page 81), recording what's happening on the screen using an app isn't possible. However, if you have access to a Mac or Windows PC, you can use a neat hack.

AirPlay is the technology built into iPads and iPhones that lets users mirror their displays on compatible devices, such as a television connected to an Apple TV.[1] However, the AirServer app turns any Mac or Windows PC into an AirPlay receiver. You can then mirror the iPad or iPhone's screen to a Mac or Windows PC and use standard screen-recording software to record it. Here's how to set it up:

1. Download and install AirServer.[2] Unless you want to buy it immediately—it costs $15—you'll first need to register for a trial-period activation code, and you'll need to enter this code when installing the app.

2. Run the app after it's installed. The app runs in the Windows system tray or the Mac's menu bar, and in both cases runs as a background service, so you won't see anything until you connect from an iPad or iPhone.

3. On the iPad or iPhone, drag up Control Center from the bottom of the screen, then tap the AirPlay button. In the list of devices select the Mac or Windows PC, which will be identified by name, activate the Mirroring switch below, then tap Done.

4. The iPad or iPhone will be instantly mirrored on the computer's screen. AirServer might default to full-screen view, which you can override by moving the mouse until the toolbar appears and clicking the shrink button (the arrow icon at the right).

---

1. https://www.apple.com/appletv/
2. www.airserver.com

5. Because iPads and iPhones have higher resolutions than most PC and Mac monitors, you might need to resize the AirServer window in the usual way: by clicking and dragging its edges. This will scale the content without any loss of quality.

The connection will be lost should the iPad or iPhone go to sleep, and you may need to repeat the preceding steps to reestablish it.

Once the content of the iPad or iPhone appears on the Mac or Windows PC screen, you can use screencasting or screen-recording software such as CamStudio on a Windows PC,[3] or the built-in QuickTime Player on a Mac (click File > New Screen Recording).

A second method of capturing an iPhone or iPad screen is to use an HDMI capture device, although this involves the use of specialized hardware.[4]

Tip 11

Take better HDR pictures

High dynamic range (HDR) is a technology that aims to produce perfect pictures (see *High-Dynamic-Range Photography*, on page 44). If you find yourself unable to get a good snap even with HDR enabled, try this trick, which isn't guaranteed to work each time but is certainly worth a try: when lining up the shot, tap and hold the darkest area of the picture for a few seconds. This will lock the focus and exposure. Then take the picture.

You may find the picture is better exposed, and it happens because you're giving iOS's HDR software a helping hand in learning about the exposure range of the image.

Of course, this will work only if the area you select isn't too close to your iPad or iPhone, because you're also locking focus and might therefore cause the main subject in the image to be blurred. But for a general shot of objects some distance away, or a landscape shot, what you focus on won't make any difference to the overall quality of the shot.

---

3. http://camstudio.org
4. http://www.iphonelife.com/blog/177/elgato-game-capture-hd-review

Tip 12

Type on the iPad keyboard with your thumbs

The iPad keyboard usually occupies the bottom half or third of the screen, depending on screen orientation. However, you can also move it up to the middle or top area of the screen, or split it into two halves that can be similarly positioned anywhere on the screen. This can be very useful if you want to hold the iPad with your hands at either side and type with your thumbs, which can be more comfortable.

Undock the Keyboard

To move the keyboard so it automatically occupies the middle band of the screen each time it's activated, make the keyboard appear by tapping in a text-input field, then tap and hold the keyboard button at the bottom right. A menu will appear, and you should slide your finger up to the Undock option.

The keyboard will move to the middle of the screen; to reposition it elsewhere drag the keyboard button up or down. The keyboard will move with it, and remain in the position where you release.

To restore the keyboard to the bottom of the screen, tap and hold the keyboard icon until the menu appears, but this time select Dock.

Split the Keyboard

To split the keyboard but leave it docked at the bottom of the screen, place your thumbs on the center of the keyboard and drag them apart. To merge the keyboard back into one, simply reverse this gesture—place a finger or thumb on each half of the keyboard and draw them together.

Split and Undock the Keyboard

To split the keyboard into two halves and undock it from the bottom of the screen, tap and hold the keyboard button at the bottom right of the keyboard, then slide your finger to the Split option on the pop-out menu. The keyboard will automatically split and move roughly to the middle of the screen. By tapping and then dragging the keyboard button you can reposition the keyboard, as the following figure shows, although beware that if you drag it to the bottom it will attempt to merge back into a single keyboard.

Another way to split the keyboard is to tap and then drag the keyboard button upward when it's docked.

To restore the split keyboard to its default mode of being merged into one at the bottom of the screen, either drag it to the bottom of the screen as described earlier, or tap and hold the keyboard icon until the menu appears and select Dock and Merge.

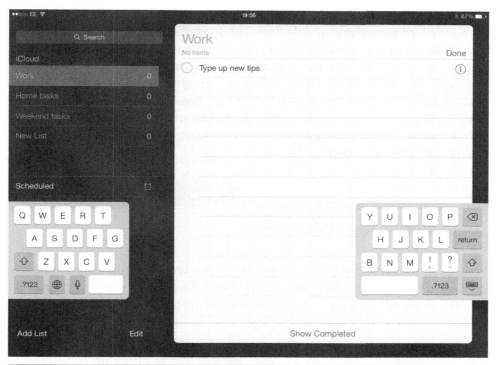

Figure 24—Using the split keyboard on an iPad

Using the Split Keyboard

A very useful feature of the split keyboard is that it includes "overtype" areas—tap in the empty space to the left of the H key, for example, and you'll type a G. Similarly, type in the blank space to the right of the T key, and you'll type a Y. The intention is to accommodate people who don't stick strictly to the "home keys" method of typing.

Note that if none of the preceding options appear, or if it seems impossible to split the keyboard, you may need to open the Settings app, tap the General heading then the Keyboard option, and tap the switch alongside Split

Keyboard. Note that this doesn't actually split the keyboard. It merely makes it possible to do so in the ways described in the preceding text.

Tip 13

Rotate clips in iMovie

Did you record something upside down, or do you simply want to make a clip in your iMovie project look like it was filmed in Australia? Move the playhead so that it's in the middle of the clip, then use the usual rotate gesture within the playback window—the same gesture you might use in the Photos app to rotate a picture (which involves rotating one finger around another). You'll rotate each picture 90 degrees each time, so to turn the picture upside down (180 degrees), perform the gesture a second time. To return it to the way it was, perform the gesture four times.

Tip 14

Get more weather information

By tapping the large temperature display in the Weather app on the iPhone, you'll switch the display to show details about the humidity levels, chance of rain, wind speed, and what the temperature feels like. Tapping again will restore the simple temperature display.

Tip 15

Know when iMessage is being used

iMessage is the name of the underlying technology that lets you text-chat and share files with other people who have Apple iPhones, iPads, iPod Touches, and Macs running OS X Mountain Lion (10.8) or later. iMessage is very like text messaging except it works entirely over the Internet. Because Apple maintains a database of iMessage users' phone numbers, iOS will always default to iMessage if possible—even if you're contacting somebody for the first time. And you can tell if iMessage is being used because once you've typed your message, the Send button will be colored blue, as will the recipient's cell number or email address. If these are colored green, then standard text messaging is being used (that is, SMS or MMS). The same applies to the bubbles displaying messages already sent—blue indicates iMessage, while green indicates regular SMS/MMS.

Tip 16

Use autoplay variations in GarageBand

Whenever the Autoplay dial appears as an option within GarageBand, such as with the Smart instruments, pressing a chord bar with two fingers will play a variation of the standard Autoplay riff. Tapping with three fingers will play another variation.

These variations are different from the choices offered by simply rotating the Autoplay dial. Instead, they modulate the basic riff or melody slightly, with three fingers often introducing slightly discordant notes. To return to the default riff or melody, just tap the note heading above each of the chord bars.

Tip 17

Undo and redo quickly in iWork and iLife

Although the standard methods of undoing an action work in the iWork and iLife apps (see Tip 47, *Shake to undo*, on page 84), there's also an Undo button in each app—in the iWork apps it's labeled Undo and is usually located at the top left of the screen, while in iLife apps the icon is an arrow turning back on itself (imagine a U-turn sign, and you're pretty close), which is usually located in the right half of the app window (under the video-playback preview in iMovie, for example).

However, unlike elsewhere in iOS, Undo in iWork and iLife has magical powers—it remembers more than the most recent task, so you can step backward through your recent changes using the Undo button.

Alternatively, to redo an action you've just undone, tap and hold the Undo button until the redo option appears beneath it.

Tip 18

Hide the keyboard when messaging

When replying to an SMS or iMessage you can tap one of the message bubbles then drag down to dismiss the onscreen keyboard, allowing you to view messages above. Just tap in the message field to restore the keyboard if you want to type.

Tip 19

Gain extra exposure within iPhoto

The Exposure tool in iPhoto lets you drag the brightness and contrast stops left and right to adjust the shadows and highlights in an image. Less obvious is that you can also drag the left- and right-end stops on the brightness/contrast scale into the shaded border area. This has the effect of making the brightest objects brighter in the case of the right stop, and the darkest objects darker in the case of the left stop. It's not always a useful thing to do and can lead to detail being lost or washed out, but it can help rescue photos that were taken in less-than-ideal circumstances.

Tip 20

Lock your iPad or iPhone with a long PIN

By default all iPads and iPhones other than the iPhone 5s require you to enter a four-digit PIN passcode every time they wake. However, four-digit PINs can be pretty easy to guess—certain easily typed number combinations are more common than others (1234, 1111, 1212, and 0000, for example). And how many of us use our date of birth or that of a loved one? A thief may well know these dates.

To negate this risk, iOS lets you create complex passcodes, as described in *Security*, on page 30.

Complex passcodes are more secure, but it can be irritating to type such a passcode each time you want to wake your device, especially if you're in transit at the time.

What would be ideal is if you could create and enter longer numerical PINs using the standard numerical onscreen keyboard rather than a full QWERTY keyboard, and there's a hidden way of doing so. Here's how to set it up:

1. Open the Settings app, then tap General > Passcode Lock. You'll be prompted to type your existing passcode, so do so.

2. Tap the Simple Passcode switch so that it's deactivated.

3. You'll be prompted to type your existing PIN, then immediately prompted to type a new passcode via the full onscreen keyboard. However, *don't* type any letters or symbols! Instead switch to the numbers/symbols keyboard (bottom-left button marked .?123, or 123 on some iPhone keyboard layouts) and type a numeric PIN, as the following figure shows. This can be however long you want it to be—just don't type anything other than numbers! Tap Next when you're finished.

Figure 25—Creating a long passcode on an iPad

4. You'll have to type the sequence once again to confirm it, and tap Done when you've finished.

That's all that's required. From now on, whenever you wake your iPad or iPhone, you'll be prompted to type the new long PIN via a large and simple onscreen numeric keypad. Once you've done so tap the OK button at the right of the PIN display area.

Tip 21

Navigate without spoken directions

Spoken directions when traveling a route worked out by the Maps app can be useful to give you warnings when a turn is coming up, but if you're happy to just keep an eye on the screen (without taking your eyes off the road, of course!) then you can tap the volume icon at the bottom right to select No Voice from the pop-up menu (you may need to tap the screen once to make the icon bar visible). To make this change permanent, open the Settings app and scroll down to the Maps heading. Tap it, and then select No Voice from the Navigation Voice Volume list. Repeat this step to enable the voice, should you wish to.

Tip 22

Group shapes, photos, and text boxes in iWork

Items placed on the page in iWork apps can be grouped together, which will mean that moving one will move the others, and resizing one will also resize the others. To group items, tap and hold one of them, then tap the others you wish to add to the group. When you lift your fingers, tap the Group option on the pop-out menu. The objects will be surrounded by a single frame, by which you can move and resize them.

To ungroup the items, tap one of them and tap the Ungroup option on the menu that appears. This will ungroup all the objects, rather than remove the single object you've selected. Unfortunately, this is the only way the iWork apps let you ungroup items.

Tip 23

View Map pins that are close together

Sometimes two pins are close together on a map, and tapping each to view their pop-up information can be tricky. One way to do so is to zoom in so that the pins appear farther apart, but an easier way that works at any zoom level is to tap and hold one of the pins so its pop-up appears, and then, *without lifting your finger*, slide it toward the other pin. That will switch the pop-up to show information about that pin, as we see in the following figure. In fact, this will even work if the pins are far apart—sliding your finger around on the surface of the iPad or iPhone will cause pop-ups to appear above whatever pin is currently beneath your finger.

Incidentally, another way to view the search results is to tap the list button at the bottom of the screen. Selecting any entry in the list will switch back to the map view with the pin for that location selected.

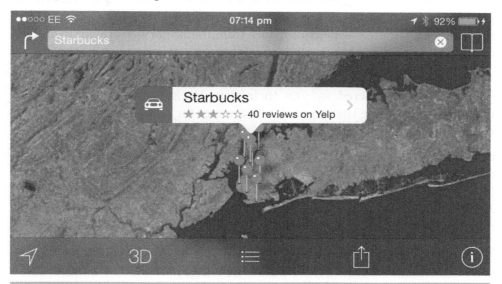

Figure 26—Viewing pins that are close together on an iPhone

Tip 24

Jump to the top of any page or list

If you're browsing down a website or email and want to quickly return to the top, just tap the status-bar area directly above the list. You'll instantly scroll back to the top. (You might find that this trick works in many third-party apps as well as the built-in iOS apps.) Note that this doesn't work the other way around—tapping the bottom of the screen won't make the page scroll downward.

Tip 25

Enable two-step verification for extra security

Anybody with knowledge of your Apple ID password has a huge amount of power. Assuming the device is registered with the Find My iPhone/iPad service a person can remotely wipe your device from the Apple website, for example, by reporting it as being stolen.

A sad fact of modern life is that passwords—even sophisticated ones—should no longer be considered safe on their own. Hackers not only show great ingenuity in cracking them, but the technology for doing so is getting better every day.

Because of this, Apple offers optional two-step verification. This means that managing your Apple account—performing tasks such as adding a new device, for example, or remotely wiping another—isn't possible without both your Apple ID password and a PIN, which is sent to your iPad or iPhone, or which can be sent by SMS to any phone.

Other than for account administration, however, two-step verification is unobtrusive—it's not used when purchasing apps, for example, or when viewing your iCloud email online.

Setting up two-step verification is easy. Here's how—it's best done on a desktop computer.

1. Log in at the Apple ID website and click Manage your Apple ID, then log in when prompted.[5]

2. Click the Password and Security section at the left, then click the Get Started link under the Two-Step Verification heading.

3. After reading about the benefits of two-step verification, clicking Continue each time, you'll be shown a list of Apple devices registered on your account. By clicking the Verify link alongside a device, you can set it up as a "trusted" device, meaning that in the future you'll be able to choose to send a PIN to it as part of two-step verification.

4. Verification works by sending a PIN to the device, which you should then enter at the website when prompted, as the following figure shows.

5. When registering an iPhone, you'll also be prompted to enter its phone number to act as a backup should there be a problem sending the verification code. You can skip this step if you wish, but it's a good idea to type in your number. (Those living outside the United States with phone numbers beginning with zero should leave off any opening zero from the number.) To confirm the cell-phone number you'll be sent a PIN by SMS, which you should confirm by typing into the website as prompted.

    Alternatively, if you don't have an iPhone you can click the Add an SMS-Capable Phone Number link to set up a different device. Again, you'll need to enter the PIN on the website after it's sent to the phone. If somebody you know well has a cell phone, it's worth considering adding that phone's number here as an insurance policy in case you lose your Apple devices—obviously that person will need to be available when you set up two-step verification because he'll have to confirm the PIN he receives.

6. When you click Continue you'll see a recovery key. If you lose your Apple devices, you can use this key to reset all the security details. For this reason, you should keep the key in a very secure place. My favorite way of recording details like this is to write them on the back page of a favorite book that lives on my bookcase. Only I know which book, and burglars have very little interest in books!

7. When you click Continue you'll be asked to confirm the code by typing it, so do so.

---

5. https://appleid.apple.com

8. After checking the box to confirm that you understand the implications of two-step verification, and how it works, click the Enable Two-Step Verification link to activate it.

Figure 27—Setting up Apple ID two-step verification

To deactivate two-step verification at a later date, repeat the preceding steps to log into the Password and Security section of the Apple ID website and click the Turn Off Two-Step Verification link.

Tip 26

Take photos while shooting video

If you're shooting a video on an iPhone 5, 5c, or 5s, you can tap the white button at the bottom left to take a snapshot (top left if the phone is being held in landscape mode). This won't affect the video, which will continue to be recorded as if nothing had happened.

It's important to note that all you're really doing is saving a still from the movie, rather than taking a photo. The resulting snapshots will be at 1080p resolution (1920×1080, or 2.1 megapixels), and far short of the 8 megapixel capability of the iPhone's camera when taking photos ordinarily.

Tip 27

Move email addresses in the Mail app

Ever entered an email address in the CC: field of an email but then decided it'd be better to use BCC:? Tap the address so it's highlighted, then drag it down to the BCC: field. In fact, this trick lets you switch around email addresses between any of the To:, CC:, and BCC: fields!

Tip 28

See a list of all upcoming calendar events

Although the Calendar app offers various ways to view upcoming events, sometimes you might want a basic list. This way you won't have to scroll across any days that don't have events, for example. The solution is surprisingly uncomplicated—tap the search icon (magnifying glass) at the top right of the screen (you must hold an iPhone in portrait mode to see the icon).

Typing anything into the search field will filter the list—if you want to see only upcoming appointments with John, for example, type his name into the search field (assuming the title of each event mentions his name or he's listed as one of the invitees). You can also drag the list up and down to move through the weeks and months.

Tip 29

Quickly rip your CD collection for your iPad or iPhone

Converting your CD collection for storing on an iPad or iPhone is always going to be a slow task, but iTunes on your computer can make it a little easier by automatically importing and then ejecting any CD you insert. This way you can keep feeding the computer CDs until the entire collection is ripped, with no need to continually click dialog boxes.

To set this up on a Windows PC, click the small icon at the very top left of the iTunes window and select Preferences from the menu that appears. On a Mac click the main application menu, then Preferences. Then click the

General tab of the dialog box that appears and next to the When You Insert a CD heading, select Import CD and Exit. Then click the OK button.

Not only will iTunes need to be running when you insert the CDs (although it can be minimized at the time), but you'll need to ensure iTunes is set as the system default app for handling audio CDs. On a Mac you can do this by opening System Preferences, clicking the CDs & DVDs icon, and selecting Open iTunes from the drop-down list alongside the heading that reads When You Insert a Music CD. On Windows open the Start menu (or return to the Start screen on Windows 8), then type autoplay into the Search field. In the list of results tap Change Default Settings for Media or Devices. Under the Audio CD heading of the dialog box that appears, choose Import Songs Using iTunes, then click the Save button.

Tip 30

Move backward and forward when giving a Keynote presentation

When giving a Keynote presentation tapping the screen will advance forward in the presentation. However, you can also swipe from right to left to move to the next slide, and left to right to return to the previous slide.

Tip 31

Control the Ken Burns effect in iMovie

When you insert a photo into an iMovie project, iMovie automatically applies the Ken Burns effect. This is where the camera appears to pan and slowly zoom into (or out of) one area of the photo, adding visual interest. It's named after the documentary filmmaker of the same name, who created the effect.[6]

To control the degree of the Ken Burns effect, or even remove it entirely, double-tap the photo within the iMovie timeline. This will highlight it. Then move the playhead to the beginning of the photo and use the pinch-to-expand and drag gestures on the playback preview window to resize the photo or focus attention on a particular area. Then move the playhead to the right of the clip, where you should make a similar adjustment. By matching the

---

6.   http://en.wikipedia.org/wiki/Ken_Burns

"before and after" positioning of the photo, and the zoom level, you can remove the Ken Burns effect entirely and the picture will appear to be stationary when it's displayed within the movie. The changes are applied instantly, so tap the play button to see what effects your edits have had.

Tip 32

Forward an SMS/MMS message or iMessage to another person

Although it's easy to forward an email you receive to somebody else (just open the email then tap the reply button, choosing Forward from the pop-out menu), it appears to be impossible to forward an SMS or MMS message or iMessage you've received.

If fact, it is possible, although it requires a little extra work. Locate the message you want to forward, then tap and hold it. Alternatively, you can double-tap the message. A menu will appear (see the following figure). Tap the More button, then tap the forwarding button at the bottom right (the icon is a curved right-facing arrow). A new message window will appear, where you can enter the recipient's details into the To: field, and then tap Send. Note that, unlike when forwarding an email, there will be no "header" information that illustrates that the message has been forwarded. Therefore you might want to edit the message before sending to explain that you're forwarding something you've received.

Figure 28—Forwarding a message to another person

Tip 33

Create folders in the Dock

Creating a new folder for apps is easy—just press and hold any app until the icons begin to wobble, then drag one app icon on top of another. Yet trying to create a folder in the Dock at the bottom of the screen seems impossible—either nothing happens when one app icon is hovered over another, or the app icon slides out of the way as if you want to merely place the icon there.

It is possible for the Dock to contain folders, however. Just create a folder in the main home-screen area, then drag it down onto the Dock, having first made space by removing one of the existing icons. See the following figure for an example taken from an iPhone.

Figure 29—A folder in the Dock of an iPhone

Tip 34

Stop the phone's ringing, but still take the call

There's nothing worse than finishing a real-life conversation with somebody while your phone is ringing. You're going to answer it, but you just need a few more words with the other person. Yet the phone's ringing is impossible to ignore!

The solution with an iPhone is to press the Lock/Sleep button once. This silences the ringer but doesn't reject the call, so you can answer it as usual as soon as you're able to.

This works for FaceTime calls too, on both an iPhone and an iPad.

Tip 35

Trim movies you record

If you record video you might be used to having that bit at the beginning where people are messing around before they realize the camera is pointed at them, and that bit at the end where you decide to stop filming and there's a resultant camera wobble as you tap the stop button.

To make for cleaner, more professional clips, iOS lets you trim clips you record. To do so, open a clip after recording (or via the Photos app) and then—without starting it playing—tap and then drag the left or right side of the frame display at the top of the window. If you do it properly, the frame display will turn yellow and show a grayed-out area to the left or right, which indicates the discarded footage. See the figure here for an example taken from an iPad.

Figure 30—Trimming a movie

At any time you can tap the play button to see how the new clip looks (when playback has finished tap the screen again to bring up the controls once more).

When you're happy, tap the Trim button. You'll be asked if you want to over-write the original (Trim Original), or to save the trimmed video as an entirely new movie (Save as New Clip), in which case it'll be added to the same camera roll as the original.

Tip 36

Instantly align maps with north

You can rotate maps by tapping and holding two fingers on the screen, then rotating one fingertip around the other. To return the map's orientation to north, tap once on the compass icon at the top right of the screen.

Tip 37

Easily rearrange home-screen icons

You can rearrange icons on the iPhone and iPad home screens by tapping and holding them until they wiggle, then dragging them to their new positions. This is a great way of moving one or two icons, but for major restructuring of the home screens it's a lot of hassle.

Assuming you sync with iTunes running on your Mac or Windows PC, there's a faster way of rearranging icons, as follows.

Setup

Attach your device to your computer or join the same Wi-Fi network if you've activated wireless syncing on the device, then select your phone from iTunes's device list at the top right. Click the Apps tab. You'll see your device's home screen(s) reproduced on the right of the iTunes program window, complete with whatever wallpaper you use.

After taking any of the following steps be sure to click the Apply button at the bottom right, which will sync the device and apply the changes.

Moving Icons and Creating Folders

Double-click one of the home screens, then click and drag any of the icons with your mouse to new positions (including onto other home screens). As when doing this on your iPhone or iPad, holding one icon over another will create a new folder.

Installing and Deleting Apps

To delete an app, double-click to open the relevant home screen for editing, then hover your mouse cursor over its icon and click the small X icon at the top left. It will disappear instantly, although you'll be warned of its deletion when you click the Apply button to sync the changes with the device.

If you've purchased apps using iTunes on your Mac or Windows PC, you can drag and drop them from beneath the Apps list at the left of the window straight onto the home-screen position where you'd like them to appear. This will also install them on the device.

Creating New Home Screens

To create a new home screen, click the plus (+) icon to the top right of the Home Screens heading. Note that if you don't add any icons to this new screen, it won't be synced with the device, so won't appear there.

Tip 38

Put your photos online instantly for non-Apple users

As discussed in *Photo Stream*, on page 20, any iPad and iPhone user can create a shared photo stream that other iPad or iPhone users can access. Unfortunately, shared photo streams are an Apple-only technology. There is, though, a way to share a photo stream with just about anybody who has a computer—whether that's a desktop PC, a phone, or a tablet created by any manufacturer.

Here's how it's done:

1. Create the shared photo stream in the usual way—tap the Select button at the top right when viewing an album in the Photos app, tap the photos you wish to be included, then tap the share button before tapping iCloud.

2. Create a new shared photo stream by tapping the Stream heading at the bottom right of the dialog box and tapping New Shared Stream.

3. Give the stream a name and tap Next.

4. You'll be prompted to add invitees, but there's no need to add people—just tap Next without filling in any details. (Note that any previous invitees will be suggested, but you can ignore this.)

5. Tap Post to create the photo stream.

6. Select the new share by tapping the Shared button in the Photos app, then tapping the name of the stream above the thumbnails of the photos it contains.

7. Tap the People button (top right on an iPad and bottom right on an iPhone) and then activate the switch alongside Public Website.

8. Tap the Share Link button to create messages or social-media postings listing the website's link. If you want to get the link for yourself without sharing it, send the message or email to yourself.

You can turn off the website share by repeating the preceding steps but this time deactivating the switch alongside the Public Website heading.

Tip 39

Type rather than speak Siri questions

Here's a useful trick if Siri is having one of those days where it doesn't understand what you're saying. When Siri shows your question and its response, tap your question. The question box will then have a cursor in it and you can overtype or correct whatever's there, as the following figure shows. Tap Done on the keyboard when you've finished. This also works if Siri shows its "I'm thinking..." comment.

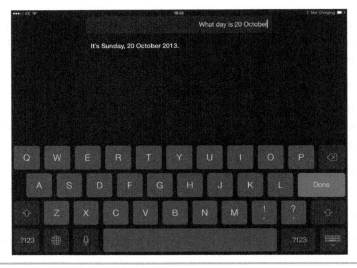

Figure 31—Typing a question for Siri to answer

To bring up Siri so you can type a question without having to speak it, hold down the Home button and then say, "Hello." Siri will greet you as you might expect, but you'll then be able to overtype the "Hello" speech bubble with whatever you want, and Siri will act upon it once you've pressed the `Done` key.

Take a snapshot of the screen

You can take a snapshot of the screen at any point, and it will be saved to your camera roll for viewing later.

To do so, simultaneously press the Lock/Sleep button at the top of the device and the Home button near the bottom. This can take a little practice to get right, but you'll know it's worked when the screen flashes white and you hear a shutter-release sound.

It won't work in a handful of apps that prohibit the taking of screenshots, such as Snapchat.[7]

If viewing the snap on a computer, remember that screenshots taken on a Retina-equipped iPhone and iPad will be larger than you might expect because Retina models have a higher pixel density than most computer screens.

To create a screencast (that is, a movie recording of what you're seeing), see Tip 10, *Record the screen of an iPad or iPhone*, on page 60.

Copy and paste a text style in Pages

Although Pages offers many different readymade text styles, you may end up creating your own text formatting, or perhaps modifying a readymade style after it's been applied to text. But Pages offers no way to add your own styles to its list of defaults. In other words, applying a homemade style to other areas of the document is difficult.

There is a solution. Select a word styled how you wish, then on the pop-out menu that appears select Style (on an iPhone you may need to tap the right-facing arrow on the pop-out menu to scroll the menu to the Style option).

---

7.   http://www.snapchat.com/

Then tap Copy Style. Highlight the text that you'd like your text formatting to be applied to, then tap Style > Paste Style.

Bear in mind that Pages differentiates between styles applied to paragraphs and styles applied to words and sentences. In other words, you won't be able to apply a style you created for a word/sentence to a paragraph or vice versa.

Tip 42

Quickly scroll through home screens

Although you can swipe left and right to move through the various home screens, you can also tap the small dots just above the Dock at the bottom of the screen. On an iPhone this can take dexterity and it's hard not to accidentally start an app, but on an iPad's larger screen it's somewhat easier.

Tapping to the left of the white dot—which indicates the home screen you're currently viewing—will scroll the list left, while tapping to the right of the white dot will scroll the list right. In fact, you don't even have to tap the dots; you can tap the empty space to the left of the dots at either side to achieve the same thing. Give it a try and experiment a little!

Tip 43

View lyrics while listening to music

Here's a nice trick that'll let you view song lyrics while listening to music on your iPad or iPhone using the Music app. Because it relies on iTunes it works only if you sync your iPad or iPhone to your Mac or Windows PC, although it works equally well with songs you've ripped from CD and those purchased through the iTunes Store.

1. Within iTunes on your Mac or Windows PC, find the first of the tunes for which you'd like to view lyrics during playback. Right-click it and select Get Info.

2. In the dialog box that appears, switch to the Lyrics tab, then switch to your web browser.

3. Use a search engine to find the lyrics for the song. Select and copy them, then switch to iTunes and paste them into the Lyrics dialog box.

4. Click OK to dismiss the dialog box. Then sync your iPad or iPhone in the usual way.

5. Repeat the preceding steps for any other tracks for which you'd like to add lyrics.

To view the lyrics during playback on your iPad or iPhone, switch to the Now Playing view within the Music app, then tap the cover-art image when the track is playing. Tap again to hide the lyrics.

Tip 44

Access your email drafts

If you tap the Cancel button when creating an email, you'll see two options appear: delete the email or save it as a draft. But if you save it as a draft, how do you find it again? The solution is simple. Tap and hold the compose-email button (the pencil-and-paper icon) at the bottom right of the screen. The draft email listing will slide up from the bottom of the screen, and you can tap any of the drafts to continue working on them (and send them if you wish, although you can again tap Cancel to save them as drafts).

With web-based email services like Gmail you'll find that any drafts you create are synced with the server, so any drafts you create at the Gmail website will be synced with your device.

Tip 45

Snooze an alarm quickly

If an alarm goes off when you're not using your device you can press the iPhone or iPad's Lock/Sleep button or volume-control buttons to snooze —provided you created the alarm with the snooze option enabled, of course. This saves the effort of tapping the small snooze button on the screen, which can be challenging when waking bleary-eyed!

Snoozing gives you another nine minutes of dreaming before the alarm sounds again, by the way, and you'll see the countdown displayed on the lock screen beneath the current time. Why nine minutes? It's an industry standard among alarm-clock makers and has been for hundreds of years!

Should you find yourself unable to drift back to sleep, you can subsequently cancel a snoozing alarm by waking the phone, opening the Clock app, switching to Alarm view, and deactivating the Alarm (if the Alarm is set for daily repeat you should immediately reactivate it).

Tip 46

Delete shared photo-stream comments

When adding photos to a shared photo stream you can add comments, but what if you add a comment that you later regret or that contains something inaccurate? Tap and hold the comment until a pop-up menu appears offering the chance to delete.

Tip 47

Shake to undo

Just made a typo? Simply shake your iPad or iPhone to bring up a button you can tap to undo any recent typing, as we see in the following figure. Note that the shake might have to be quite vigorous to register!

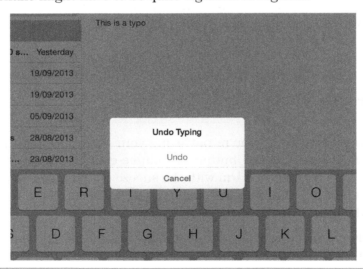

Figure 32—The "shake" Undo dialog box

Note too that this isn't quite the same as undoing typing on a Mac or Windows PC by pressing `Ctrl`-`Z` or `Cmd`-`Z`; you'll likely lose the entire last sentence you typed rather than the last word or letter. However, you can restore the text by shaking the iPhone or iPad again, and this time selecting Redo Typing. Additionally, iOS tends to remember only one event to undo, unlike a desktop computer, which might remember hundreds.

For what it's worth, shaking isn't the only way to undo—switch to the numbers/symbols keyboard (that is, tap the `.?123` button, or `123` on some iPhone keyboard layouts) and you'll find an Undo button at the bottom left. Tap to switch to the alternative symbol keyboard (that is, tap the `#+=` key), and the Undo button will switch to Redo.

Tip 48

Quit multiple apps in one gesture

As mentioned in *Multitasking and Switching Apps*, on page 14, you can quit apps by double-clicking the Home button and then flicking the window preview of any app upward.

Less obvious is the fact that if you use two fingers on the screen (or even three or four if they'll fit!), each on a different app window preview, you can flick all of them to the top of the screen and thus quit multiple apps at the same time. Give it a try! It takes a little getting used to, but can be a real time-saver if you want to quit all the apps on the device!

Tip 49

Always quit GPS apps to save battery life

If you use any apps that access the device's GPS functions, such as route planners, be sure to terminate any navigation and quit to the home screen when you've finished with those apps and before locking the device. This is because many such apps continue working if they're running when the device enters sleep mode, and the power needed for the GPS functions can drain the battery quickly.

Apple's Maps app will tell you it's still working via a status bar at the top of the screen, but third-party apps may not. Remember that a symbol appears on the status bar whenever GPS is being used—see Figure 4, *The iOS 7 status-bar icons*, on page 9.

Depending on the app, you might need to quit the app completely by opening the multitasking bar by double-clicking on the Home button, then flicking the app toward the top of the screen.

Tip 50

Quote only part of a message in an email reply

If you tap the Reply button when reading a message within the Mail app, the entire message will be quoted beneath the cursor in the new mail. However, if before tapping Reply you select just part of the message, only the selected text will be quoted in the new email.

Tip 51

Quickly switch to large or small fonts in Pages

Rather than tapping the bigger and smaller font-size buttons on the format bar above the keyboard in Pages, tap the point-size number in between the two buttons. This will show a list of typical font sizes. Tap one to apply it.

Tip 52

Use the built-in dictionary to look up definitions

Don't buy an expensive dictionary app! Did you know that your iPhone or iPad has the Oxford English Dictionary built in? In fact, it also has British English, French, Spanish, German, Dutch, Italian, Korean, Simplified Chinese, and Japanese dictionaries (plus English translation dictionaries for Korean, Japanese, and Chinese).

Looking Up Words

To get a word definition, just tap and hold a word in a compatible app such as Mail, Safari, or Notes, then select Define from the menu that pops up. You might have to tap the right-facing arrow to expand the menu to see the option.

On an iPad the definition will appear in a pop-up window, which you can dismiss by tapping outside of the window; on an iPhone it appears in a new window that slides up from the bottom of the screen, which you can dismiss by tapping Done.

In addition to words, the dictionary includes basic encyclopedia-like features, such as biographies of notable individuals. To look up short phrases and names, simply drag the selection handles around the phrase and then tap Define.

Sadly, you can't copy and paste definitions from the dictionary, or even cross-reference words that you find there. However, for infrequent look-ups it's a valuable tool.

Note that you might be prompted to download the dictionary if this is your first time using this feature.

Adding Other Dictionaries

The New Oxford American Dictionary is installed by default for US English speakers, but you can also install other languages' dictionaries. To do so, highlight a word, then choose the Define option as described previously, then tap Manage at the bottom left. Then in the list that appears tap the cloud-download button (the cloud with the down-facing arrow) alongside the dictionary you want, as the following figure shows.

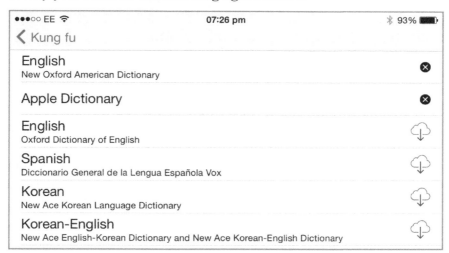

Figure 33—Adding dictionaries to an iPhone

Two or more dictionaries can be installed at the same time, although the ones other than that for the default language can only be used to find word definitions, in the way described previously. Typing in German after installing the German dictionary will cause iOS to underline most words as misspelled, for example. To write in a second language in iOS you'll need to configure a second keyboard language, as described in Tip 146, *Be multilingual*, on page 151.

To uninstall a dictionary, again bring up the dictionary-management component and tap the black circled X alongside the dictionary you want to remove.

Tip 53

Have directions repeated

If you're driving or walking a route worked out by the Maps app and you want to hear the spoken instructions again for your next turn, just tap the top part of the screen where the instruction is listed.

Although of limited use when driving because it would involve taking your attention off the road, when on foot this can be a useful trick if you're unable to study the map.

Tip 54

Listen to just the audio of a music video

Downloaded a music video to your iPhone via iTunes and want to listen to just the audio while you do something else? You could leave it playing and leave the screen active while you pocket your device, but the chance of accidentally tapping something onscreen is high. Instead, here's a trick you can use: start the video playing, then lock the screen by pressing the button on top of the device. The music will stop but if you wake up the device and tap Play on the controls that appear on the lock screen it'll start again, and this time continue when you once again click the Lock/Sleep button.

This trick also works on iPads, where you might want to deactivate the display to save battery life, for example.

Sadly, on either device it works only for music videos, and not movies or TV shows that you might download, although it does work if you're viewing a video file within Safari on a site like YouTube (but not in the YouTube app)—simply start a video file playing in Safari, lock the screen, then wake the device and tap the play button on the lock screen.

Note that this tip is essentially an extension of Tip 232, *Listen to the audio of videos—even after switching away from them*, on page 204.

Tip 55

Make maps orient to the direction you're facing

Virtually every map is drawn so that the vertical axes align with north. In other words, when looking at a map of the United States, Alaska is the state that's highest on the map and Texas is the one that's lowest.

The Maps app aligns maps in the same way. However, if you're walking from one place to another it's useful and potentially less confusing if the map orients the vertical axis to the direction in which you're traveling. In other words, if you walk up a street, the map shows the street as a vertical line, with the street aligned to the direction in which you're walking.

Luckily, the Maps app can do this. Just double-tap the current-location button at the bottom left. This causes the app to align the map to the direction in which the iPhone or iPad is pointed, but this is usually the direction in which you're walking.

To return the map to default north orientation tap the compass icon at the top right.

Tip 56

Cancel Siri

Accidentally started Siri? It's easy to do and there are a handful of ways of canceling it:

- Press the Home button once. This will return you to the app you were using before you started Siri.

- Tap the waveform display at the bottom of the Siri interface. This will stop Siri from listening for your query, but will leave it running.

- When Siri is listening for your query, say, "Goodbye."

Tip 57

Forward just an email's attachment

Did you receive an email with an attachment that you want to forward without quoting any of the email message? Just tap and hold the attachment until the share list appears (tap and hold the preview of the document, if one is shown). Then tap the Mail icon. This will start a fresh Mail message with the file attached. The subject line of the new message will be the filename of the attachment, but you can easily overtype this.

If you want to include the original sender's name and email address when forwarding the attachment, without forwarding all of the original message, highlight just one word in the original email then tap the Reply/Forward button (at the bottom of the screen on the iPhone, and top of the screen on an iPad). Then tap Forward, and select to include the original attachments. Then delete from the message the word you highlighted.

Another method when you wish to forward a picture attachment is to tap and hold it within the original mail, then select Copy before composing a new email and pasting the image into the new email in the usual way (double-tap a blank space in the message of the email and select the Paste option).

Tip 58

Be notified of only important emails

A fact of life is that some emails are more important than others, and some people who send you emails are also more important than others! To help make sure messages from important individuals are always read, iOS offers the VIP mailbox functionality, which can filter mail from certain individuals and provide special alerts. Mac users might already be aware of the VIP mailbox feature because it's also part of the OS X Mail application; note that any VIP entries are automatically synced between your iOS devices and that application.

Setting Up a VIP Mailbox

To make use of it, you'll need to view your mailboxes. Open the Mail app, then swipe in from the left side of the screen. The Inbox mailbox (or All

Inboxes if you have several mail accounts) is where all incoming mail resides, and you can activate the VIP mailbox by tapping the Edit button at the top of the screen and putting a check alongside it by tapping. Tap Done at the top of the screen when you've finished.

To add people to your VIP list, tap the VIP mailbox, and then tap Add VIP. You'll then be able to select the individual from your list of contacts. (Unfortunately, there's no way to add somebody for whom you don't have an existing contact.) Repeat as many times as necessary to add as many VIPs as you need, and tap Mailboxes to return to the main mailboxes listing when you've finished.

Using VIP Mail

To filter your mailbox to show only messages from VIP senders, access the mailbox list by swiping from the left edge of the screen, then tap the VIP entry.

To return to the standard inbox, just swipe in again from the left edge of the screen and select Inbox or All Inboxes in the list of mailboxes.

Setting Up VIP Notifications

VIP comes into its own with the Notifications feature of iOS, because you can configure iOS to show only specific alerts when messages arrive from VIP senders—even if you don't otherwise have Notification Center set to alert you about emails.

To do so, open the Settings app, then navigate to Notification Center > Mail. Scroll to the bottom and tap the VIP heading, and then set what type of alerts you'd like to see and hear.

Tip 59

Use vocal or guitar tracks for sampling in GarageBand

GarageBand includes the ability to record your own electric-guitar-playing as well as vocals (or indeed anything that you can record with a microphone). It also includes a sampler that lets you record audio and play it back at different pitches on a keyboard.

But what if you'd like to turn one of your existing vocals or guitar tracks into a sample?

You can do this by switching to the track-listing view, then dragging the blue audio or guitar recording to the bottom of the track listing, where there's the icon of a synthesizer on a stand (if the icon isn't there you may need to first switch to the Sampler instrument, even if you don't use it to create anything; this activates it as a track within the listing). Although it looks like you're moving the track when you drag it, when you release your finger you'll be asked if you want to import the track. The Sampler instrument will then open and you can record a new track using the newly created sample sound. Crucially, however, the vocal track will still be present when you switch back to the track listing.

Tip 60

Move from right to left when taking a panorama shot

The panorama function lets you take a long landscape shot showing anywhere up to 180 degrees around your current position. To access it on compatible phones (iPhone 4s and later), start the Camera application and swipe from right to left several times until the Pano option is selected.

By default the Panorama feature assumes you want to take a picture by starting at the left and panning to the right, but this isn't always convenient. The solution is to tap the arrow on the panorama display—this will switch it around so the camera expects you to start from the right and pan to the left. Tap the arrow again if you change your mind!

Tip 61

Default to walking directions in Maps

There's a belief that satellite navigation systems are useful only to drivers but, in fact, they can also help when walking from one place to another. The Maps app in iOS includes knowledge of paths and pedestrian areas that aren't accessible to vehicles.

You can choose walking directions when asking the Maps app to figure out a route, but to make the app default to walking instructions rather than driving, open the Settings app on the main screen and then scroll down to the Maps heading. Tap it, and then select Walking under the Preferred

Directions heading on the right. Repeat this if you later wish to make Maps default to driving instructions.

Group slides in Keynote

Individual slides can be grouped together in Keynote. This has no bearing on the eventual presentation, but it can help you keep track of slides that relate to each other, and you can move groups of slides around together within a presentation if you need to reorder things. However, groups can consist only of contiguous slides. You can't group the first, third, and tenth slides, for example. It is possible to create groups within groups, however.

Grouping Two Slides

To group a slide with the one above it, simply tap and hold until the slide enlarges, then drag it to the right. A bar will appear at the left and when you release, the slide above will have a small triangle alongside it that indicates it's the top slide of a group. Tapping the triangle will expand and hide the group.

Alternatively, to create a group drag the second slide on top of the first until a bar appears. This can be difficult to get right, however, because dragging also repositions slides within the running order.

Grouping Two or More Slides

To group several slides together, tap and hold the slide beneath the one you wish to head the group. When it enlarges—while still holding the first slide—with a second finger tap the slides you wish to include in the group. The selected slides will turn blue. Lift your finger and then drag one of the selected slides to the right. A bar will appear at the left. When you lift your finger the slides will be grouped and a small triangle will appear at the left of the head slide. Tapping this triangle hides and reveals the slides within the group.

It's also possible to drag slides onto another slide to create a group—just hover the slides over the first until a bar appears at the left. However, as before, this can be difficult to get right and it's easy to accidentally move slides rather than group them.

Removing a Slide from a Group

To remove a slide from a group, tap and hold it so it enlarges, then drag it to the left. To ungroup several slides at once, tap and hold the first of them until it enlarges, then tap the others using a second finger. Upon lifting your finger, drag any of the selected slides to the left.

Tip 63

Quickly type a period

You might already be aware that tapping the `Space` key twice on the onscreen keyboard inserts a period and a space at the end of a sentence. However, instead of tapping twice, you can tap it with two fingers, or perhaps with both your thumbs if you're using an iPhone. This will insert a period, then a space, and you can start typing again immediately.

Tapping the `Space` key with two fingers at times when a closing period isn't required (that is, when the cursor isn't following a word or sentence) will insert two spaces rather than one.

If you use three fingers to tap the `Space` key, then you'll insert a period followed by two spaces, or just three spaces if typing when a closing period isn't required.

Tip 64

Import contact photos from Facebook and Twitter

iOS likes to make use of contact photos within the phone app and other places, but manually assigning a snapshot to each contact within the Contacts app can be a drag. It's quicker and easier to import the user ID photos from Facebook and Twitter for each of your contacts who have an account with either service. The following steps explain how, and assume you've already logged into Facebook, Twitter, or both—see *The Settings App*, on page 37.

1. Open the Settings app, then scroll down to the Facebook heading and select it.

2. Scroll down the following screen until Update All Contacts is visible. Tap this. Note that downloading of information will take a few minutes.

3. Tap the Settings link at the top left to return to the earlier menu, then tap the Twitter button. Again scroll down and tap the Update All Contacts button.

Assuming you've activated iCloud, you should find that the photos for your contacts are shared among all your iOS devices, as well as any Mac computers you own.

As a bonus, you should also find that your contacts who have Facebook or Twitter accounts also have the a new field added to their contact card showing their Twitter or Facebook name. Opening the Contacts app and tapping one of these entries will show the person's most recent Facebook wall posts or tweets.

You should repeat this tip every few months to keep up to date with the latest contact photos.

Tip 65

Get free stuff from Apple

Apple is understandably keen to have its customers try new things, so frequently gives away commercially sold apps, ebooks, music, and videos. It does this in two ways—via its Apple Store app and in the Christmas/New Year period via its 12 Days of Xmas app. Both are available in the App Store.

To see what if anything is available in the Apple Store app, just tap the first icon on the toolbar then look within the list for any free offers. Tapping an offer will show some details of the item, and a link that will open the App Store or iTunes Store app with a voucher code already filled in—just tap the Redeem button, which will complete the "purchase" and download and install the item.

The 12 Days of Xmas app exists only to offer a free gift for the 12 days after Christmas, and activating the app each day during that period will again show a link that—when tapped—opens the App Store or iTunes Store app with a filled-in voucher code.

It's a good policy never to turn down a free app, even if you don't have enough room on your device—see Tip 212, *Get free apps even if your device doesn't have the space*, on page 191.

Tip 66

View the number of items on your iPad/iPhone via iTunes

You can use the Settings app on your iPad or iPhone to see how many apps, photos, movies, and songs you have, but getting to the information can be cumbersome and involve quite a lot of tapping.

If you sync the iPad or iPhone to iTunes running on your computer, you can discover the same info in a much more accessible way (see the following figure). To do so, attach your iPad or iPhone to your computer or ensure the two are on the same network if you've configured Wi-Fi syncing, then open iTunes and select the device in the drop-down list at the top right of the screen. Select the Summary tab and move the mouse to the bar chart at the bottom, which shows how much space is occupied. Hover the mouse over each section to see a pop-up display showing the number of items in each category.

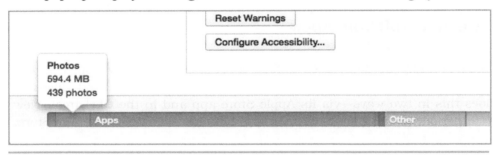

Figure 34—Viewing the number of apps via iTunes on a Mac computer

Tip 67

Store PDFs

The iBooks app, which you can install for free via the App Store, can also act as a library for any PDF files you receive via email or iMessage or that you find on websites. Tap to download the PDF if you haven't already, then tap and hold the file icon (or the preview of the document if one is shown). Select Open in iBooks from the list of choices that appears. The file will instantly be added to iBooks's virtual shelves, and you can access it in the future by selecting it there.

Note that PDFs get their own virtual bookcase (separate from that for ebooks). Swipe left or right to switch between the bookcases, or tap the drop-down heading at the top of the screen and select PDFs from the list.

Tip 68

Repeat calendar events on the first or last day of each month

The Calendar app lets you create events that repeat periodically on particular days in the month, but it doesn't let you repeat events on the first Friday of each month, for example, or the last Saturday—dates that can vary depending on which month it is.

For Windows PC users who use iCloud to synchronize and back up data, the solution is to visit the iCloud website using a Windows PC and use its browser interface to access your calendar, as follows:[8]

1. Log in at the iCloud website using your Apple ID, then click the Calendar icon.

2. Click the plus sign (+) at the bottom right to add a new calendar event.

3. Fill in the calendar events as you would normally on an iPhone or iPad. In the Repeat drop-down list, select Custom.

4. In the new dialog box that appears, click the Monthly tab, then at the bottom click the radio button alongside "On the" and select on which day you'd like the event to repeat.

5. Click OK when done.

If you have a Mac but don't have it logged into iCloud, you can also follow the preceding instructions to visit the iCloud website. However, if you have a Mac computer that's logged into the same iCloud account as your device, start the Calendar app, switch to month view by clicking the tab at the top of the program window, then double-click on the first day you wish the event to happen to create a new event. This will open a dialog box where you can edit the event, after which you should follow the preceding list from step 2 onward (note that you should click the Frequency drop-down and select Month instead of clicking a tab option).

---

8. https://icloud.com

Tip 69

Activate Siri using your headphones

If your iPhone earbuds are plugged into either an iPhone or iPad, you can activate Siri by clicking and holding the middle of the in-line remote, just like you would click and hold the Home button.

Tip 70

Save time when typing numbers and symbols

The usual method for typing numbers or symbols is to tap the corresponding button on the onscreen keyboard—the key marked either `123` or `.?123`—and then type, before tapping the `ABC` button to return to the standard QWERTY keyboard. However, to save time if you want to type a single number or symbol, tap and hold the symbol and number button and then slide your finger or thumb up to the number or symbol you want without lifting it. Then release your finger. This will type the number or symbol and return the keyboard to the standard QWERTY keyboard, removing the need to switch back manually.

Tip 71

Create fancy email signatures

A *signature* is text automatically added to the end of email messages you create. It can save you typing your name each time, but the default signature is "Sent from my iPhone" or "Sent from my iPad." To change this if you haven't already, open the Settings app, then tap the Mail, Contacts, Calendars heading and tap Signature. Tap the text and edit it or delete it if you don't want a signature to appear. By tapping Per Account if you have more than one email account set up, you can use a different signature for each.

A little-known fact is that signatures can include text formatting such as bold and italics. To use such formatting, type some text then highlight it and select the BIU icon (for "bold, italics, underline") from the pop-up menu that appears; you may need to tap the right arrow on the pop-up menu to see this option.

Signatures within the Mail app can also include hyperlinks, but there's no way to add them when typing an email signature in Settings. Instead you must copy the hyperlink from a website or email by highlighting the link text and tapping Copy on the menu that appears, and then pasting it into the signature field within the Settings app. The full text and underlying link are pasted in and work as a link when your email recipients click or tap it.

One of the simplest ways of creating a complex signature involving formatting and hyperlinks is to create a new email message containing the signature, then send it to yourself and open the email on your iPhone to copy the signature for pasting into the signature field of the Settings app as described previously. Note that any text coloring is stripped out when the text is pasted. This means iOS email signatures can only be black text against a white background.

Although the Settings app allows you to paste images copied from apps such as Photos into the signature field, in my tests the images weren't attached to any email messages I sent.

Tip 72

Remotely view the remaining charge of your Apple devices

Ever wanted to know what battery charge is remaining in your iPad without finding it and checking? Or on your iPhone? If the device is registered with the Find My iPhone/iPad service, you can use the Find My iPhone app or visit the iCloud website on a Mac or Windows PC to see this detail.[9] You'll also see the battery life of any MacBook computers you've registered.

Start Find My iPhone or visit the page at https://icloud.com and click the Find My iPhone button, and wait for it to locate your equipment. Then do one of the following:

- iCloud website: Click the All Devices heading at the top and select the device for which you want to view the battery life.

- iPhone: Select the device from the list in the lower half of the screen.

- iPad: Tap the My Devices heading at the top left, then tap the device for which you want to view the battery life.

---

9.   https://icloud.com

In each case, the map will scroll to show the location, and at the top right of the screen will be a battery symbol showing how much charge is left or a symbol indicating that the device is attached to its charger. See the figure for an example from the iCloud website.

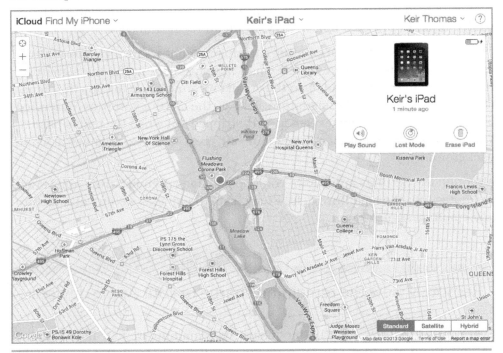

Figure 35—Remotely viewing an iPad's battery charge

Tip 73

Why can't I use a tune with iMovie?!

When attempting to insert a track in an iMovie project you might find that it simply won't show the insertion icon. What's going on? One of two things is probably happening:

- You've purchased the song but haven't downloaded it to your device. To remedy this, open the Music app, locate the song, then tap the iCloud-download icon alongside it.

- The song has been purchased via iTunes and is protected by digital rights management, which means it can't be inserted into a creative project. Unfortunately, there's no way around this other than to acquire the song from a different source (ripping it from a CD via iTunes, for example).

Copy contact photos

Ever wanted to add a photo of friend or colleague to an email or message—perhaps if you're setting up two friends on a blind date? If you already have a picture of an individual within your address book, iOS makes it easy. Just go to the entry within the Contacts app for the person concerned, then tap and hold his photograph until a pop-up menu appears. Tap Copy. Then switch to the Messages or email app and, where you want the picture to appear, double-tap so another pop-up menu appears. Tap Paste.

It's unlikely the picture will be of very high resolution—so printing a large copy probably won't work very well—but it should be enough for the recipient to see what the person looks like.

This process also works in reverse, meaning you can paste a photograph into a person's entry within your address book. Just open the Photos app and copy a relevant photo, then go to the desired entry in the Contacts app and tap Edit before tapping and holding the circle where the photo should appear, and tapping Paste. This works even if the individual's entry in your contacts book already has a photo.

See also Tip 64, *Import contact photos from Facebook and Twitter*, on page 94, to learn how to quickly and easily populate your contacts list with photos!

Send map locations from iPad to iPhone

Ever looked up a location on your iPad, then wanted to view it on your iPhone so you could create a walking or driving route? One way to do this is to add the location as a bookmark and then wait a few seconds for the two devices to sync via iCloud. However, this means your bookmarks list can become cluttered, and it won't work if you don't use iCloud.

Instead, try the following:

1. On the iPad, tap and hold the location within the Maps app so that a pin is dropped.

2. Tap the Share icon at the bottom of the screen when viewing the location and—if prompted—tap Selected Location on the menu that appears.

3. If both the iPad and the iPhone are compatible with AirDrop and have the feature activated, tap the AirDrop icon and select the iPhone in the list.

4. If either of the devices isn't AirDrop-compatible, on the menu that appears select the Message icon and type your own iMessage address (or phone number) into the address field and tap Send.

5. Once the AirDropped location or the new message has been received on the iPhone, tap the Dropped Pin preview. This will open the location in a map window that, although it looks like the Maps app, isn't the real thing.

6. Tap the (i) icon in the pop-out balloon. Then tap the Map URL link on the next screen. This will open the location within the Maps app.

Tip 76

Tap to shrink Control Center

You can make Control Center appear by dragging upward from the bottom of the screen, but to make it disappear you don't necessarily have to drag it down again. Instead you can tap the small triangular handle at the top of Control Center, which will cause it to retract immediately. Unfortunately, this trick doesn't work with the notification area, which must be dragged upward just as it was dragged down in the first place!

Tip 77

Bow strings in GarageBand

GarageBand offers a variety of ways to play its stringed orchestra instruments, but at the most basic you can go it alone with a fingerboard as if playing the real thing—just tap the Notes button at the top right to activate it (on the iPhone tap the dial icon at the top right first). With the fingerboard onscreen, tapping a string plays it as if it were being bowed, but what if you want to emulate the technique of *spiccato*, where the bow is quickly bounced off the string, making a short bowed noise?

GarageBand has you covered. Just tap and hold the metal plate at the top of the neck. This usually activates pizzicato mode (that is, where tapping an onscreen string plucks it) but if you brush your fingers across a string you'll hear a spiccato sound. But beware: it takes a little practice to get right!

Tip 78

Less obvious things to say to Siri

Siri can do and answer more than you might think. Try the following:

- "What's trending on Twitter?" (Also try asking what one of your Twitter friends is saying.)
- "Roll dice." (Also try "Flip a coin" or "Pick a number between 1 and 5000.")
- "Turn off Bluetooth."
- "Make the screen brighter."
- "How much is $500 in Euros?"
- "What day was April 3rd, 1973?"
- "Stop navigation."
- "What's in my inbox?" (Also "Check email.")
- "Find images of London."
- "Post to Facebook." (Or Twitter.)
- "Write on my wall: Arrived home OK" or "Tweet: Arrived home OK."
- "What does the rest of my day look like?"
- "Play more songs like this one!"
- "What planes are above me right now?"
- "How long is *The Empire Strikes Back*?"
- "Take me to John Smith." (This assumes that both you and John Smith are using the Find My Friends app.)
- "What type of Pokémon is Pikachu?"

- "Take a picture." (This will only launch the Camera app, but you can then take a picture using the volume buttons—useful if you're wearing old-fashioned gloves and can't tap the screen!)

- "How much should I tip on $76?"

Tip 79

Access a hidden "field test" iPhone mode

iPhones contain a hidden engineering test mode that reports technical details about the cellular connection. You can access it by opening the Phone app, switching to the keypad, then typing *3001#12345#* before tapping the Call button.

Most of the details presented are too obscure for the nontechnical layperson to understand, and the level of detail you see depends on what your carrier configures its network to report. Perhaps the most useful feature is that the signal-strength blobs at the top left of the screen are replaced by the received strength indicator figure, measured in decibels per milliwatt. In simple terms, this shows the strength of the cellular signal in negative figures, with a larger number indicating a stronger signal—so -60 is better than -104, for example. The scale is also exponential, which again means larger numbers indicate significantly stronger signal strengths. The very strongest signal will be in the order of -40 to -60dBm. (If you don't see the signal figure, try tapping the signal bars at the top of the screen, which will cycle between bars and signal dBm strength indicator.)

Switching away from the field-test app will automatically cause it to quit.

Tip 80

Lock out notifications while using an app

The Do Not Disturb feature of iOS lets you suspend incoming phone calls, messages, and Notification Center updates. But it's meant to be used for long periods, such as while you're sleeping. It's not the right tool if you want to play a game for 20 minutes without being disturbed, for example. For that you can use a component of iOS's useful Guided Access tool to "lock" the phone to a particular app so that nothing can disturb you while you're using it. You just have to remember to repeat the trick afterward to unlock the app!

Here's how to set it up:

1. Open the Settings app, then tap the General heading, and then scroll down to Accessibility.

2. Scroll to the bottom of the list and tap Guided Access before tapping the switch alongside the Guided Access heading on the next page.

3. Activate the Accessibility Shortcut switch beneath this. Once done, quit the Settings app.

To turn on the lock feature for an app you're using, triple-click the Home button, then carefully tap the Start button at the top right of the screen, being sure not to tap anywhere else on the screen. The first time you do this you'll be prompted to set a passcode for Guided Access, which is the function you're using to make this happen. Reusing the same passcode as the one you set for the iOS lock screen is fine.

Once the app is locked you won't be able to switch out of it, or even turn off the phone, without triple-clicking Home again, entering the passcode you typed earlier, and tapping the End button.

Beware that this feature really will turn off other features of your iPad or iPhone. You won't be able to alter the volume, for example, and incoming calls will be sent straight to voicemail.

To permanently deactivate this feature, repeat the preceding steps to access the Guided Access settings, but this time tap the switch to deactivate it.

Tip 81

Print to any printer connected to a Mac or Windows PC

In order to print from iPads and iPhones, you'll need a printer compatible with AirPrint. As its name suggests, AirPrint prints over Wi-Fi to compatible printers on the same network. More and more new printers are compatible, but this isn't much help if your existing printer isn't, or if you happen to have just bought a printer that isn't compatible!

Luckily there's a solution—you can install software on PCs or Macs that emulates AirPlay, making it possible to print to any printer attached via USB.

Of course, for this to work you'll need to ensure the Mac or Windows PC is turned on before you print.

Setting Up Mac AirPrint

Adding AirPrint to any Mac with a printer connected by USB or Wi-Fi is simple. Start by downloading and installing the latest version of handyPrint.[10] Once it's installed, open System Preferences, then click the handyPrint entry under the Other heading at the bottom. Click the slider to On.

Note that handyPrint comes with a trial period, after which you're invited to make a donation by clicking the License button in the bottom left of the handyPrint dialog box. Deciding the donation amount is up to you, although apps with similar functionality on a Mac cost $5-10.

To uninstall handyPrint, right-click the icon in System Preferences and select Remove handyPrint Preference Pane.

Setting Up PC AirPrint

Here's how to share a printer attached to a Windows PC so iPads and iPhones can use it. These instructions are written for Windows 7.

1. Ensure that the latest version of iTunes is installed. You'll find it at http://www.apple.com/itunes/download/. You should also install Apple's Bonjour Printer Services, if you haven't already—do this using Apple Software Update, which installs alongside iTunes, or by clicking the link at the right of this Apple support page: www.apple.com/support/bonjour/.

2. Share the printer on the network by clicking the Start button, then Devices and Printers. Right-click the printer you want to AirPrint to and select Printer Properties from the menu. Then select the Sharing tab and ensure there's a check mark alongside Share This Printer.

3. Download and install Presto from www.collobos.com. This comes with a free trial that watermarks any pages it prints. To remove the watermarking, you'll need to subscribe to the software for $1.95 per month.

4. Once Presto is installed it will automatically share any printer attached to the PC for AirPrint, but running the program will let you choose which printers you want to share. Presto runs in the background, so there's no need for the main program window to be open in order to print.

---

10. www.netputing.com/handyprint

You can uninstall Presto in the usual way using the Uninstall a Program feature of Control Panel.

Printing from an iPad or iPhone

After ensuring the Mac or Windows PC sharing the printer is turned on, tap the share button on the toolbar of the app you want to print from, then tap the Print button and tap Select Printer. The printer attached to your Mac or Windows PC will appear. Tap to select it, then tap Print.

Tip 82

Prune your contacts list without going insane

Over time you'll find your contact list grows and grows, because any email address you reply to is automatically added.

Pruning contacts on your iPad or iPhone is an involved procedure—after opening the Contacts app, you must find the contact, then tap the Edit button, the scroll down to the very bottom of the listing where there's a Delete Contact button.

The solution is to visit the iCloud website using a Mac or Windows PC (assuming you've activated iCloud syncing of contacts) then log in with your Apple ID.[11] Click the Contacts icon, then hold down Ctrl (Cmd on a Mac) while selecting entries you want to delete. When you've made your selection, click the cog icon at the bottom and tap the Delete button.

Beware that you can't undo a deletion—there's no Trash for your contacts.

Tip 83

Transfer photos from a Mac or Windows PC

Upon purchasing an iPad or iPhone you own one of the best digital photo frames in existence—not only can you show pictures in high definition to others (and in award-winning color accuracy!), but you can also edit them to a very high standard with apps like iPhoto. Because of this you might choose to transfer photos from your Mac or Windows PC to your iPad or iPhone. The following are the easiest ways of doing so.

---

11. https://icloud.com

Syncing Photos on a Mac or Windows PC

iTunes can sync with your iPad or iPhone photos contained within a particular folder on your Mac or Windows PC, or photos within the libraries of certain apps (the Mac version of iPhoto, or Aperture, Photoshop Elements, and others).

To do so, attach the iPad or iPhone via USB (or ensure it's within range if you have Wi-Fi syncing activated), then select it from the list of devices at the top right of the iTunes window. Click the Photos tab at the top right of the iTunes window, put a check mark alongside Sync Photos From, and choose the application or folder from the drop-down list. Depending on the app you choose, you'll be able to select between syncing all photos (which will likely eat a lot of storage space on your device) and syncing selected albums or folders. Note that you may have to check any Albums or Events entries beneath this listing.

When you're finished, click the Apply button at the bottom right, which will immediately sync the photos to the device. If you leave the Sync Photos box checked, every time you sync your device in the usual way, any new photos that have been imported into the app or folders you chose will be synced automatically.

After the sync, you can find the photos on the device within the Photos app, in a new album named after the event or album.

Transferring Photos to iPhoto via iTunes

If you have iPhoto installed on your iPad or iPhone and you use iTunes to sync with the device, you can follow these steps to import pictures directly into iPhoto's library.

To do so, attach the iPad or iPhone via USB (or ensure it's within range if you have Wi-Fi syncing activated), then follow these steps:

1. Click the Apps heading, then scroll down to the File Sharing heading near the bottom.

2. In the list of apps beneath the File Sharing heading, click iPhoto.

3. On the right of the screen, in the box marked iPhoto Documents, drag and drop from your hard disk any photos that you want to put on your iPad or iPhone.

4. On the iPad or iPhone, open iPhoto. If it's already running, temporarily switch away to the home screen, then switch back to the app.

5. You'll see a dialog box on the iPad or iPhone saying that iTunes wants to import some pictures. Click the Import button to start the process going.

6. The image will open immediately for editing, but will be listed in a special album called iTunes.

Tip 84

Use the Calculator app's scientific mode

The iPhone's Calculator app has a hidden scientific mode, offering many more math functions. To access it, rotate your phone to landscape mode (assuming you haven't activated rotation lock via Control Center). See the following figure for an example. You can access even more math functions in scientific mode by tapping the button marked "2nd" at the top left, which will switch some of the existing buttons to show related functions.

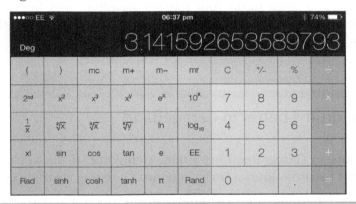

Figure 36—Accessing the Calculator app's scientific mode

Tip 85

Read manuals online

Apple is renowned for its "unboxing experience," and to keep things simple the company doesn't include full manuals. That isn't to say manuals aren't available, though. Just visit http://support.apple.com/manuals/ipad/ and http://support.apple.com/manuals/iphone/ for detailed iPad and iPhone manuals, respectively.

Drop pins even when driving a route

Have you ever walked or driven somewhere using a route worked out by the Maps app, yet seen something interesting along the way and wanted to make a note of its location? The usual method of noting a place on a map is to drop a pin by tapping and holding the relevant spot; unfortunately, this won't work when you're following route-planning directions.

The solution is to temporarily switch to the route-overview mode. On an iPad tap the Overview link at the top right, then tap the option; on an iPhone tap the screen once until the End and Overview options drop down from the top of the screen, then tap the option.

In overview mode the Maps app works like usual—you can use the pinch-to-expand gesture to zoom in on your current location, then tap and hold to drop the pin. Once you've finished, tap Resume at the top right of the screen to return to navigation mode.

Play the drums better in GarageBand

The drum kits in GarageBand are undoubtedly one of the app's most fun elements, but two little-known tricks can make creating rhythms even easier.

- Two-finger rhythms: Tap and hold a drum or cymbal with two fingers, and a repeating pattern will be played (usually quarter notes). Moving your fingers apart will increase the rhythm of the pattern, making it easy to create a snare roll, for example (the technique offering most control is to leave one finger stationary and move the other away from it). Moving your fingers up or down on the screen will increase or decrease the volume.

- Tap different parts of the drum: Some drums and cymbals will make different sounds depending on where you tap them. Tap the hi-hat at the left, for example, and you'll hear an open hi-hat sound. Tap at the right, and you'll hear a closed hi-hat sound. The snare drum has three sounds—tapping the rim plays a rimshot; taping the left of the skin plays a rimshot mixed with a snare; tapping the main skin area creates the usual snare sound.

- Touch sensitivity: The harder you hit a drum or cymbal, the louder it'll sound. This lets you introduce all kinds of nuances into your performance.

Tip 88

Use Bluetooth or Wi-Fi even in airplane mode

As explained in *Control Center*, on page 34, airplane mode switches off all radio communications on your iPad or iPhone—cellular, Wi-Fi, and Bluetooth. However, perhaps surprisingly, even when airplane mode is active, you can tap the Wi-Fi and Bluetooth switches within Control Center or the Settings app to reactivate those features. This means you can work using a Bluetooth keyboard on an iPad during a flight, for example, or connect to the in-flight Wi-Fi. There is no way of reactivating cellular services, however, other than turning off airplane mode.

Another use for activating Wi-Fi during a flight is to make FaceTime audio or video calls—remember that FaceTime calls happen over the Internet, and not the cellular network!

Tip 89

Save and share iWork files with WebDAV

WebDAV is a way of storing files online and is supported by the iWork apps. If you don't want to use iCloud but you do want to be able to access your iWork files on other computers and with other users, then it's a potentially useful solution. There are some caveats: WebDAV isn't as seamless as iCloud, where files are synchronized automatically, and you'll need to manually copy files back onto the WebDAV server each time you make edits, for example.

Uploading and Downloading from WebDAV

To use WebDAV you'll need an Internet-accessible WebDAV server. If you rent web space for websites, then you may already have WebDAV facilities that you can activate, but you can also purchase WebDAV-only packages. WebDAV includes no security features, so when looking for a WebDAV host you should select one that offers HTTP Secure (HTTPS) access.

- Downloading from WebDAV: Assuming the document has been saved onto a WebDAV server from a desktop computer or another iPad/iPhone, open the documents view in the iWork app, then tap the plus (+) icon at the top left. Then select Copy from WebDAV. This will open a dialog box requesting the server address, username, and password. You'll then see a listing of available files. Selecting any will copy it to your device for editing. There are a couple of important notes:

  – You've now created a copy of the original file on the server, which will join any other documents on your device and be synced with iCloud (if you have iCloud activated, of course). Any changes you make to the document won't automatically get synced with the WebDAV server.

  – Files in Microsoft Office or LibreOffice/OpenOffice file formats will automatically be converted to iWork's native file formats. This can cause problems if the file is password protected, and you may need to ask the file's author to reopen the file on a desktop computer, remove the password protection, and save again.

  – Once you've logged into WebDAV you'll stay logged in until you tap the Sign Out button in the WebDAV browser, which you can access as discussed previously, on the main Documents screen.

- Uploading to WebDAV: If you've made changes to a file and want to share it once again on the WebDAV server, or you've created a document from scratch that you want to share, open the document for editing and tap the share button at the top right on the iPad, or the Settings button (the icon is a wrench), and then Share and Print on the menu that appears on an iPhone. Then tap Send a Copy, after which you should tap the WebDAV icon. You'll be prompted for a format in which to save the file. Once you do it'll be converted, and you should tap the Send button to upload it.

Accessing WebDAV on a Mac or Windows PC

You can easily access WebDAV servers on Mac or Windows PC, as follows:

- Mac: Click the Finder icon in the Dock, then click Go > Connect to Server on the menu. Fill in the server address in the dialog box that appears (ensuring you precede the address with http or https, as appropriate). Then type your username and password when prompted. The WebDAV server will be added as an entry under the Shared heading of Finder, as when accessing a file server on the local network. You can disconnect by hovering the mouse over the icon and clicking Eject.

• Windows 7: Download and install Microsoft's Software Folders add-in,[12] then open file explorer and click Map Network Drive on the top toolbar. Mapping a network drive is like inserting a USB memory stick, in that the contents of the server will be available via a drive letter in file explorer. Therefore you'll need to select a drive letter from the drop-down list, then in the Folder field type the address of the server, including the http or https component. Put a check mark alongside Connect Using Different Credentials, then click Finish. A username and password field will appear, and when you've finished typing you'll be shown the WebDAV server contents. To disconnect, right-click the drive's entry in the Computer listing and select Delete from the menu that appears.

Tip 90

Move shapes or images precisely in iWork

Although you can move shapes, text boxes, and images in the iWork apps by tapping and then dragging, moving them precisely can be a challenge—in part because our fingers can be a little too fat and uncoordinated.

The solution is to tap and hold the image with one finger, and with another finger (or perhaps a finger on your other hand) swipe left, right, up, or down to move the image 1 pixel in those directions.

Tip 91

Use Siri to plan a route in Google Maps

Tip 256, *Get transit directions*, on page 219, explains how Siri can summon the Google Maps application, which is available in the App Store. Essentially, all you need do is ask Siri for directions to somewhere but add "via transit" or similar. The built-in Maps app is currently unable to provide transit directions, so Siri offers the choice of another app, such as Google Maps, and then passes the route information to it when you've made your choice.

---

12. http://www.microsoft.com/downloads/details.aspx?FamilyId=17C36612-632E-4C04-9382-987622ED1D64

Of course, when Siri switches to Google Maps you don't have to select the suggested transit route, and can instead tap the icons for either walking or driving, meaning that asking Siri for transit directions is actually a neat way of getting it to start Google Maps with the route already programmed into it.

Tip 92

Dial a voicemail PIN or phone extension automatically

Wouldn't it be useful if you could have your iPhone call an automated switchboard service, wait a few seconds for the call to be answered, then dial the required extension or a PIN automatically? Your iPhone can do this, or it can display a button during a call that—when tapped—will enter a PIN or extension, which can be useful for automated switchboards that have varying greetings that you can't predict.

Entering Voicemail PINs Automatically

Here's how to make your iPhone automatically enter a voicemail PIN. Although these instructions discuss voicemail services, this should work for any service that requires you to enter a PIN. Obviously, this represents a security risk because this effectively removes the voicemail security protection for anybody who has access to your phone. Remember, depending on how Siri is configured it's possible to make calls without first unlocking the phone.

1. Find out the direct-dial number for your voicemail service by searching online or calling your carrier (or see the first step of Tip 101, *Divert all iPhone calls straight to voicemail*, on page 121, to see how to discover it on an iPhone).

2. Open the Contacts app and tap the plus (+) button at the top right to create a new contact. In the First Name field, type Voicemail.

3. Tap the Add Phone entry, then enter on the keypad the direct-dial number for your voicemail service.

4. When you've finished typing the number, tap the `+*#` key at the bottom left. This will reveal new options on the keypad. The two we're interested in are Pause (on the left) and Wait (on the right). Pause will cause the iPhone to wait two seconds during calls before dialing the PIN, and Wait will show a button during the call, which, when tapped, will dial the PIN.

5. Tap whichever choice you want. If you tap Pause, a comma will appear after the number. If you tap Wait, a semicolon will appear after the number. Type the PIN straight afterward, and don't forget to add the pound symbol (#) at the end if your voicemail service requires it to confirm entry (to access the pound key you'll again need to tap +*#). See the figure here for an example from an iPhone.

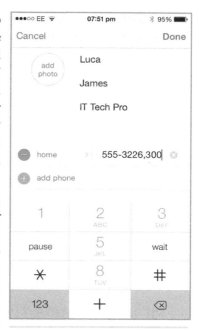

Figure 37—Entering a pause and extension number in a contact card on an iPhone

In the future just select the Voicemail entry in your contacts link to connect to voicemail. If you find the PIN is dialed too soon, repeat the preceding steps and choose to edit the new contact, this time pressing the Pause button twice (inserting two commas). This will cause the phone to pause for four seconds before dialing the PIN. Pressing Pause three times when editing the contact will cause the phone to pause for six seconds, and so on.

Because Siri associates the word "voicemail" with the feature of your iPhone to check the number of messages, if you wish to use Siri to autodial and autoenter the PIN for your voicemail, then you should choose a different title for the contact. The title is up to you, but bear in mind that Siri recognizes words like "messages" too.

Auto-entering Extension Numbers

Here's how to have your iPhone automatically enter an extension number for automated phone systems.

1. If you already have an entry in your address book for the phone number, open it within the Contacts app, and then tap the Edit button at the top right of the screen.

2. Tap the end of the phone number so the cursor is positioned after the numbers, then tap the +*# button at the bottom left of the numeric keypad that appears.

3. This will show two new buttons—Pause and Wait. Assuming the number you're dialing has an automated operator that lets you dial the extension

as soon as the call is answered, tap the Wait button. You'll notice a comma appears after the number (see the following figure).

4. Type the extension number, followed by the pound sign (#) if it's required by the automated system to confirm entry (to access the pound key you'll again need to tap +*#).

5. Tap Done to save the contact.

Try dialing the new contact. You'll find that the number is dialed as usual, after which the phone pauses for two seconds before dialing the extension number. If two seconds isn't long enough, edit the contact again and add another pause between the number and the extension (that is, so that two commas are inserted). This will pause for four seconds. Three pauses inserted will pause for six seconds, and so on. If the time interval is unpredictable, tap Wait instead of Pause when editing the number. This will cause a button to appear during the call, which will dial the extension number when you tap it.

Incidentally, you can insert pauses and waits when dialing numbers straight from the keypad in the Phone app. Just tap and hold the star (*) button to insert a pause, which will again appear as a comma, and tap and hold the pound key to insert a wait, which will appear as a semicolon. Follow each with the PIN or extension number.

Tip 93

Take long and tall shots using Panorama mode

A secret feature of the Panorama mode within the Camera app is that it works for more than panoramas! Hold the camera in landscape mode, and you can use the Panorama feature to photograph things that are tall, such as Big Ben, the Leaning Tower of Pisa, or a tall friend!

Activate the Panorama mode by swiping down until PANO is highlighted, then point the camera at the top of the subject. Tap the shutter-release button in the usual way to start the photograph, and pan the camera downward until you've taken in the whole subject.

Alternatively, to start from the bottom and pan upward, tap the arrow to make Panorama mode switch directions (see Tip 60, *Move from right to left when taking a panorama shot*, on page 92).

Tip 94

Take photos like you would with a point-and-shoot camera

When taking photos or recording movies you don't have to tap the button on the screen to take a photo or start/stop recording. Instead, press either of the volume-control buttons, which will do the same thing. This can make for steadier, less blurry photos, and makes using an iPhone held in portrait mode more like using a regular camera—just point and click!

Burst mode also works when using the volume buttons—see Tip 1, *Take photos in burst mode*, on page 53.

Tip 95

Use Bluetooth devices

You can use a variety of Bluetooth add-ons with your iPad and iPhone. Using a Bluetooth keyboard with an iPad turns it into a very useful laptop replacement for office work, for example, while using a Bluetooth headset is a necessity if using your iPhone while driving. Unfortunately, the only common Bluetooth item you can't use is a mouse—iOS is touch-only!

To add a Bluetooth device, start by setting it into discovery mode. The process varies from device to device—you may need to hold a certain key combination on a keyboard, for example, but many devices have a small recessed button specifically for the purpose. Sometimes this is hidden within the battery compartment.

Once the device is in discovery mode, open the Settings app and tap the Bluetooth heading. Switch Bluetooth on, if it isn't already on, by tapping the onscreen switch. Once you do this your iPad or iPhone will start searching for nearby devices.

When your device appears in the list, tap it and then respond to any onscreen queries. You may need to type a passcode on a Bluetooth keyboard, for example (don't forget to press Enter at the end!). See Figure 38, *Setting up a Bluetooth keyboard on an iPad*, on page 118 for an example.

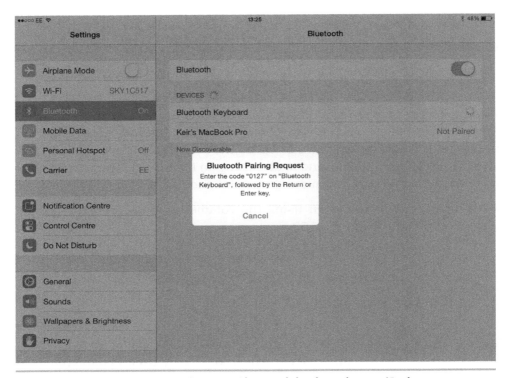

Figure 38—Setting up a Bluetooth keyboard on an iPad

Once you've added a device in this way, it'll work in the future automatically whenever it's in range and switched on.

To remove a device so that automatic connection doesn't happen, open the Bluetooth section of the Settings app, tap the (i) button alongside the device's entry in the list, and tap Forget This Device.

Tip 96

Easily type capital letters when needed

Usually we type capital letters by tapping Shift (⇧) on the onscreen keyboard, and then a letter. However, there are other methods, as follows:

- Use one finger to tap and hold the ⇧ key, and another finger to tap the letter—rather like when typing on a standard keyboard. Obviously, this can be difficult on the small screen of an iPhone!

- Tap and hold the ⇧ key, then *without lifting your finger* slide it across the screen to the letter you want to be capitalized. When you lift your finger the capitalized letter will be typed.

- Activate Caps Lock mode, as described in Tip 161, *Type in all capital letters*, on page 160.

Tip 97

Undo photo edits—even after you've saved them

Photo editing in iOS 7 is nondestructive, which is to say a copy of the original is kept alongside the edited version. This means that if you crop an image during editing, for example, the part you've deleted sticks around in case you want to restore it in the future. Try this now—open a picture in the Photos app, tap Edit, then use the Crop tool. Save the image, quit the Photos app, then open it again and repeat the steps so you're using the Crop tool—you'll see the part of the image you removed is still there, and you can restore it by dragging the edges of the crop box over it.

The same applies to using the Auto-Enhance tool or filters while editing a photo—they can all be turned on and then turned off, even after a photo has been saved back to the camera roll.

Tip 98

Add words to the spelling dictionary

Like most computing devices, your iPad or iPhone will underline in red any words it thinks are misspelled. Unlike with most computers, however, you can't tap a word that's actually correct in order to have it added to the dictionary. iOS simply doesn't allow this.

You may have noticed that iOS doesn't underline the names of your contacts as being misspelled, no matter how strangely their names might be spelled. This is because it automatically adds the names on Contact cards to its spelling dictionary, and you can exploit this function to create a personal dictionary of odd words you use frequently that would otherwise confuse iOS.

Choose one of your contacts at random in the Contacts app and tap Edit at the top right. Scroll down and tap the Add Field box and, in the list that appears, tap Notes. Then, in the new Notes field, type all the words that you want your iPhone to learn, as the following figure shows.

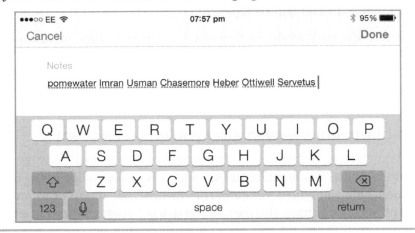

Figure 39—Creating a personal spelling dictionary on an iPhone

This can include people's names, proper nouns, swear words, vernacular, or just about anything. Once you've finished, tap the Done button. The new Notes entry added to the contact won't affect anything else and will be essentially invisible in everyday use.

Your iPad or iPhone will now consider the words you added as unquestionable whenever you're typing in any application. In fact, it will even attempt to autocomplete them, just like it does with other words!

Tip 99

Help iOS type contractions ("we'll," "I'll," and so on)

iOS is keen to help when you're typing and sometimes will automatically correct "well" to "we'll," for example, or "ill" to "I'll." If you actually meant to type "well" or "ill" this can be annoying. On the other hand, iOS has an uncanny knack for *not* autocorrecting "well" to "we'll" when that's what you actually want!

Forcing Contractions

Continuing with our example, should you find yourself typing "ill" with the hope of it being autocorrected to "I'll," and you find iOS doesn't fix it for you, simply type an extra l at the end: "illl." Then tap the `Space` key. This gives iOS a sufficient clue that you want "I'll." The same applies for "we'll"—typing "welll" followed by space will make iOS substitute "we'll."

Refusing Contractions

Again continuing the example, if you type "well" and find iOS wants to auto-correct it to "we'll" against your wishes, you can simply tap the autocorrect pop-out. This will cancel the autocorrection.

However, if you don't want to move your fingers from the keyboard area, just type an extra l at the end—"welll"—then *delete the last "l" and tap the* `Space` *key*. This is enough to tell iOS not to autocorrect the word.

Tip 100

Let people iMessage a specific iPad, iPhone, or Mac

Tip 3, *Let people FaceTime-call a specific iPad, iPhone, or Mac*, on page 54, explains how you can configure your iPad, iPhone, or Mac so that people can FaceTime-call that specific device without having the call "ring" on all your Apple devices and Macs. With a little adaptation, you can apply the same trick to iMessage.

Select Messages instead of FaceTime within the Settings app during the setup steps of the aforementioned tip, and select the Send & Receive heading to assign a specific email address or cell-phone number for iMessage.

Once the individual has created the new contact specific for your device, as described in the earlier tip, she can send an iMessage specifically to it by starting a new message and then typing the contact name (for instance, "Keir Thomas iPad" or "Keir Thomas Mac").

Tip 101

Divert all iPhone calls straight to voicemail

If you don't want to be bothered by phone calls, you can use your iPhone's call-forwarding feature to divert them straight to voicemail. Here's how:

1. Open the Phone app and switch to the keypad by tapping the icon at the bottom. Then dial *#67# and tap the Call button.

2. This will display data about call-forwarding settings for your carrier, but at the top will be the number that voicemail calls are forwarded to. Make a note of this.

3. Tap the Dismiss button, then open the Settings app and tap the Phone heading.

4. Tap Call Forwarding, then tap the switch to activate the feature, tap the Forward To heading, then type the voicemail number you noted earlier. A new icon will appear to the right of the Wi-Fi symbol in the status bar at the top of the screen, indicating that call forwarding is now in operation.

Note that Verizon users might not see a Call Forwarding option within the Settings app. However, Verizon offer a special call-forwarding service you can use.[13]

Should you wish to completely deactivate your iPhone's ability to receive calls—essentially turning it into a high-spec iPod Touch—you can forward calls to an unobtainable number, such as those beginning with 555 used in movies.

Don't forget to repeat the preceding steps to disable call forwarding when you wish to receive calls again.

Tip 102

Apply EQ to individual tracks or albums

Although you can set overall audio equalization (EQ) for music or audio tracks played through the iPad or iPhone (see the Music heading within the Settings app), you can't set EQ for individual tracks. You might wish to do this if you play mixed playlists featuring heavy rap as well as folk acoustic, for example—one might benefit from bass boost, while the other won't!

If you sync your iPad or iPhone with iTunes on a computer, however, you can individually set the EQ for either individual tracks or a selection of tracks, such as a complete album. When you sync, the settings will be carried across and will override the global EQ setting for the device (if one has been set).

To do this, right-click any track within iTunes on your computer, or use Ctrl /Shift (⇧) to select a handful before right-clicking one of them, then select Get Info. Ensure the Options tab is selected in the dialog box that appears,

13. https://insidersguide.vzw.com/tech-smarts/verizon-call-forwarding/

and select whichever EQ setting you want from the Equalizer Preset drop-down list.

Click OK to dismiss the dialog box, then sync your device as usual using iTunes.

To undo the EQ, repeat the preceding steps but select None from the Equalizer Preset drop-down list.

Listen quietly at night

Just like with a hi-fi system, you can set the audio equalization (EQ) for the speaker or headphones of your iPad or iPhone when playing music. To do so, open the Settings app and select Music > EQ, and choose from the list.

While the settings are mostly obvious and similar to those found in other audio apps, the Late Night option deserves a special mention. This "flattens out" the audio so that sudden loud passages within music don't explode out of the speakers, potentially waking up your neighbors! It can also be useful if you're on a plane listening through headphones and don't want to annoy fellow passengers.

Start Safari ultraquickly in "clean" mode

Whenever you tap the Safari icon on an iPad or iPhone, it'll display the page you were last viewing. This can be annoying because sometimes the page is reloaded and this can take a few seconds to complete. To get around it, you can create your own home-page shortcut to Safari that starts it instantly in a "clean" way with a blank new tab. Any tabs previously open in Safari will remain, however. Here are the steps:

1. Start Safari in the usual way and, in the address field, type about:blank. This will display a blank screen, but don't worry—that's what we want.

2. Tap the Share icon, then tap Add to Home Screen.

3. You're about to make a new home-screen bookmark, so you'll be prompted to type a name. On my iPad and iPhone iOS suggested calling

it Favorites, but you may see a different suggestion. Tap the name field and delete what's there, then call it something like Browser. Then tap the Add button.

And that's all that's required! You'll now have a new home-screen icon that, when tapped, will start Safari quickly with a new blank tab.

To delete the new home-screen icon, just press and hold its icon on the home screen until it begins to wobble, then tap the X at the top left.

Tip 105

See if it's dark somewhere

Ever wanted to make a phone call to a colleague or friend overseas, yet not known whether it's too late in the evening to do so? The Clock app can help. Add the location after tapping the World Clock icon—tap the plus (+) icon and type the name of the nearest big city—and if the clock face is black then the sun has set in that location. If the clock face is white then the sun has risen! (If you don't see a clock face, tap the time display alongside the location until it appears.) See the following figure for an example.

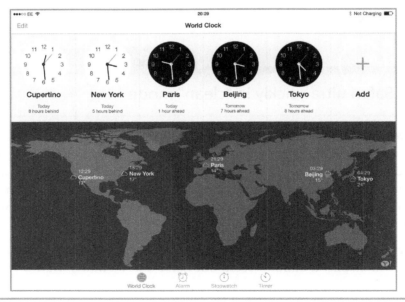

Figure 40—Seeing if it's dark in various parts of the world, via an iPad

You can also use the Map app to judge if somewhere is dark. Open the app, switch to satellite view—tap the (i) icon at the bottom then select the option—then zoom out until the entire globe is visible. You'll see the wave of darkness as it covers the earth!

Tip 106

Get your longitude and latitude

Although the Maps app can locate your position on a map, it won't tell you your longitude and latitude, which can be helpful when hiking, for example. The iPhone-only Compass app will come to the rescue, however, and the values will be shown at the bottom of the screen. Tapping the figures will open the Maps app and plot the values on a map—which will essentially display your current position!

Tip 107

Use kaomoji emoticons

Tip 7, *Use emoji—full-color emoticons*, on page 57, describes how to use Japanese emoticons called emoji, but there's another lesser-known series of Japanese emoticons, called kaomoji. Unlike full-color emoji, kaomoji are constructed from ordinary Japanese symbols, lettering, and punctuation. Usually they're pictorial in nature and perhaps one of the most popular on the Internet is the angry table flip, which is used to indicate ironic anger at something. Admittedly, some kaomoji can be a little hard to interpret unless you've previously encountered them, but they're fun to send to friends who are aware.

Adding a Kaomoji Keyboard

Follow these steps to add a kaomoji keyboard on the iPhone or iPad:

1. Tap the Settings icon and then tap the General heading.

2. Scroll down to the International heading and tap it. In the menu list that appears, tap Keyboards.

3. Tap Add New Keyboard and in the list of languages, select Chinese - Simplified (Pinyin). Then close the Settings app.

Using the Kaomoji Keyboard

Here are the steps to use each time you want to access the kaomoji keyboard:

1. Switch to any app that uses the onscreen keyboard, like Messages or Notes.

2. Tap within the message area or open a new or existing document so the onscreen keyboard appears. Tap the globe icon at the bottom of the screen, and you'll switch to the Chinese keyboard (you can tell because the Return key will now use Chinese writing). Tap the .?123 button (or the 123 button on some iPhone keyboard layouts), and then the #+= key. Both are located at the bottom left.

3. On the symbols keyboard that appears, tap the bottom middle key, which will look like a smiley face. This will bring up a submenu above the keyboard showing kaomoji. Tapping the up arrow at the right of this will open a larger menu from which you can tap to select the kaomoji you wish to insert at the cursor position, as the following figure shows.

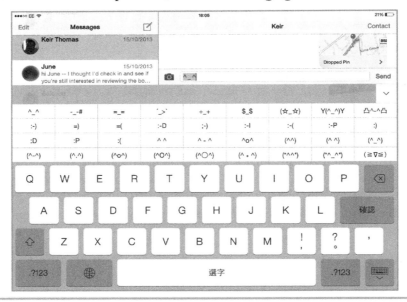

Figure 41—Typing kaomoji emoticons on an iPad keyboard

Scroll up and down the list in the usual way by tapping and then dragging, or dragging and then flicking to scroll the list quickly. Tap any you wish to insert and they'll appear at the cursor position.

4. To cancel the menu, tap the down arrow at the top of the extended keyboard. To return to the English keyboard when you've finished, just press the globe icon again.

Because kaomoji are nothing more than a series of characters, you can delete them just like any other text using the backspace key on the onscreen keyboard.

Deactivating the Kaomoji Keyboard

Repeat the steps in *Adding a Kaomoji Keyboard*, on page 125, to open the International Keyboard section of the Settings app. Then slide your finger left on the Chinese (Pinyin) entry until the red delete button appears. Tap this to delete the keyboard.

Tip 108

Share and print "moments" photo albums

In addition to sharing individual photos via AirDrop, shared photo streams, and social-media sites like Facebook, you can share "moments," which are collections of photos gathered around a particular day at a particular location. To view a moment, open the Photos app and tap the Photos icon at the bottom. Scroll so the heading for the one you want to share is at the top of the screen beneath the status bar, then tap the Share link at the top right. You'll be asked if you want to share some or all of the photos, after which the same sharing options will appear as if you've tapped the standard share button when viewing a single photo. Tapping the Print button will output the entire "moment" album via AirPrint (see *AirPrint*, on page 50).

Tip 109

Jump to the Music app from Control Center

By bringing up Control Center you can not only start and stop music—if the phone is unlocked, you can tap the artist or band name under the name of the track to switch instantly to the Music app and the Now Playing component of it, where you'll have better control over what's playing.

Getting around a broken Home button

If you find your Home button has become unreliable to the point of being useless, then you can use the AssistiveTouch feature to access a virtual Home button that you can tap onscreen. AssistiveTouch is designed to help out people with limited mobility by reproducing onscreen an icon panel offering one-tap access to various functions usually offered by the Home button, such as Siri, the multitasking bar, and so on.

To activate AssistiveTouch, open the Settings app, then tap the General heading. Tap Accessibility > AssistiveTouch. Then slide the switch to activate it.

A white dot will appear at the bottom right of the screen. This is the menu button and, when tapped, it will open an onscreen menu with quick-access icons for the Home button, Siri, Favorites (which relates to gestures you can record using AssistiveTouch), and Device, which offers various additional functions. See the figure here for an example from an iPhone.

The virtual Home button on the menu works just like the real one—tapping it will switch back to the home screen, while tapping and holding will start Siri and double-tapping will open the multitasking bar.

To deactivate the menu when you've finished with it, tap anywhere outside of it.

You can move the menu button by tapping and then dragging it to a new location. The bottom right of the screen is a good location that doesn't get in the way of other functions.

Figure 42—Getting around a broken Home button on an iPhone

The AssistiveTouch blob will also appear when you wake the phone from sleep using the Lock/Sleep button on top of the device, so there'll be no need to tap the Home button ever again.

To deactivate AssistiveTouch, follow the preceding instructions, and this time deactivate the switch alongside its heading within the Settings app.

Tip 111

See where suspicious links point

A favorite trick for people who browse on desktop or laptop computers is to hover the mouse cursor over a link, then look at the status bar to see the address. This can help you avoid following links that lead to scam sites. On an iPhone or iPad, hovering over a link is obviously impossible. Instead, you can tap and hold any link for a few seconds. A menu will pop up, showing the link address at the very top above the buttons.

Tip 112

Delete app folders and put apps in alphabetical order

Rearranging your icons so they're in alphabetical order and removing folders makes finding apps a little bit easier, but it's an almost impossible task to do by tapping and dragging. However, iOS offers a hidden solution.

Open the Settings app, then tap the General heading and tap the Reset entry within the list. Tap Reset Home Screen Layout. This will restore the first home screen to a "virgin" state, showing all the Apple apps as if you've booted for the first time, then it will rearrange all your other apps into alphabetical order, removing any and all folders in the process.

Tip 113

Automatically stop music or videos playing after a time

If you want to listen to music or watch a video on your iPhone or iPad when dropping off to sleep, you can set a hidden timer than will stop playback after any period between 1 minute and 24 hours.

Start the Clock app, and tap the Timer button. Then set a time and tap the musical-note button on an iPad or the heading that reads When Timer Ends on an iPhone. You'll see a list of tones you can use, but scroll down to the bottom, where an entry reads Stop Playing. Select this and tap the Set button. Tap the Start button, then switch out to the Music or Video app and start playback as usual using the Music or Video apps. When the timer ends, not only will the music or video stop playing, but the device will return to the lock screen and then go into sleep mode after a few seconds, as usual.

You can cancel the timer at any time by switching back to the Clock app and tapping the red cancel button.

This will work in some third-party applications that play back audio and video, such as the YouTube app. To discover which ones it works with, you'll need to experiment by setting a timer for a minute and starting playback in the app.

Tip 114

See your own number quickly

Got a new phone with a new number that you've yet to memorize but want to share with somebody? Start the Phone app in the usual way, tap the Contacts button, and scroll to the very top. Your own number will be listed above the A entry in the list.

Another way of seeing your number, which is slightly more involved, is to open the Settings app then tap the Phone heading. The number will be listed at the top. Here you can even edit the number should you ever need to (just tap it and type)—such as if you swap SIM cards at some point or your cellular provider changes your number.

Tip 115

Use nicknames for people

You might know your friend Rebecca Smith as "Becky," but it's unlikely your iPhone or iPad will make the connection. Yet changing the contact card for the individual to read Becky Smith can cause problems when emailing—emailing Becky's business address, for example, could lead to confusion or even embarrassment for recipients.

There are two potential solutions. The first is to start Siri and say, "Rebecca Smith is Becky." Siri will confirm the change with you. You can use any noun, in fact, and could even say something like, "Janet Colgan is my better half" or "Jane Munday is my youngest daughter." From then on you can use the name or phrase with Siri, and this name rather than the person's full name will appear within the Messages list. You'll also be able to search within Spotlight for the individual's contact details using the nickname.

Unfortunately, Siri might struggle with more esoteric words or names, so another solution is to manually add a nickname to the contact card for the individual. Siri will then know to whom you refer should you use the nickname.

Here's how to add a nickname to a contact:

1. Open the Contacts app then open the contact to whom you want to add a nickname.

2. At the top right tap Edit, then scroll down the individual's entry until you see Add Field. Tap it.

3. From the pop-up list, tap Nickname. Then enter the nickname in the new field that appears.

4. Tap the Done button at the top right.

Removing a nickname is a matter of following the preceding steps and deleting it from the individual's contact card.

Tip 116

Stop advertisers from tracking you

Many desktop browsers now include the so-called Do Not Track switch. This is a way to tell advertisers that you don't want them to track what websites you visit, something they do to more effectively target ads that you might be interested in. Some people consider tracking to be an invasion of privacy.

Advertisers don't have to take any notice of Do Not Track, but many do, and you can activate the feature on your iPad and iPhone (although it works only in Safari; you'll still be tracked if you use other web browsers).

To activate the feature, open the Settings app, then tap Privacy and then tap Advertising, and finally tap the switch alongside Limit Ad Tracking so that it's activated.

While on the same settings screen you can select to reset Apple's own advertising tracking system, which is based on a unique anonymous identifier. While activating the Limit Ad Tracking switch deactivates this feature, tapping the Reset button will remove the old tracking identifier completely.

Tip 117

Open browser tabs in the background

The browsing experience has always been built on the idea of clicking a link and then having that link open in front of you. However, wise web users open links in the background so they can switch to the page later on to read it.

In Safari on the iPad you can do this by tapping and holding a link until a menu appears, and then selecting Open in New Tab.

On an iPhone a little one-off setup is necessary to use the same trick—open the Settings app, tap the Safari heading, and then tap Open Links and change the setting to In Background. Subsequently within Safari you should select the Open in Background option on the menu that appears after you tap and hold a link.

Tip 118

Have iBooks read to you

Although iTunes offers audiobooks for download, it's not possible to convert books bought via iBooks into speech...unless you use a secret technique that relies on an accessibility feature of iOS. It's not a perfect solution because you can only read at most a chapter at a time before you have to once again select new pages for reading, but it's better than nothing.

Here's how it's done.

1. Open the Settings app, then tap General > Accessibility.

2. Tap the Speak Selection entry in the menu that appears, and then tap the Speak Selection switch so it's activated.

3. Drag the Speaking Rate slider beneath. This will cause your iPad or iPhone to start speaking, and dragging the slider left or right will cause the voice to speed up or slow down. Choose a speed you're happy with.

4. Open iBooks, then open the book that you want to have your iDevice read aloud.

5. Tap the font icon at the top right (its icon is two *As* next to each other) and then tap the left font-size icon several times so the lettering shrinks to its smallest possible size.

6. Still within the font-size pop-out window, tap the Fonts heading and select Georgia from the list. This crams the most text onto the screen compared to the other font options.

7. Activate the Scrolling View switch in the pop-out window. This will switch the iBook to scrolling mode rather than showing pages, so that more text is included on each screen. Once done, tap outside the pop-out window to dismiss it.

8. Select as much of the text as possible by tapping and holding a word at the top of the screen, then dragging the right handle from top to bottom, as the following figure shows.

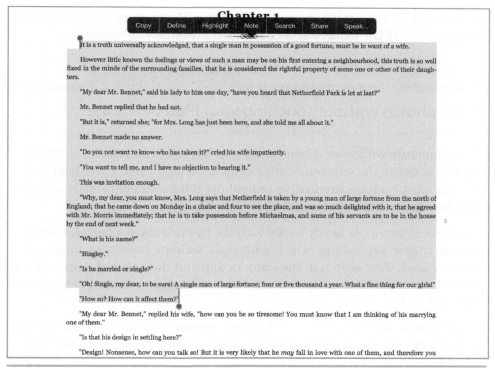

Figure 43—Selecting text in iBooks on an iPad so it can be read aloud

9. Scroll the screen up so more of the chapter is shown. This can be tricky because a menu appears each time you tap the screen, and you'll have to be careful not to select an option on it or to accidentally cancel the selection. Drag the selection handle to the bottom of the screen once again to extend the selection. Repeat this step as many times as possible until you've highlighted as much of the text as you want to read. It usually isn't possible to highlight more than a single chapter.

10. When you release your finger for the last time, tap the right-facing arrow at the right of the menu, then select Speak. Speech will commence immediately.

To stop the voice once it's started speaking, again tap to select some text and then tap the Pause button on the menu that pops up. Beware that this will cancel speaking, so if you want to continue reading you'll need to repeat the preceding steps to highlight the chapter text afresh. An alternative way of turning the voice off is to tap the Home button, which will return you to the home screen.

You can speak text anywhere, not just in the iBooks app. You could read emails in exactly the same way as described previously, for example.

Tip 119

Take photos without touching your iPad or iPhone

Taking a picture with your iPhone or iPad in low light can result in blur. This happens because the exposure time needs to be long when there isn't much light, yet most humans are unable to hold the iPhone or iPad steady enough. Even the slightest movement will blur a photograph.

If you have some Apple headphones with the in-line remote control, however, you can trigger the taking of a photograph without having to touch your iPhone or iPad. Just switch to the Camera app and then click the up or down volume button on the remote control. (This is similar to a cable release you might use with a DSLR camera.)

If the Camera app is set to record video, clicking the up or down volume button on the remote control will start and then stop recording. Don't press the middle remote-control button, though, because that will start music playing!

If you have a Bluetooth headset paired with your iPad or iPhone (see Tip 95, *Use Bluetooth devices*, on page 117), and it includes a volume button, this trick should work there too—giving you a hands- and cable-free remote control! Tapping the up or down volume button on a Bluetooth keyboard also should work.

Tip 120

Know your pins in the Maps app

Two types of pin can be dropped on locations within the Maps app. The first are red pins, which the Maps app itself will drop whenever you search for a location. These are temporary and will disappear as soon as the search field is cleared, although the pin indicating the destination of a route you ask Maps to plan will also be red and will disappear once you reach the destination or should you tap the End button to terminate the route planning.

The other type of pin is purple. These are pins you drop by tapping and holding a location. They'll stick around forever until you choose to delete them (by tapping them, then tapping the (i) icon and selecting the Remove Pin entry from the menu that appears).

Tip 121

See larger thumbnail previews when browsing photos

The Photos app arranges any pictures you take into a hierarchy of albums. First there are yearly albums, which show all the photos taken in a particular year. If you tap one of these then you'll see Collections, which are albums based on photos taken at locations at certain times. Finally, tapping a collection will show "moments," which are albums that further split out pictures into times and places.

Although the pictures are too small to view when clustered together in Years or Collections views, tapping and holding any photo will cause a thumbnail preview to pop up under your fingertip, as the following figure shows. Sliding your finger around will show other previews.

When browsing "moments," the pictures are already thumbnailed so they can be seen, but you can briefly make them bigger using the pinch gesture (place a thumb and finger together and then move them apart slowly). If you release while doing this, the picture will fill the screen for viewing, but you can also reverse the gesture to restore the image to its original size.

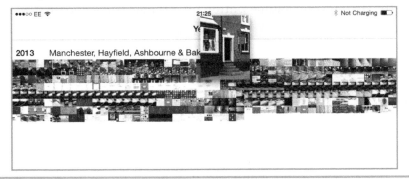

Figure 44—Viewing thumbnails of a yearly album on an iPad

Tip 122

Hard-reboot your iPhone or iPad

If your iPhone gets jammed so that no buttons respond and you can't even turn it off, hold down the Lock/Sleep and Home buttons together for about seven seconds. The device will switch off, and you can then restart it in the usual way by holding the Lock/Sleep button. Note that there's a serious risk that any files you've edited in apps might be lost, so the hard reboot should be a last resort!

Tip 123

Find out which apps understand which kinds of files

Ever wondered which apps installed on your iPhone or iPad can read Word documents, for example, or display PDFs? To find out, open an email that has an attachment of the kind you want to know about (if you can't find one, just send a new email to yourself with a file attached), then tap and hold the file attachment. The share menu will pop up, but with a difference—you'll be offered a choice of apps that can open the attachment (which means they can read that kind of file). With some popular filetypes, like PDFs, there might be several apps that are compatible, and to see them all you might have to scroll through the list by dragging your thumb left and right.

Tap Cancel when you've learned all you need from the list or, in the case of an iPad, simply tap outside the pop-up window.

Tip 124

Make Siri less loud!

Broadly speaking, there are two separate volume controls for your iPad or iPhone—the ringer/alerts volume (which, as you might have guessed, controls how loud the phone rings) and the main volume (which controls how loud music and videos play, as well as the sounds in some games). The headphone volume can also be set independently when headphones are attached, but that is essentially the same as the main volume.

You can change the main volume by sliding up Control Center from the bottom of the screen, and set the ringer and alerts volume by opening the Settings app and selecting the Sounds heading.

You might think Siri's volume is changed along with the main volume control, but that's not the case. You can set Siri's volume independently. To do so, start Siri in the usual way, by holding the Home button, then use the volume controls on the left of the iPad or iPhone to adjust the volume. You can't turn the volume all the way down, but you can reduce the volume level to one bar, which is pretty quiet. See the figure here for an example.

To silence Siri completely, you'll need to open the Settings app, then tap General, and then the Siri heading. Then tap Voice Feedback and put a check mark in the Hands-Free Only section. Unfortunately, this means Siri's voice will still

Figure 45—Adjusting the volume of Siri's voice on an iPhone

be heard if you're using headphones or if Siri is connected to your in-car entertainment system, although during general use Siri's voice won't sound. You will still hear the beeps whenever its activated and deactivated, however.

Tip 125

Jump to the beginning or end of an iMovie project

To instantly jump to the beginning of an iMovie project, tap and hold the very left edge of the screen anywhere within the timeline area beneath the playback window. To scroll to the end, tap and hold the very right edge of the screen.

Tip 126

Turn off in-app purchases

Many apps use a "freemium" revenue model, which is to say that the basic app is free but users are invited to upgrade by making small purchases when the app is running. Games, in particular, prefer this way of working.

Each in-app purchase prompts a password-confirmation dialog to appear, although some apps may ask you to input your password as soon as they start, to avoid the need for this. However, despite this it's not hard to make a purchase in error or that you later regret, and there have been horror stories about people loaning their iPad or iPhone to family members who knew their Apple ID password and who subsequently ran up hundreds of dollars worth of purchases!

Turning off in-app purchasing is easy, however.

1. Open the Settings app on the device, then tap General > Restrictions.

2. Tap the Enable Restrictions heading at the top. You'll be prompted to enter a specific four-digit PIN to control who can access the restrictions screen. It's a good idea to make this different from your main PIN, which people you loan your iPad/iPhone to may already know and so might choose to enable in-app purchases when you're not looking.

3. Once you've set up the PIN, scroll down to the In-App Purchases section and tap the switch so that it's deactivated.

To restore in-app purchases at any time, repeat these steps and tap the switch again so it's activated. You might also wish to deactivate app restrictions by tapping the Disable Restrictions button at the top of the screen.

Tip 127

Download from foreign App Stores or iTunes Stores

A fundamental limitation of the way Apple offers apps, music, and video is that each country has its own online stores. This is often a stipulation of copyright holders, but can be very annoying for Canadian users who live 10 miles from the US border, for example, or anybody who has noticed how apps tend to be released in the US App Store before they're released worldwide (if they ever are!).

Perhaps surprisingly, this limitation is easy to bypass on an iPad or iPhone. All you need do is create a new Apple ID registered within any country whose app store you want to download from. Following this, you can log into the iTunes Store or the App Store using the new ID.

In other words, it's entirely permissible to have items bought using different Apple IDs on the same device.

Here's how to set up a new ID and make purchases (note that the new ID must be set up as follows, and not using the Apple website):

1. Open the App Store, ensuring the Featured screen is showing, then scroll down to the bottom. There'll be a button showing your Apple ID. Tap it.

2. In the dialog box that appears, tap Sign Out.

3. Choose any free app that you haven't already purchased, then tap to purchase it.

4. A dialog box will appear, asking if you wish to log in with an existing Apple ID or create a new one. Opt to create a new one.

5. Follow the registration wizard from start to finish, but be sure to select the country whose app store you want to join, as shown in Figure 46, *Creating a new Apple ID registered in a different country, using an iPad*, on page 140. Note that the United States appears at the top of the list rather than in alphabetical order.

6. Select the None option when asked to add a credit card.

7. Unless you have a friend in that country whose address and phone number you can use, you're going to have to make up those details when you're prompted for them. Note that you'll need to use an email address

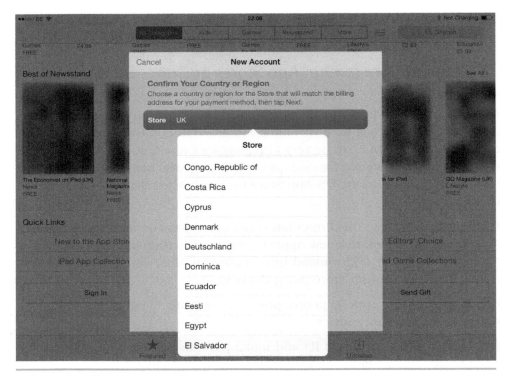

Figure 46—Creating a new Apple ID registered in a different country, using an iPad

not already known to Apple, and you'll have to reply to a confirmation email at that address to finish registration.

8. Once the new Apple ID is created, again scroll to the bottom of the App Store and log in as that user.

You can now select and download apps in the usual way, with the difference being that you'll be viewing the selection of apps used in the country that the Apple ID was registered within.

You can switch Apple IDs in exactly the same was as described previously within the iTunes Store app—just scroll down to the bottom and tap the Apple ID button, logging in with the new ID.

Purchasing items that aren't free is difficult because you won't be able to register a credit card against the account without providing a corresponding address. One solution is to buy iTunes gift cards for the country in which the Apple ID is registered. These can usually be purchased on eBay, for example.

Tip 128

Deal with photo-stream warnings when importing images

With the use of a Camera Connection Kit you can import to your iPad (although not to your iPhone) pictures you've taken with a digital camera.[14] But if you import many pictures in one go you might see an error saying that you've reached Photo Stream's limitation. There's nothing to worry about, however. You've merely hit the limit for uploads to Photo Stream, which is set at 1,000 pictures per hour, 10,000 per day, and 25,000 per month.[15] As soon as that time period has passed (that is, an hour, day, or month) your pictures will once again be uploaded and shared via Photo Stream.

A better way to import images, and which avoids them being uploaded to photo stream (and is compatible with the iPhone and iPad) is to follow Tip 83, *Transfer photos from a Mac or Windows PC*, on page 107.

Tip 129

Find a lost password for an iTunes backup

If you back up your iPhone or iPad using iTunes you might've made use of the encrypted backup feature that protects the backup with a unique password. And if you set up the password some time ago you may have forgotten what the password is, which will mean you're unable to restore the backup.

There's no way around this unless the backup was made on a Mac computer, where you can use the Keychain Access application to discover the password. Of course, this will work only if you opted to use Keychain Access to store the password when creating it (it's usually set as a default option).

Here are the steps required:

1. Open the Keychain Access app on your Mac (it's in the Utilities folder of the Applications list within Finder), then in the search field at the top right type either *iPad* or *iPhone*, depending on which device backup you're trying to discover the password for.

---

14. https://support.apple.com/kb/HT4101
15. https://support.apple.com/kb/HT4858

2. In the list of results double-click the backup file (it'll be called either iPad Backup or iPhone Backup), and put a check mark in the Show Password box of the dialog that appears. Then type your Mac login password when prompted, and click the Allow button. The password will now be revealed.

For what it's worth, this same trick will reveal passwords within other Mac applications—you could use it to reveal a password for your Mac instant-messaging app, for example.

Quit the Keychain Access app as soon as you've finished, because it's a powerful app and misclicking anywhere can cause serious problems!

Tip 130

Discover the IMEI and UDID

Sometimes you might be asked to quote the IMEI number of your iPhone, especially if you're filling out insurance forms. IMEI stands for International Mobile Station Equipment Identity number. It's a unique number identifying the cellular components of your device.

You can discover the IMEI on the iPhone itself by opening the Phone app and entering *#06#, which works with most phones from any manufacturer, but you can also discover it using iTunes if the iPhone has been set up to sync with that application. Attach the phone, then select the device from the drop-down list at the top right. On the main Summary screen, click the Phone Number field at the top left. It will instantly change to show the IMEI. Click again, and you'll see the ICCID (Integrated Circuit Card Identifier), which is the unique number that identifies the SIM card.

Similarly, clicking the Serial Number field beneath the phone number in iTunes will show the unique device ID (UDID) number, which is a unique number identifying the entire device, with the bonus that if you type Ctrl-C on a Windows PC or Cmd-C on a Mac, the UDID will be copied to the clipboard for pasting elsewhere. You might be asked for the UDID if you contact Apple's technical support or that of an app vendor.

Following these steps with an iPad will show a Serial Number field, and clicking it will also show the UDID. Clicking again if the iPad has cellular capabilities will show its cell-phone number (if the SIM card it uses was assigned one), plus the ICCID.

Tip 131

Insert the ellipsis character

Ellipsis is the name given to the three periods often used to indicate something is missing or to give a sense of...suspense—just like in this sentence, in fact!

Although you can type three periods, there's actually a dedicated ellipsis character that you can type by switching to the numbers/symbols keyboard, then tapping and holding the period key. The ellipsis symbol will appear in a pop-out window, and you can select it by tapping it.

Tip 132

Instantly create a calendar event

In addition to speaking to Siri or tapping the plus (+) button at the top right of the Calendar app screen to create a calendar event, you can tap and hold any particular day during Day, Week, or Month view to create an event (note that only the iPad Calendar app offers Month view). In the case of Day and Week view, this will create an hourlong event. In Month view on an iPad, tapping and holding will automatically create an all-day event.

Tip 133

Make images and shapes the same size in iWork

If you've inserted several images or shapes on the page or spreadsheet in an iWork app, you might want to make them all the same size. You can try to do this by dragging the handles of each and estimating, but there's a better way. Adjust one of the images or shapes to the size you want all of them to be. Then select one of the other shapes or images and begin to resize it by dragging its handles. With another finger (possibly using your other hand), tap the first shape or image. The second shape or image should instantly resize to match the first one. Finally, lift your finger from the second image, then lift the finger from the first.

Tip 134

Copy Calculator results

To copy to the clipboard any numbers or results in the Calculator app, just tap and hold (or double-tap) in the results area (the "LCD screen" on the calculator) and select Copy from the menu that appears. To paste them when typing within another app, double-tap where you want the data to go, then select Paste from the menu that appears.

You can also paste into the Calculator numbers you've copied from elsewhere, such as from an email—again, just tap and hold (or double-tap) the "LCD screen" and select Paste from the menu that appears. Note that the numbers must not have a gap between them—copying and pasting 123.45 will work fine, but if you copy 123 45 only 123 will be pasted in.

Tip 135

Move the browser pane in iPhoto

If using iPhoto in landscape mode on your iPad or iPhone, you can move the photo browser thumbnail grid that appears at the left side to the right—along with the various tools listed beneath it—by tapping and then dragging the heading that lists how many photos are in the current album. This works only in landscape mode, however.

Tip 136

Rip CD tracks in the very best audio quality

Music fans can debate the quality of MP3 and Apple's native AAC audio-file format until the cows come home, but one thing is for certain—they're "lossy" formats, designed to discard musical data in order to shrink file sizes.

This is ideal for devices like iPads and iPhones that have limited storage space, but depending on the quality of the headphones you use (and your ears) it might be a step too far.

If you rip tracks from CD on your Mac or Windows PC rather than buying them from the iTunes Store, iTunes offers a way of encoding tracks so that all the data from the disc is retained with zero quality loss. The downside is that each ripped track takes up a lot of space—whereas a standard iTunes track might occupy 3–4MB, you can expect a lossless track to take up 20–30MB. Large file sizes won't be an issue for your computer, but they may prove challenging for a 16GB device.

If you decide lossless is for you, open iTunes and, if using a Windows PC, click the menu button at the top left and select Preferences from the menu that appears. If using a Mac, click the Preferences entry on the main application menu. In the dialog box ensure the General tab is selected, and click the Import Settings button. Then select Apple Lossless Encoder from the Import Using drop-down list.

Any tracks you import from this point onward will be encoded losslessly and will be synced with your iPad or iPhone in the usual way.

Tip 137

Avoid wearing out the Home button

The Home button on an iPhone or iPad can withstand thousands of presses but will eventually break, as all mechanical devices do. After all, it's used several times whenever the device is accessed, which can add up to hundreds of presses a week!

Here are a few tricks to work into your routine, each of which avoids the need for at least one press of the Home button. See also Tip 110, *Getting around a broken Home button*, on page 128.

- Wake an iPad or iPhone from sleep by pressing the Lock/Sleep button on top rather than pressing the Home button.

- Use an Apple Smart Cover, the cover of a Smart Case, or the cover of competitor product to wake an iPad from sleep—this will mean that whenever you open the cover the iPad will automatically wake from sleep.

- When rearranging icons, rather than clicking Home to deactivate rearrangement mode, briefly pull down the notification area from the top of the screen or pull up Control Center from the bottom. This will automatically cancel the mode.

- Use the "hand pinch" gesture on an iPad to return to the main app listing. Similarly, on an iPad swipe left and right with three or four fingers to switch between open apps. See *Gestures*, on page 29.

- On an iPad bring up the multitasking bar to switch apps by swiping upward using four fingers. See *Multitasking and Switching Apps*, on page 14.

- Activate Siri's "Raise to Speak" mode on an iPhone, which—provided the iPhone is not in sleep mode—will cause Siri to automatically activate when you raise the phone to your ear. This avoids the need to press and hold the Home button. To activate Raise to Speak mode, select the General heading in the Settings app, then select the Siri option.

- Start Siri as described previously, then launch apps by saying the word "open" or "launch," followed by the name of the app (that is, something like "open Mail").

- Quit Siri when you've finished using it by tapping the microphone icon and saying "goodbye" rather than clicking the Home button.

- To switch to an app, rather than tapping its icon on the main app listing, bring down Notification Center and tap any of the app's entries (if it has any, of course). For example, if you want to access the Calendar app, open the notification area and tap a calendar alert.

Tip 138

Cancel an app download

Started an app download but changed your mind and want to stop it from being installed? Or do you have an app that seems to have gotten jammed while it's installing, and it's showing nothing more than "Loading" or "Waiting"? Just tap and hold the app icon on the home screen until it begins to wobble, then tap the X icon at its top left to delete the app. The app will be removed even if it's still being installed. If it's a new app you've purchased, however, this won't cancel or refund the purchase, and the app will remain available for you to download. Tip 163, *Get a refund for an app*, on page 161, explains how it's sometimes possible to get a refund for an app bought in error.

Tip 139

Create your own wallpaper from images

Creating your own wallpaper for use behind your app icons on an iPad or iPhone is surprisingly easy.

Using the Camera's Macro Mode

Arguably the best kind of wallpaper behind your app icons is a texture of some kind, and creating your own using the macro mode of the built-in camera is surprisingly effective. In a well-lit room find a texture you like—perhaps some patterned cloth, for example, or the fabric cover of a hardback book, as the following figure shows. You might even choose some real-life wallpaper! Then put the camera as close as it can go without losing focus. This will probably be a few inches away. Don't forget you can tap the screen to force the camera to focus. Then take a picture. For what it's worth, woolen and cotton-based fabrics seem to work very well as wallpaper back-drops, especially on devices that have Retina displays.

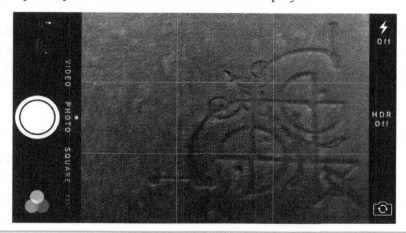

Figure 47—Creating a wallpaper image from the cover of an old book, using an iPhone

Creating "Bokeh" Light Blurs

Bokeh describes the visual effect of photographs that are deliberately out of focus. A good example is a photograph taken of a city landscape at night, where the picture is deliberately focused "incorrectly" so that the points of light in the distance look pretty. The same technique can be applied to taking pictures of other myriad light sources, such as the lights on a Christmas tree.

The iPad or iPhone Camera app would appear to make bokeh impossible because it always wants to focus on what you're looking at. The trick is to use the focus-lock feature to force blurriness. Start by lining up the shot in the usual way so that it's in focus. Then hold your hand in front of the lens so that it fills most of the screen yet isn't so close that your camera can't focus. Tap and hold the screen for a second. When you lift your finger the words "AE/EF Lock" will appear at the bottom of the screen. This means the focus and exposure are both locked. Remove your finger, and then take your picture.

I've posted a gallery of wallpapers I made this way at http://applekungfu.com/wallpapers. Take a look and download any you like!

Tip 140

Instantly redial a busy line

Just dialed a number and reached nothing but a busy tone? Rather than typing the number again after hanging up, press the green Call button. This will bring up the last number you dialed (whether manually or after selecting an entry in your contacts list), and you can tap the Call button a second time to dial it.

Tip 141

Move images, shapes, or text boxes in straight lines in iWork

You can move shapes, text boxes, and images within the iWork apps by simply tapping and then dragging them, but it's extremely hard to move them in a perfectly straight line. You may want to move an image up, for example, but not left or right for fear of damaging the overall layout.

To move an item in a straight line, drag it a small amount in the direction in which you want it to move, then tap and hold another finger (possibly from your other hand) on the screen. This will lock the item to a horizontal, vertical, or 45-degree path for movement. In other words, it will only move in a straight line.

Although the movement will be locked, you can in fact switch to a different line (from vertical to horizontal, for example) by pushing the finger that's dragging the item in that direction. In other words, if you've locked an item to a horizontal path, then pushing some distance in a vertical path will alter the path lock to vertical.

Tip 142

Personalize the Music app

You can reconfigure the icon row at the bottom of the Music app on the iPhone by tapping the More icon and then tapping the Edit button at the top left. Then drag whatever icon you wish from the selection over one of the four existing icons at the bottom to replace it.

Note that on the iPad's screen all the icons are visible all the time, so this isn't necessary.

Tip 143

Scroll text boxes on web pages

If there's a scrollable text box on a web page (that is, a list of options contained within a box with a scrollbar), then you should be able to scroll up and down by tapping and then dragging. However, this won't work on certain web pages, and tapping and dragging will instead scroll the web page. The solution is to tap and scroll in the box with two fingers bunched together.

Tip 144

Trim audio tracks to remove nonsense

Some tracks you rip from CD might include extra audio at the end or beginning, especially if they're live performances. Alternatively, you might find that the last track on a CD includes several minutes of deliberate silence in order to hide an "Easter egg"—an extra song or joke material at the end of the album. When these tracks are included as part of larger playlists the extra bits can prove annoying.

There's no way to trim tracks using the iPad or iPhone alone, but if your device syncs with iTunes on a Mac or Windows PC, then you can set a start and stop time for the track so that it plays only the parts you want. This won't edit the track in any way. It merely tells the Music app on your iPad or iPhone to play and stop playing at certain points.

Here's how to put this in place:

1. Open iTunes on the computer, then locate the track. Listen to it carefully on the computer and note the start point and/or end point, in minutes and seconds, where you'd like to start or end the track.

2. Right-click the track and select Get Info from the menu. In the dialog box that appears, select the Options tab.

3. Put a check mark in either the Start Time or Stop Time box (or both), and enter the time (again, in minutes and seconds) at which you'd like the song to start or end (that is, 1:10 for one minute, ten seconds).

4. Click OK and then sync as usual with your iPad or iPhone.

From now on, no matter where you play the track it will start and/or end as you specified.

To restore the track to playing in its entirety, repeat the preceding steps but this time remove the check marks alongside Start Time and/or Stop Time box.

Tip 145

Send map locations to a desktop PC

Tip 75, *Send map locations from iPad to iPhone*, on page 101, explains how to send a map location between an iPad and an iPhone, but what if you'd like to send the link to a Mac or Windows PC?

Sending Locations to OS X Mavericks or Mountain Lion

If the Mac's running OS X Mavericks (10.9) then you can follow the instructions in the aforementioned tip to send the link to yourself via the Messages app, where it will open in the desktop Maps app. If you're using OS X Mountain Lion, in Messages double-click the Dropped Pin.loc file received from the iPad. This will open a Quick Look preview, and clicking the Maps URL link will open the address within Google Maps in a web-browser window.

Sending Locations to PCs Running Windows or Linux, and to Old Macs

Users of old versions of OS X on a Mac, and PC users running Windows or Linux, can use a different solution for sharing map locations between iOS and a Mac or Windows PC. It takes advantage of how the Maps app sends links to locations as contact-card files (.vcf). Follow these steps:

1. Tap and hold the location within the Maps app on the iPad or iPhone so that a pin is dropped. Then tap the Share icon at the bottom of the screen when viewing the location, and tap Selected Location on the menu that appears.

2. On the menu that appears, tap Mail. This will open a new email message. Type your own address as the destination, then tap Send.

3. Open your email client on the Mac or Windows PC, then open the email message you sent to yourself and click the file. On a Mac this will open the Contacts app and ask if you want to import the contact card. Select to do so. On a Windows 7 PC the contact card will be imported into the address-book app (or Outlook, if you have it installed). In each case the new contact will be called Dropped Pin.

4. Open the Dropped Pin contact and look for a line that reads either Map URL or Website, then click the link alongside it. This will open the location on the Google Maps website within the default web browser.

Repeat this trick as many times as needed to share a location, and in each case the Dropped Pin contact card on the Mac or Windows PC will be updated with a new link (note that the address details listed in the contact card might not change, although these can be ignored).

Linux users can import the contact file into an app of their choosing, although it's also possible to examine the file using a text editor; the map URL will be listed on a line beginning item2.URL;type=pref:.

Tip 146

Be multilingual

If you regularly communicate in multiple languages, you might find it a little frustrating that iOS always wants to autocorrect to English whatever you type. Even when you overrule the autocorrection by tapping the suggested replacement to cancel it, you'll still find foreign-language words are underlined as being misspelled.

The solution is to configure an onscreen keyboard for the other language, and then switch to it before typing in that language. Here's how:

1. Open Settings, then tap General > Keyboard.

2. Tap the Keyboards entry in the list. Tap Add New Keyboard, scroll down to the language you want, and select it.

3. You can keep confusing foreign-language layouts (such as AZERTY for French, or QWERZ for German) from appearing when you switch to the language. To do so, in the list of keyboards, tap the right-facing arrow alongside the new keyboard and select QWERTY from the layout list.

4. If you use a Bluetooth keyboard, be sure to select the US option from the Hardware Keyboard Layout list, too. This will again ensure that the foreign keyboard layout isn't used.

From now on whenever you want to type in a different language, tap the globe icon at the bottom left of the onscreen keyboard. This will switch the keyboard to the other language, and anything you type will be autocorrected and spell-checked according to that language. Just remember to tap the globe icon again to return to English when you've finished.

Should you want to remove the new keyboard at a future date, just repeat the preceding steps to access the Add New Keyboard page, then swipe left on the entry for the language you want to remove. Then tap the Delete button.

Another option if you need to insert occasional foreign-language words is to create keyboard shortcuts for the words—see Tip 270, *Create shortcuts to autotype text*, on page 229.

Tip 147

Fast-forward through music

You might already know that you can drag the playhead on the time bar when a song is playing to scrub backward and forward in a track (see also Tip 218, *Scrub properly*, on page 194). Less well known is that you can accomplish the same thing by tapping and holding the double-arrow (fast-forward and rewind) buttons to the left and right of the play button—a little like holding the rewind and fast-forward buttons on old tape recorders!

You can do this while the music is playing or when it isn't. If it isn't playing you'll hear the track being cued through, but when you lift your finger the music will again be paused.

Tip 148

Use iPod/iPhone headphones with Mac computers

If you have a Mac computer you should find your iPhone headphones along with their in-line microphone work fully once plugged into the headphone socket. This is because Macs have the same special dual input/output headphone socket as iPhones do. You can even adjust the volume by clicking the plus and minus buttons on the in-line microphone, and click the center of the microphone to start and stop iTunes playing—just like on your iPhone or iPad!

Tip 149

See more info in the Stocks app

When viewing the iPhone's Stocks app, tap the percentage-change figure, and it'll change to show the actual price increase, as the figure here shows. Tap the figure again, and it will display the current market capitalization. To set one of these as default, tap the menu icon at the bottom right and select from the choices at the bottom of the screen.

Additionally, holding the phone in landscape mode will show a growth graph, and tapping the entries along its top axis will switch the graph to showing the time period indicated. Swiping left or right will move between graphs for the various stocks and indices.

Tapping the Y! icon at the bottom left when in portrait mode will open Safari to the Yahoo! Finance page, showing all the data for your chosen stock or market.

Figure 48—Viewing additional data in the Stocks app of an iPhone

Tip 150

View and delete iCloud documents

Because of the way iOS works, the usual method of viewing and deleting an app's files that have been stored within iCloud is to do so using the app itself. If you've deleted the app on one of your devices, this is obviously impossible, however.

The Settings app can come to your rescue. Tap the iCloud heading, then scroll to the bottom and tap Storage & Backup. Then tap Manage Storage. Under the Documents & Data heading are all the apps that use iCloud for storage. Tapping any will show the files for that app, and you can swipe from right to left on each line to reveal a Delete button. Alternatively, you can tap the Edit button at the top right, in which case every entry in the list will have an icon at the left that you can tap to reveal the Delete button.

Note that deleting a file in this way will remove it from all your devices or computers that use iCloud.

Tip 151

Move calendar events easily

You can bring forward or move back the timing of calendar events by tapping and holding them, and then dragging them to a new time, day, or even month. Dragging the event to the left or right edge of the screen will scroll to the next day in Day or Week view, while on an iPad dragging to the bottom will scroll to the next month if you're using Month view.

Tip 152

Back up your contacts

If you've signed up with iCloud your address book is shared among any devices you own, as well as Macs and suitably configured PCs (see *iCloud*, on page 26). However, you might still choose to create a backup, perhaps for importing to a non-iCloud-equipped computer or device, or just for safekeeping.

Here are the steps that you can carry out on any Mac or Windows PC with a web browser:

1. Head over to the iCloud website and log in with your Apple ID.[16]

2. Click the Contacts icon, which will show your address book, then click the cog icon in the bottom left.

3. Click Select All on the menu that appears, then click the cog again, and this time click Export vCard.

4. You'll be prompted to download a .vcf file, which is a contact-card file containing all the address-book data. This is a standard file format that you should be able to import into other apps that have address-book features.

To back up just one contact or a handful of them select the contact(s) in the list (Ctrl-click on a Windows PC to select multiple entries, or Cmd-click on a Mac) and then again click the cog icon at the bottom and select Export vCard.

Tip 153

Stop iPad or iPhone backups from eating your hard disk

There are two ways of backing up iPhones and iPads—via iCloud, in which case the backup happens magically whenever the device is connected to a power source (and online), or to your PC whenever you attach the device and run iTunes.

If you choose the latter then you may well accumulate a high number of backup files. Being at least 16GB each in size, depending on the storage capacity the device you're backing up, they can start to consume your hard disk voraciously.

In theory, at least, all you need is the most recent backup. You can discard all the rest, and iTunes on your computer lets you prune the backup store. If using a Windows PC, open its preferences dialog by clicking the icon at the top left of the iTunes window, then selecting Preferences. On a Mac click the main application menu, then select Preferences. Then in the dialog box that appears select the Devices tab and look in the Devices window for the Device Backups heading. Select any backup you want to delete, then click the Delete Backup button.

---

16. https://icloud.com

Tip 154

Preview a slide in Keynote

The play button at the top right of the Keynote screen will start playing through a presentation, but you can also use it to preview the current slide full-screen. Simply select the slide at the left, then tap Play. When you're finished previewing, use the pinch gesture (pull a finger and thumb together on the screen) to return to slide-design mode.

Tip 155

Make an iPhone truly quiet

When you activate the switch on the side of an iPhone, the ringer is turned off and theoretically the phone is silenced...except that it isn't, because it'll still vibrate for incoming calls and notifications. Place an iPhone on something like a glass table, and the vibrations can be very noisy!

The solution for those who desire perfect silence is to open the Settings app, tap the Sounds heading, then tap the switch alongside Vibrate on Silent so it's deactivated. From now on the phone won't vibrate when switched to silent mode, but will vibrate as usual otherwise.

Note that even this won't silence every noise an iPhone might make, however. Find My iPhone will override it, for example (see *Security*, on page 30), as will emergency alerts.

Tip 156

Stop being nagged about missed calls or messages

If you miss any calls, your iPhone will add a number to the icon showing how many. You can clear this by opening the app and looking at the Recents list, but the world splits into two camps: those who clear the missed-call notifications immediately, and those who let them stack up until they reach three or even four digits (infuriating the former camp of users).

To turn off the missed-call icon, open the Settings app, tap the Notification Center heading, and then tap the Phone entry in the list. Finally, tap the switch alongside Badge App Icon so that it's switched off. Presto—no more numbers (although when you open the Phone app the Recents icon will have a number against it still).

This trick will also work for other apps that display numbers against their icons—just select their entries within the Notifications list.

Tip 157

Fully utilize fonts in iWork apps

Although you can easily activate bold and italics when typing or editing text in iWork apps, often the font has many other built-in styles that can help add variety to your documents. For example, the staple of many business documents—Helvetica Neue—has Regular, Medium, Light, Thin, UltraLight, and Condensed variations to choose from.

How you access the font styles depends on which app and device you're using, as follows:

- Pages: On the iPad tap the font name on the format bar above the keyboard, and then tap the (i) icon alongside the font name when the list of fonts is shown. On the iPhone, bring up the keyboard then tap the Style Inspector button (the paintbrush icon), then the font name, and the font name again in the following screen, then the (i) icon alongside the font name when the list of fonts is shown.

- Keynote: On both the iPad and iPhone, bring up the onscreen keyboard by tapping in a text box, then tap the format-inspector icon (the paintbrush). Ensure the Style tab is selected in the pop-up window, then tap the font name at the top of the list, and then the font name again in the following list (on the iPhone you may have to scroll to see the font name). Finally, tap the (i) icon alongside the font name when the list of fonts is shown.

- Numbers: Tap a cell on either the iPad or iPhone, then tap the format-inspector icon (the paintbrush) and then—ensuring the Cell tab is selected—tap the Text Options heading. Following this, tap the font name and, when the list of fonts is shown, tap the (i) icon alongside the font name.

Tip 158

Beam items using iPhoto

iPhoto includes a "beam" tool by which you can quickly and easily transfer to another iPhoto user not only photos, but also entire albums and events, as well as journals and slideshows. AirDrop can perform the same task, but beaming a file will work even with a device incompatible with AirDrop, such as old iPads and iPhones.

To beam a picture or selection of pictures, open the photo you'd like to send (or make a selection from an album by tapping one thumbnail, then tapping and holding others), then tap the share button and select the Beam option. For beaming to take place, the following conditions must be met:

- The recipient device must be running iPhoto at the time. It isn't enough to have iPhoto running in the background—the app must be visible onscreen in order to receive the file(s).

- The recipient device should be on the same Wi-Fi network as the sending device. If this is not possible, then both the sending device and the recipient device must have Bluetooth activated.

- The recipient device must have the Wireless Beaming option activated; switch to the main Library view in iPhoto, then tap the menu icon at the bottom right (the three dots). Tap the switch alongside Wireless Beaming so it's activated.

The recipient will need to accept the file(s) once sending has been initiated.

Tip 159

Play music or video on computers you haven't synced to

Although you might want to copy to your iPad or iPhone music from two or more computers, the reality is that iPads and iPhones are designed to sync with just one computer. In fact, if you try to sync to a second computer you'll be asked if you want to erase your iPad or iPhone's existing music collection. However, by opening iTunes, selecting your device from the drop-down list at the right, opening the Summary tab, and selecting Manually Manage Music and Videos, this restriction is lifted. However, it's not recommended you use this option because it can become confusing to manage music—so much so that Apple has produced a support document for those wishing to try it.[17]

Curiously, though, music and video already on an iPad or iPhone—regardless of which computer it came from—can be played through iTunes on a computer that isn't the "home" computer normally used to sync music with the device. You could play music stored on your iPhone using your work PC and the speakers attached to it, for example, even if you ordinarily use your home PC to sync music files.

To create this setup, attach the device to the second computer and start iTunes. You'll be asked if you want to authorize the computer to work with the iPad or iPhone, and you'll need to provide your Apple ID and password when prompted.

Once the device is authorized, select it from the drop-down list at the top right and then click the On This iPhone/iPad/iPod link at the top right. Choose the music or video you want to play back, and double-click it to start hearing it through your computer's speakers or viewing it on your computer screen. Music should play back seamlessly, but you might find HD video files stutter because of the limitations of a USB connection.

Tip 160

Use Pages for outlining

Through its bullet-point feature, Pages on the iPad and iPhone offers a relatively sophisticated outlining tool.

To get started, create a new document and open the format inspector (tap the paintbrush icon), then tap the List tab and select what kind of outline format you'd like (lettered, numbered, and so on).

Start typing the outline, and press Enter to add a new line. Tapping the tab button on the format bar above the keyboard will indent the new line on an iPad, while tapping and holding anywhere on the screen and selecting Insert > Tab from the pop-up menu will do the same on an iPhone. Alternatively, if you haven't started typing a line, you can swipe the outline bullet, number, or letter left or right with one finger to decrease or increase the indentation (although this is difficult to do without accidentally scrolling the page). You

---

17. http://support.apple.com/kb/HT1535

can also adjust the indentation by tapping the indent and outdent buttons in the list view of the Styles pop-up window that appears when you tap the Format Inspector button.

You can reorder lines within the outline by tapping and holding a bullet point (or number or letter) and dragging it up or down, or back or forth to decrease/increase the indentation. Beware that this is again difficult on an iPad screen, and practically impossible on an iPhone screen!

To end the outline, simply tap `Return` after leaving a line empty.

Tip 161

Type in all capital letters

Want to type in UPPER CASE? Rapidly double-tap the Shift (⇧) key on the onscreen keyboard. The key will turn dark to indicate Caps Lock mode is operating, as in the following figure. To turn off Caps Lock, just tap ⇧ again. It'll also turn off automatically when you switch to the numbers/symbols keyboard.

If this doesn't work for you, open the Settings app, then General > Keyboard and ensure the switch alongside Enable Caps Lock is active.

Figure 49—Typing in all capital letters using the iPad's onscreen keyboard

Tip 162

Quickly type accented letters

When you tap and hold some keys on the keyboard, a pop-out window appears showing alternatives, such as accented characters when you tap E. Most people simply tap one of the options to select it, but there's a slightly quicker way. Tap and hold the letter until the pop-out menu appears, then slide your finger left or right *without* moving it up to the pop-out menu. A blue highlight will appear and will select the option your fingertip is underneath. Just lift your finger to insert the character. Give it a try—it might sound like a small detail, but it can save a lot of time in the long run.

Tip 163

Get a refund for an app

Most stores you visit offer refunds of some kind, but Apple's iTunes Store and App Store are different. If you've bought something in error or if it isn't as described, according to Apple's terms of business you're out of luck—all purchases made through the App Store are final. However, you can put in a request for a refund, and if you have a valid explanation requests are usually honored—at Apple's discretion, of course.

Here are the steps required.

1. Uninstall the app on any device you own. If you're still using the app or media then clearly your claim that you don't need it will be eroded.

2. Open iTunes on your computer, then visit the iTunes store by clicking the button at the top right of the program window.

3. Click and hold the button showing your iTunes username or Apple ID at the top left of the window, then select the Account entry in the menu that appears.

4. Scroll down to the Purchase History heading, then click the See All button to the right.

5. If you've just made the purchase, click the Report a Problem button. If the purchase was made a few days ago, look for the date when you purchased it in the list and click the small arrow icon to the left of the date

(note that the app itself might not be listed). Then, in the list that appears, click the Report a Problem button.

6. A new Report a Problem link appears alongside the app within the list. Click this, and a form window will appear either within iTunes or within your web browser.

7. In the drop-down list in the form window, click the entry from the Problem heading that relates best to your issue. Then describe the problem briefly in the text area underneath. Click Submit when done.

Once you've submitted the problem you should receive a response within 24 hours.

Tip 164

Right-justify text

Dedicated word-processing apps like Pages can easily right-justify text, but the email and Notes apps can't—unless you follow this trick, which relies on a side effect of the fact that the iPad and iPhone can display Arabic text, which reads from the right to left.

Setup

Here's how to set up the tweak that will allow you to right-align any text you wish.

1. Open the Settings app.

2. Tap the following sequence of buttons: General > Keyboard > Keyboards > Add New Keyboard.

3. In the list of keyboards, select Arabic. Then quit Settings. Don't worry—we're never going to use the Arabic keyboard. It just adds a new option to the text-editing menu.

Right-Aligning a Line of Text

In any app that allows text editing, like Notes, begin typing a sentence or word, double-tap what you've typed, and then, on the pop-up menu, you'll see a new option at the right (you might have to tap the right-facing arrow to see this new option). The icon will be two arrows, one pointing to the left and the other to the right. Tapping this will right-justify the line. To left-justify it again, tap the two-arrows icon.

Most computers and devices receiving an email with text right-aligned in this way will display it correctly, including Windows PCs and Macs, as well as other iPhones and iPads.

Deactivating Right Justification

To deactivate the ability to right-justify text, repeat the steps under the preceding Setup heading until the list of installed keyboards is displayed. Then swipe left on the line for the Arabic keyboard until the Delete button appears. Tap the button.

Tip 165

Quickly adjust color and brightness in iPhoto

Although the Color and Exposure tools in iPhoto utilize sliders at the bottom of the screen, you can also tap and then drag on the screen to adjust after activating the tools. You can drag up and down or left and right, and labels will appear where you touch to show what you're adjusting.

iPhoto is clever enough to detect what you want to adjust. Tapping a shadow while using the Exposure tool, for example, will adjust the shadow slider. Tapping skin-colored objects when the Color tool is active will alter the warmth/coolness slider. Tapping the green leaves of a tree will adjust the greenery slider.

If your adjustments go wrong, you can tap the menu button (the icon is three dots) and tap Reset.

Tip 166

Make Maps show titles in native languages

If you travel abroad and use your iPad or iPhone for directions, the Maps app will very sensibly label destinations in English rather than the native language. In Germany you'll see Cologne rather than Koln, for example. As useful as it might sound, this can cause confusion when traveling—local signage won't match up with what you see in your directions, and any non-English speaker to whom you show your device might find it difficult to understand.

Luckily there's a solution: open the Settings app and scroll down to Maps on the left. Tap it, and then deactivate the switch that reads Always in English under the Map Labels heading. When you switch back to Maps you should find everything is instantly redrawn in the language of the country in question. Any pins you drop will still show English addresses, however, and regardless of the setting of the switch you should be able to search for places using both English and local names.

Repeat the preceding step if you later wish to return Maps to default to English.

Tip 167

See how long construction work will last

If you activate the Maps app's traffic mode (tap the (i) at the bottom right, then select Show Traffic) you'll see not only any potential jams, but also construction work and road closures. Tapping the icon for these will show a pop-up (see the following figure), and if you then tap the right-facing arrow you'll see details of the construction projects, including when they started and a proposed end time, if such details are available.

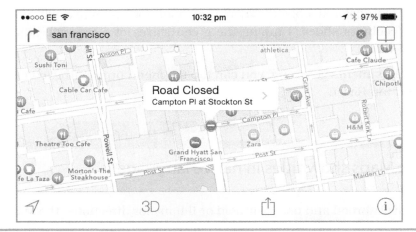

Figure 50—Viewing details about construction work in Maps on an iPhone

Tip 168

Easily move alarms on an iPad

The iPad's Clock app shows any alarms you have set as a horizontal weekly calendar, for which the vertical display shows the hours in each day. Inactive alarms are shown as gray bars, while active alarms are shown as red bars. Tapping and holding either kind will let you move the alarm in order to change its time, with each "jump" from one square to another representing 15 minutes. You'll see the display of the time above change accordingly.

Beware that repositioning an inactive alarm setting in this way will automatically set it!

Tip 169

Instantly see any unread emails

People have all kinds of policies for reading their email. Some people read all new email. Others read the important items and leave what they consider unimportant emails until later. If you fall into the latter category, then the Mail app can save you some effort.

A little-known feature of Mail is its mailboxes feature, which is accessible on both the iPad and iPhone by swiping in from the left side of the screen. The inbox is where you'll find all incoming mail, and the VIP mailbox is explained in Tip 58, *Be notified of only important emails*, on page 90, but by tapping the Edit button at the top of the screen you'll see several others that you can activate. One of these is the Unread mailbox. To activate it, put a check mark alongside it by tapping, and then tap Done at the top of the screen.

To use the new mailbox, just select it. It will show only unread messages. If there are no such messages, you'll be shown the message "No unread mail"—which means you can relax and play some Angry Birds!

To return to the usual inbox, just swipe in again from the left edge of the screen and select Inbox in the list of mailboxes (or All Inboxes if you have multiple accounts set up on the device).

Tip 170

Hide photos in iPhoto

Within some albums you might want to hide certain photos (for example, shots that are slightly blurry) without going to the extreme of deleting them. Select the photo(s) in the thumbnail album view, then tap the menu button (the icon for which is three dots). Then tap Hide Photos.

When you deselect the photos by tapping on any other, the photos will disappear.

To reveal hidden photos, tap the top of the album thumbnail listing, which usually shows how many photos are in that album. Then tap the Hidden button on the pop-out menu that appears. Note that this will only temporarily reveal the hidden photos. To unhide them, you must select them and then repeat the preceding steps to view the menu, except this time tap Unhide Photo.

Tip 171

Chat to groups of people via iMessage

An important difference between iMessage and text messaging is that you can create group chats in iMessage. Unlike when sending text messages, where each recipient you add to the message will be sent the message without knowing who else it's been sent to, group chats in iMessage will send every message to and from everybody included in the conversation—a little like in a website chat room.

To use group chat, start a new message in the Messages app and then type the name of each recipient in the To: field. Then type and send your message as usual. Replies will appear in the usual way, too, as if you're chatting to one other person, although all the group will have received them (unless the sender has trimmed the recipient list).

Unfortunately, there isn't a way to remove yourself from a group chat once you're part of one. If the messages become particularly annoying, you might choose to temporarily block the individuals, as described in Tip 224, *Block calls and messages from certain people*, on page 198.

For what it's worth, it's not possible to FaceTime with more than one person.

Tip 172

Use custom ringtones and vibrations for individual callers

Knowing who's calling or messaging you is usually a matter of glancing at the screen, but you can also assign custom ringtones to individuals so you can know who's calling by sound alone. In the case of the iPhone you can also assign custom vibration patterns, which can help identify who's calling if the phone is on silent and in your pocket.

Assigning Custom Ringtones

Open the individual's entry in the Contacts app, then tap the Edit button at the top right. Scroll down to the Ringtone section and tap it, then select the ringtone from the list. (Don't forget Tip 220, *Create your own ringtones*, on page 195, which explains how to create custom ringtones from MP3s.)

Creating Custom Vibration Patterns

To assign a custom vibration pattern on your iPhone, open a contact's details as already described, then tap the Vibration entry in the list. Choose a pattern from the list that appears, or scroll down and tap the Create New Vibration entry. Following this, tap the screen to create the pattern (recording will start on the first tap), and then tap the stop button when you're done. Tap the play button to "hear" the vibration played back to you, and tap the Save button at the top right when you're done, after which you'll be prompted to give the new pattern a name—choosing the name of the individual concerned should be fine. From then on the new pattern will be found under the Custom heading when you choose vibration patterns, as described previously, so you could use it for two or more people if you wish.

Tip 173

View "invisibles" in Pages

Some word processors offer the ability to view where carriage returns and tabs occur in a document. They do this by showing them as characters on the page, and collectively such symbols are known as *invisibles.* To view invisibles within Pages, simply highlight text by selecting it: double-tap anywhere, then tap Select All from the menu that appears.

Tip 174

Choose the order in which notifications appear

You can swipe from the top of the screen to view the notification area. It's designed to provide at-a-glance viewing of what apps want you to know about—everything from a news headline to a change in the weather or when it's your turn in a game.

With a lot of notifications, however, it can become hard to discern what's actually important. One way of getting around this is to manually adjust the order of notifications so that a notification of a new email message will always be placed above a notification that there's a new Facebook message, for example—regardless of then they were received.

Here's how it's done.

1. Open the Settings app, then tap the Notification Center link.

2. Under the Notifications View heading, tap Sort Manually.

3. Tap Edit at the top right, then scroll down to the Include heading, where the apps shown in the notification center are listed. At the right of each will be three bars. Drag this to reorder the apps—those at the top will have their notifications appear first, and so on. See Figure 51, *Rearranging the order in which notifications appear on an iPad*, on page 169 for an example from an iPad.

4. You can also remove an app's ability to appear in the notification center by dragging its entry to the Do Not Include heading (drag any apps already in that list into the Include section if you wish them to be able to show up in the notification area). Note that this doesn't alter the app's ability to show notifications when you're using your iPad or iPhone. It merely removes the notifications' ability to appear in the notification-area list.

5. When you've finished, tap Done. The changes will be reflected instantly in Notification Center, although remember that the heading for an app won't appear there unless there's currently a notification for it.

To return to the default setting of notifications being shown in the order they're received, repeat the preceding steps but this time tap Sort by Time under the Notifications view heading.

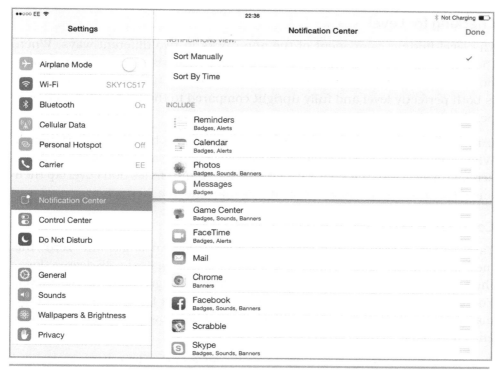

Figure 51—Rearranging the order in which notifications appear on an iPad

Tip 175

Find level surfaces with your iPhone

The Compass app on the iPhone is impressive, although perhaps not entirely useful in everyday life. However, it has a secret ability to check surface level-ness, like a carpenter's level used in construction work.

When the phone is laying on its back, look at the small crosshair within the larger crosshair of the compass display. If this smaller crosshair is perfectly centered, then the surface is flat.

However, there's also a decided level-finding tool within the Compass app, which can be accessed by starting the app and then swiping left. This is much easier to use, as follows.

Checking for Level

The level-finding component of the app works in two different ways. When the iPhone is rested on one of its edges it will show via black and white sections whether the iPhone is level. When the display turns green the iPhone is both perfectly level and fully upright compared to the surface (that is, perpendicular to the surface).

If the phone is laid flat on its back, two circles will be shown overlapping. When they overlap entirely with each other, creating a single circle, and the screen turns green, the phone is perfectly flat. If the circles don't overlap then one edge of the phone is lower or higher than the one facing it.

Comparing Different Angles

Tapping the screen at any time when measuring an angle will "zero" the measurement. In other words, if you hold the phone against a 45 degree slope, then tap the display, the iPhone will consider 45 degrees as the base level. You can then hold the phone against other surfaces to see if they precisely match the angle. If the angle is different you'll be shown the degree of difference onscreen.

Tapping the screen again will reset the measure to the default.

Tip 176

Search for businesses in Maps

The search field within the Maps app isn't just there to search for streets or zip codes. You can also enter the names of businesses. Want to know where your nearest Starbucks is? Just type that into the search field, and you'll find pins dropped wherever a Starbucks is found nearby. To see a text list of all the results, tap the list icon at the bottom middle of the screen.

It's not only names of businesses that you can search for. If you urgently need a gas station, for example, type that into the search field.

Of course, another way of searching for destinations is to ask Siri—you could say, "Where's the nearest Starbucks?" but you could also ask, "Where can I get coffee?"

Tip 177

Access photo-stream pics on a Windows PC

Apple Macs sync automatically with iCloud, although you'll need iWork installed on a Mac to sync documents, and iPhoto or Aperture to sync with your photo stream.

Believe it not, users of Windows-based computers have an advantage over Mac users because they don't need to buy any extra software to sync photo-stream pictures—even those that aren't in shared galleries. All they need to do is download the free iCloud Control Panel application.[18]

Once that application is installed, start the iCloud application, then ensure the Photo Stream option is checked and click the Apply button to start syncing. You'll find a new favorites entry in Windows Explorer that'll take you straight to the folder showing your main photo stream along with any that are shared by you or with you.

Perhaps strangely, any photos you manually add to this folder aren't synced with your account's main photo stream. However, you can right-click any photo anywhere within the Windows file system and select Add to a Photo Stream, then choose a shared photo stream. There'll also be an option to set up a new shared photo stream. To delete the photo from the shared photo stream, select the stream within Windows Explorer and delete in the usual way.

Tip 178

Answer or decline calls when wearing headphones

If you're wearing Apple headphones when you receive a phone call, clicking the center of the in-line remote control will answer the call. Pressing it again will hang up the call. Pressing and holding the center button until you hear two beeps will decline the call and send it straight to voicemail—the equivalent of tapping the Decline button on the screen.

18. http://support.apple.com/kb/DL1455

Tip 179

Save website images for viewing later

Most pictures on a website can be saved for later viewing by tapping and holding on them, and then selecting the Save Image option that appears. The image will be saved to your default camera roll and photo stream, and you can access it in the usual way using the Photos app.

Tip 180

See the time of messages at a glance

When viewing texts on an iPhone or iMessages on any Apple device, the time and date of each conversation is shown above it. But have you ever wanted to see at a glance when each individual message was sent, free of other details? Just drag any messages to the left. This will show the times in the right border of the screen.

Tip 181

See the full video frame when recording

If you create video using an iPad or iPhone 4s, you won't see the entire frame when recording, although the full video frame will still be recorded. What you see will have the sides chopped off.

This happens because the iPad and the iPhone 4s record video at a 16:9 screen ratio while their screens have a boxy 4:3 ratio. This isn't a problem on the iPhone 5 and later because the taller screen has an aspect ratio of 16:9.

There is a solution for iPad and iPhone 4s users, however—just double-tap the screen. This will show the full frame. Black borders will appear at the top and bottom of the screen—a bit like watching certain movies on a high-definition TV—but these won't be recorded. Double-tap again to switch back to the clipped view.

Tip 182

Get curly quotes

Whenever you type, iOS defaults to "straight" quotes like the ones I used there—quotation marks that don't look like miniature floating 6s and 9s (which are often referred to as curly quotes). If you're typing a business document or email this can look amateurish, especially considering most desktop operating systems add them automatically. The solution is to tap and hold the quotation-mark key on the onscreen keyboard. Via a pop-out menu you'll be able to choose curly quotes, as well as guillemets used in French and other languages.

The same applies to the single-quote (apostrophe) key, which when held will show curly varieties.

Tip 183

Alter the 3D maps angle

The Maps application includes a function that shows buildings as 3D models, allowing you to "fly through" areas to get a better visual idea of their layout before visiting. Activate the function by tapping the buildings icon at the bottom left of the screen when viewing in Satellite mode. (If the buildings icon is replaced with an icon that reads *3D*, then Apple hasn't yet provided 3D modeling for the area you're in.)

When using the fly-through view you can move around in the usual way by tapping and then dragging. You can alter the angle of the 3D perspective by dragging two fingers up and down on the screen, but ensure the fingers are bunched together—if they're wide apart iOS might assume you want to zoom in or out, or rotate the map.

Tip 184

Fix crashes

Sometimes an app crashes hard, so that it refuses to function any longer. It might even appear to jam your phone so that the Home button doesn't work.

There are two ways to quit apps like this. If the Home button is still working, press it twice to open the multitasking screen. When you see the list of open apps, flick the preview window for the crashed app to the top of the screen. This will quit it.

If this doesn't work, or if you can't even get the Home button to respond, try holding down the power button until the Slide to Power Off message appears. Then press and hold the Home button until the Slide to Power off message disappears. A split second later the app will quit and then restart almost instantly, when hopefully it will be better behaved.

If the device has entirely locked up, so that it doesn't respond to any button presses, press and hold the Home and Lock/Sleep buttons together until the screen goes blank, which may take 5–10 seconds. The device will then reboot.

Neither of these methods should be used casually; use them only when you have no other choice.

Tip 185

See how much data was used in a FaceTime call

Got only a small data allowance with your cellular provider and want to see know much of it that FaceTime call just ate up? Tap the phone icon, then tap Recents. Locate the call in the list and carefully tap the (i) symbol alongside the individual's name (be careful not to tap the full entry, because that will attempt to restart the call). On the screen that appears, you'll see details of the call, including its length and, in brackets afterward, the total amount of data sent and received. According to my calculations, you should allow roughly 8–9MB per minute of a call.

Tip 186

Quickly access your browsing history

Want to see what sites you've visited recently? Just tap and hold the back button in Safari until a page appears listing the sites in order. Then tap one of the entries in the list to visit that site.

Should the forward button be visible after you've browsed back, the same trick will work if you tap and hold it—you'll see a list of sites you viewed after the one you're currently looking at.

Tip 187

Find the serial number of a stolen iPad/iPhone

If you lose your iPhone, iPad, or iPod Touch, or have it stolen, then the police or insurance company might ask for its serial number. But there's a problem: although this info is visible in iTunes when the device is attached or within Wi-Fi range, and viewable on the device itself by opening Settings and tapping About, it won't be visible when the phone is in the back pocket of a thief across town!

Luckily there's a solution, although it varies depending on whether you're using a Mac or Windows PC. Additionally, it won't work unless you've synced your device with your computer at least once.

Finding Serial Numbers on a Mac

To find the serial number of your Apple device(s) using a Mac, follow these steps.

1. Install Xcode via the Mac App Store. This is free of charge but a multiple-gigabyte download, so install it when you have a good Internet connection.

2. Close iTunes, then open a Finder window, hold down Shift-Command-G, then type the following in the dialog box that appears:

   ~/Library/Preferences

3. Look for the file that reads com.apple.iPod.plist (even if you don't actually have an iPod!), then double-click it. This will open it in Xcode's plist editor. A plist is simply a configuration file.

4. Under the Devices heading will be one or more strings of hexadecimal characters. Click the triangle next to an entry to expand it. Alongside the Device Class heading will be the type of device (iPad, iPod, etc.) and under the Serial Number heading will be the info you're looking for. Be careful not to modify the plist file while you're viewing it. Just close it when you've finished, and quit Xcode.

Finding Serial Numbers on a Windows PC

Here's how to find the serial numbers using a Windows computer.

1. Open a file-browsing window, then navigate to the following folder (replacing USERNAME with your own username).

   ```
   \Users\USERNAME\AppData\Local\Apple Computer\iTunes
   ```

2. Double-click the file that reads iPodDevices. This will open it in Internet Explorer.

3. There will be lists for each device you've used on that computer, and you can tell which list is for which device by looking under the Device Class heading.

4. Look for the line that reads Serial Number, then look beneath it to see the serial number.

There's a small drawback to viewing serial numbers in the ways described here. Entries for old devices will still be in the list, as will entries for iPads and iPhones that weren't yours but have been attached to the computer (those of family members, for example). On one of the Macs used for testing this tip there was an entry for an iPad that was sold more than a year ago. If you find the list includes such items, you'll have to use another clue to find which are currently used devices—look at the Connected field, which shows when a particular device was last connected to your Mac.

Tip 188

Insert commonly used currency symbols when typing

Press and hold the dollar sign on the onscreen keyboard, and a submenu will appear showing various currency symbols from around the world, including the pound-sterling symbol (£) and the Euro symbol (€). You'll also find the cent symbol (¢) listed. Just slide your finger over to one and lift your finger to insert it at the cursor point.

To add lesser-known currency symbols to the pop-out menu, add the corresponding language's keyboard by following the steps in Tip 164, *Right-justify text*, on page 162. For instance, for the Saudi riyal you would add the Arabic keyboard, and for the baht symbol you would add the Thai keyboard.

Tip 189

Add another person's Touch ID

Although the Touch ID setup might've given you the idea that only you can be authorized to use your phone, the truth is that Touch ID can recognize up to five separate fingerprints. This means you can give four more people access to your device.

To do so, open Settings, then tap General and scroll down to Passcode & Fingerprint, then tap Fingerprints > Add a Fingerprint, and have the other person follow the wizard steps to add her own print to the Touch ID system.

For what it's worth, the other user doesn't even have to be human—people have been able to add their cats and dogs as Touch ID users!

Tip 190

Choose a serendipitous destination

Ever wanted to spin a globe and stick a pin in it to choose a travel destination? Well, if you're about to visit a country and want to surprise yourself with the exact destination, the Maps app can do something very similar!

Start by zooming out within the Maps app so you can see the globe, and then zoom in a little so the country in question is in the center of the screen. Then tap and hold somewhere beyond the country's border until a pin is dropped. If you wanted to visit Mexico, for example, you might tap and hold in the Gulf of Mexico. Tap and hold the pin before flicking your finger toward the country. This will "throw" the pin, and where it lands depends on the force with which you flicked but is essentially random. And *that* will be your travel destination! Send us a postcard!

Tip 191

Zoom in further to pictures

If you open an image in the Photos app and use the pinch gesture to zoom in, you'll see that there's a limit on how much you can zoom into the image.

If you absolutely need to zoom in beyond this range, you can call on a rather odd trick. Open the image in Photos, then tap the share button and select to add it to a new Messages conversation. Then send it to yourself (that is, type your own email address or cell number in the recipient field). Switch to the Messages app, and the photo will be waiting for you as if you've just received it from somebody else, but if you double-tap to view it, you will find that you're able to zoom into it via the pinch gesture much more than you can within Photos. For an example, see the following figure.

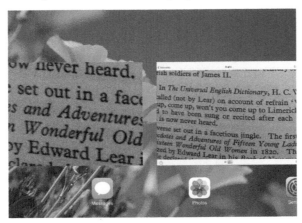

Figure 52—The iPad's multitasking bar showing the different maximum zoom levels of the same image when viewed in the Photos app and as a Messages attachment

Tip 192

Remove a photo filter

If you've shot a photo with one of the filters applied on an iPhone 5/5c/5s, you might change your mind later on. The black-and-white Noir filter looked great when you shot the photo during the party, but in the cold light of morning it just makes your guests look weird.

Perhaps surprisingly, photo filters are removable even if they were applied while the image was taken. Just open the picture in the Photos app, then tap the Edit button. Tap the effects button and scroll the list of effects to the left so that None is selected. Tap Apply, then Save.

Of course, if you change your mind a second time and decide the effect is indeed what you want, you can repeat the preceding steps and reapply the effect!

Tip 193

Look up a phone number

Have you ever gotten home and found that the caller display on your landline shows a number, but nobody's left a message?

The Contacts app lets you search by phone number as well as name. Just type the phone number into the search field at the top of the screen, and see if it matches one of your contacts.

Tip 194

Crop a photo for printing

A standard photo taken on an iPad or iPhone is squarish. It doesn't take a genius to realize that, but in fact the aspect ratio is roughly 4:3, which means that the images are a quarter wider than they are tall if the photo is taken in landscape mode, or a quarter taller than wide if taken in portrait mode.

Unfortunately, the papers used by photo-printing outlets aren't quite the same size because they're based on the older 35mm film sizes. This leads to the edges of images being chopped off. Usually this is done automatically once the photos are downloaded to the printer, but you can prepare in advance and crop the images yourself according to the size of print you want. This could mean the difference between the top of somebody's head being lost and not!

Here's how it's done:

1. Open the picture in the Photos app and then tap the Edit button.

2. Tap the Crop button (its icon is a square with corners that extend out), and then tap the Aspect Ratio button at the bottom of the screen on an iPad, or the Aspect button on an iPhone.

3. You'll be shown a handful of aspect-ratio choices—choose the one you need based on the print size listed in the following table.

4. Once you've chosen a ratio, you'll be able to drag the photo around to reposition it within the new frame size, as the following figure shows. You can also use the pinch gesture to zoom in or out.

Figure 53—Cropping a photo for printing

5. Tap Crop when done, and then Save to record the changes. Remember that any edits you make to a photo aren't permanent—see Tip 97, *Undo photo edits—even after you've saved them*, on page 119.

Print size	Aspect ratio
2×3 inches	3×2
4×6 inches	3×2
5×7 inches	5×7
8×10 inches	8×10
10×15 inches	3×2

Table 1—Aspect ratios for commercial photo printers

Tip 195

Refer to the page number in a Pages document

Ever wanted to have the current page number referred to in a paragraph of a Pages document? You can insert page numbers easily into the footer of a document (see Tip 207, *Create footnotes in Pages*, on page 189), but there's seemingly no way to insert them into the body of a document.

As you might expect, you can do so via a quick hack. Switch to Doc Setup view by tapping the wrench icon, then Document Setup. Tap the footer area so the cursor appears there, and double-tap a blank spot, then select Page Numbers on the pop-out menu that appears. Choose which style of page number you want, then once it's been inserted, highlight the text that's been inserted into the footer, and cut it to the clipboard.

Switch back to the main document view by tapping Done twice, and you can then paste the page number right into the document itself. Crucially, the page number will retain the same magical properties it had when used in the footer, and will always reflect the current page number. So if you paste it in on page 4, it will show 4. Paste it in on page 500, and it will show 500—and it will instantly change to reflect any pages being added or removed (so if page 500 becomes page 503, the number will change to reflect this).

Tip 196

Export high-res edited images in iPhoto

Whenever you edit one of your camera-roll images in iPhoto, the app will automatically save the edited version back to your camera roll, seemingly replacing the original. However, iPhoto is lying a little because it actually saves a low-resolution edit to the camera roll.

For example, if you edit a snap using iPhoto, then open it in your camera roll and send it as an iMessage via the share button, you'll send an image that's less than 1 megapixel in size!

The original high-resolution photo is still stored within iPhoto, though, and you can make iPhoto output a full-resolution edited image. To do so, open the edited image within iPhoto, then tap the share button and select Camera Roll under the Apps heading, then tap the Selected (1) heading to start the export. Once you do, the edited photo will be added to the camera roll as a new, high-resolution image that will mirror the original's megapixel resolution.

Tip 197

Sort documents in iWork apps

Dragging down in the document listing of the iWork apps will reveal a Date and Name heading, and tapping either will sort the documents according to either date of creation or last edit (Date), or alphanumerically (Name).

Tip 198

Get pictures off your device without iCloud

Although iCloud provides a way to get photos off your iPad or iPhone and onto a Windows PC, waiting for your pictures to download can be annoying if you're in a hurry. Of course, if you lack an Internet connection then picture syncing is impossible.

By connecting your iPad or iPhone to your Mac or Windows PC using the USB cable, you can download photos just like when using a digital camera, although you will only gain access to pictures on the camera roll, and not photo-stream pictures taken with a different device.

Here's how it's done.

Downloading Photos on a Mac

The process of downloading images via a Mac is the same as for other digital cameras that lack dedicated software for the purpose, in that the Preview app is used, as follows.

1. Attach your iPad or iPhone, then close iTunes if it opens automatically. Instead, open Preview, which you can find in the Applications list of Finder.

2. Click File > Import From, and choose the option representing your device.

3. A window will open showing thumbnail previews of all the images on the device's camera roll. Click and drag the slider at the bottom right to enlarge or shrink the thumbnail size if you need to see more details.

4. Hold down Cmd and select the photos you want to import. Click in a blank area to undo the selection if necessary.

5. When done making your selection, click the Import button. Alternatively, click the Import All button to import all photos from the camera roll.

6. A file-save dialog box will appear asking where you want to save the pictures. Once you've selected a folder (or made a new one using the New Folder button at the bottom left), click the Choose Destination button.

7. The images will then be imported, and Preview will show them as a series of thumbnails. You can opt to tweak the photos within Preview if you wish, or close the app.

Note that you can also click and drag images to the desktop or a Finder window when you opt to import from the device.

Downloading Photos on a Windows PC

The process of downloading photos on a Windows PC is the same as for any other digital camera or storage device, in that your iPad or iPhone will appear under the Portable Devices heading of the Computer view of File Explorer, and you can drag and drop files from the DCIM folder to a location on your hard disk. Here are the steps:

1. Attach your iPad or iPhone, then close iTunes if it opens automatically. If this is the first time the device has been attached, Windows will search for and install drivers automatically, which might take a minute or two.

2. Open the Computer view of the file explorer, which you'll find on the Start menu.

3. At the bottom of the drive listings will be a Portable Device heading, showing your iPad or iPhone. Double-click this, then double-click the Internal Storage icon that appears.

4. Open the DCIM folder and you should see your images, which you can drag and drop to your hard disk.

Tip 199

Easily send emails to groups of people

Although it's possible to create groups of contacts (see Tip 251, *Create contact groups*, on page 216), iOS offers no way to send email messages to a contacts group. However, it is possible to quickly and easily email a group of people using a small hack. The solution is to create a single contact card with several addresses.

Setup

Here's how to create the card that we'll use to send group emails. You only have to do this once for each group you want to create.

1. Using a Mac or Windows PC, visit the iCloud website,[19] then log in with your Apple ID.

---

19. https://icloud.com

2. Tap the Contacts icon and then, when your list of contacts appears, click the plus (+) icon and select to create a new contact (*don't* select to create a new group!).

3. In the First Name field, type a name for the group. Something like Family or Office Colleagues will be fine.

4. In the first email field (Home), type the first email address, then a comma, then the next address. Repeat until you've entered all the addresses, and click Done. You can now quit the iCloud website.

Sending Group Emails

To send a group email, open the Contacts app on your iPad or iPhone, then search for the group contact you created. When it opens, tap the email-address field. This will start a new email with the addresses automatically filled in. If you have multiple email accounts set up on the device, tap the From: field twice to choose the account from which you'd like to send the email.

Alternatively, rather than using the Contacts app to start a new email, you can compose a new email in the Mail app (or via the share button in other apps) and type the group contact name into the address field. When you tap the Send button you'll be warned that the email address is invalid. Clicking the Send option in the dialog box should send the message anyway, however. Additionally, in my tests sending email from an iCloud account in this way doesn't work, although sending via Gmail, Outlook.com (aka Hotmail), Yahoo!, and AOL all work fine.

Tip 200

Be reminded of birthdays

Being notified of people's birthdays in the Calendar app is a great way to avoid potential embarrassment. Rather than create an individual calendar event for each person, however, iOS lets you add birth dates within your Contacts app. The individuals' birthdays will then automatically appear as calendar events each year—complete with an icon representing a present—and you'll be shown their age, too, if you entered a birth year in Contacts.

Here's how to add birth dates to contacts:

1. Open the Contacts app, then search for the person in question and open the contact.

2. Tap the Edit button at the top right, then tap the Add Birthday field.

3. Enter the date by adjusting the dials. You can leave off the year, but if you do, you won't be told the person's age on the birthday notification.

4. Tap Done.

The changes will be reflected in the Calendar app immediately. The events are part of a special Birthdays calendar created for the purpose, so to instantly hide all birthdays deselect this calendar in the Calendars list view (which you can see by tapping the Calendars button at the bottom of the screen).

Tip 201

Reduce the space your music collection takes up

iTunes on the PC and Mac offers a way of shrinking the file size of any music files it syncs with your iPhone or iPad, allowing you to cram in more tunes. This can be extremely useful if you own a 16GB device, for example, which is easily filled with music, movies, and apps. Crucially, although the music will be shrunk when synced to your iPhone or iPod, the full-sized versions will remain on your computer's hard disk.

You shrink the file size by reducing the bit rate of the song—essentially, removing detail from the audio waveform. This sounds worse than it is, and whether it actually affects audio quality is open to debate. The consensus is that it takes a true audiophile to spot any quality compromises, and in several listening tests listeners have actually preferred lower bit-rate settings!

Here's how to reduce the bit rate of songs on your device:

1. Attach the device (or ensure it's within Wi-Fi range if Wi-Fi syncing is enabled), then open iTunes and select it from the drop-down list at the top right of the iTunes window.

2. Select the Summary tab, and look under the Options heading near the bottom. You'll see an entry that reads "Convert higher bit rate songs." Put a check mark alongside it, and choose 128kbps from the drop-down list.

3. Click the Apply button at the bottom right of the iTunes window. Your music collection will be copied to your device afresh, at the altered bit rate, and replace the existing tracks.

Depending on the size of your music collection, it may take some time for the tracks to be shrunk and copied across to your device.

Of course, should you find the audio quality difference unacceptable, you can repeat the preceding steps but uncheck the box, which will resync your tracks at their original bit rates.

Tip 202

See links from Twitter buddies

iOS features full Twitter integration and you can use the Share feature of apps like Photos to instantly share and upload photos along with a tweet.

Even if you don't want to tweet from your device, there is a good reason to sign into Twitter: Safari will scan the recent postings of your Twitter friends and show all the postings that have links.

Here's how to sign into Twitter and access the links list:

- To set up Twitter on your iPad or iPhone, open the Settings app then tap the Twitter heading and fill in your details.

- To view tweets that contain links, open Safari then tap the bookmarks icon (overlapping squares). A new column will be visible, with an "@" heading. Tapping this will show tweets involving links.

- Tapping a link will cause you to visit the link in Safari, and the tweet will be listed at the top of the web page so you can reference it. Unfortunately, there's no way to respond to a tweet without using the official Twitter app, which is available in the App Store.

Tip 203

Create a "lost or stolen" lock-screen message

Here's a basic but sensible tip that could see your iPhone or iPad quickly returned to you if it gets lost. It involves creating a special wallpaper image detailing your contact details, which you then set as the lock-screen wallpaper. Subsequently, anybody who tries to wake the device will see this message. This might not help if a device is stolen, but it can aid quick recovery if the device is misplaced at an office or school, for example.

The Find My iPad/iPhone service will theoretically display a message you send to a lost or stolen device (see *Security*, on page 30), but it relies on the iPhone or iPad being able to receive a network connection. This might not always be the case.

Here are the steps required to create a lock-screen message, which require the use of an image-editing program of some kind:

1. Create a new file in your favorite image editor using the following dimensions, depending on what device you have (each device requires a separate wallpaper):

   - iPhone 4 and 4s: 640×960
   - iPhone 5, 5c, and 5s: 640×1136
   - iPad and iPad Mini: 1024×768
   - iPad Air, iPad Retina, and iPad Mini Retina: 2048×1536

   Rather than creating a file, you might choose to open an existing digital-camera image and crop or shrink it to these dimensions.

   The *iPad and iPhone Kung Fu* website provides several ready-made template files you can adapt within Adobe Photoshop or a compatible app.[20]

2. Roughly in the middle of the image, use the text tool to type something similar to the following. Substitute your personal details and use a font and point size that's not too large but will be readable (remember that whatever you write must appear between the time/date and the "Slide to unlock" message):

```
Property of
[your name]

If you're reading this
then this phone [or iPad] is
lost or stolen. Please phone

[a non-cell phone number]

to arrange return.
```

   You might also add a section about a reward for return. It's not a bad idea to add a small snapshot of yourself, because then if you're reclaiming the phone after it's lost or misplaced there'll be no need to prove who you are—you can point to the picture!

---

20. http://applekungfu.com/lockscreen.html

3. Optionally, add a background color that ensures the text is legible.

4. Save the file in PNG format, then transfer it to your device so that it's imported into the camera roll. You can do this in a variety of ways—send the image to yourself via email, for example, then open the email on the iPad or iPhone and save it to your camera roll. On a Mac running OS X Mountain Lion or later you can send the image file to your own iMessage address using the Messages app.

5. Open the Settings app, then select the Brightness & Wallpaper option. Choose the new wallpaper in the usual way, and move and scale it so that the message is visible. In the case of the iPad, be sure to choose the wallpaper in portrait mode, then rotate the device to ensure the text is still readable in landscape mode.

6. Finally, set the image as your lock-screen wallpaper.

Tip 204

Get a visual cue when notifications appear

Want to know of new notifications when you're across the room from your iPhone, or when it's face-down? Just open Settings, tap General > Accessibility, and tap the switch alongside LED Flash for Alerts under the Hearing heading.

From now on whenever you get a notification, the LED flash on the back of your phone will blink briefly. Beware that it's a very bright light and in a dark environment it will not fail to draw attention!

To deactivate the blink, repeat the preceding steps, but this time deactivate the switch alongside LED Flash for Alerts.

Tip 205

Zoom when recording video or taking photos

To zoom when recording video, or to zoom in before taking a shot, just use the pinch gesture on the screen—finger and thumb pinched together, then expanded. Reverse the gesture to zoom out again.

Alternatively, if the pinch gesture is too difficult, use the gesture to start the zoom and then drag the circle on the bar display that appears showing how much you're zoomed in.

The zoom that happens is digital. When taking photos this can make for poorer-quality images, but there's little if any sacrifice in image quality when shooting video because the image sensor in an iPad and iPhone is large enough to record sufficient detail.

Tip 206

Bounce to activate the lock-screen camera

You can start the camera from the lock screen by sliding up the small, faint camera icon at the bottom of the screen. Although it serves no practical purpose, you can also "bounce" open the camera by sliding the camera icon to about halfway up the screen, then quickly firing it back down to the bottom of the screen. If you do it right, the lock screen will bounce to the top of the screen, revealing the camera.

This is easier to do on an iPhone than an iPad, but it's a great trick for impressing friends!

Tip 207

Create footnotes in Pages

You can add individual footnotes to pages in the following ways, depending on which device you're using:

- iPad: Tap the plus (+) symbol on the format bar above the keyboard when editing text, then select Footnote.

- iPhone: When the keyboard is visible tap and hold anywhere on the page, then from the pop-up menu select Insert, and tap the Footnote entry in the list that appears.

To apply headers and footers to the entire document you'll need to tap the Settings button (the icon is a wrench), then Document Setup, then the Tap To Edit Header or Tap To Edit Footer areas on the Doc Setup view that appears.

Tip 208

Type apostrophes and quotes quickly on an iPad

When you tap and hold the comma or period key on the iPad's main keyboard, a pop-up option will appear allowing you to type an apostrophe on the comma key, and a quotation mark on the period key. However, there's no need to tap and hold to insert the characters. Instead you can tap and then drag upward immediately. The pop-up will appear and be instantly selected, and when you lift your finger the symbol will be inserted. Have a try—it's a small trick that can really speed up typing.

Tip 209

Make Siri pronounce names correctly

If Siri can't seem to pronounce a name right, all you need do is tell it. Whenever the name is mentioned, say, "Siri, that's not how you pronounce that name." It will then prompt you to say the name, and subsequently ask you to choose from several variations of its own pronunciation—just tap the play icon alongside each to hear how they sound, as the figure here shows.

To force Siri to learn how to pronounce your own name correctly, start it and then say, "Siri, who am I?" Siri will respond by showing you your own contact details, along with a quip involving your own name. You can then tell it that its pronunciation is wrong, as described previously.

Figure 54—Correcting Siri's pronunciation on an iPhone

Tip 210

Easily select paragraphs in iWork apps

iWork apps include a magical way of selecting entire paragraphs that isn't available elsewhere in iOS—tap the paragraph three times. You can also tap once with two fingers, as described in Tip 6, *Easily select paragraphs, sentences, and lines*, on page 57.

Tip 211

Instantly dismiss notifications

If a notification folds down from the top of the screen while you're working, there's no need to wait for it to go away. Just drag it back up to the top of the screen. In fact, you can use a flick gesture to send it back to the top of the screen, which is even quicker!

Tip 212

Get free apps even if your device doesn't have the space

You might find that an app is being offered for free or at a reduced price for a limited time. Or you might be offered a free app as described in Tip 65, *Get free stuff from Apple*, on page 95. But what if you lack storage space on your iPad or iPhone to install the app?

The advice is simple: don't ignore the offer. Instead, tap to "buy" it anyway. You'll be told right away that there isn't space to install the app on your device, but the key thing is that as far as Apple is concerned, you own the app—even if you didn't install it. You can therefore install it at a later date and/or on other devices by opening the App Store and tapping the Purchased link (on an iPhone tap the Updates button and then tap Purchased at the top of the screen).

Tip 213

See more detail when viewing Safari tabs on an iPhone

It's a small detail, but one worth knowing—when you view the tabs within Safari on an iPhone, the "cards" that represent each website exist in 3D space. If you angle your phone down, you can see more detail at the bottom of each card.

This doesn't work on the iPad, because the iPad uses a more traditional system of tabs at the top of the Safari user interface.

Tip 214

Turn the first home screen into a picture frame

Here's a useful trick if you want to see the wallpaper without any app icons in front of it each time you unlock your phone, as the figure here shows. This might be desirable if you have a family photograph set as the wallpaper, for example. Your app icons will still be accessible on the other home screens, which you can access by swiping in the usual way. The Dock will be visible at the bottom of all home screens.

The trick is simple: move all the icons from the first home screen onto the other home screens. You do this in the usual way: by tapping and holding until the icons wobble, then repositioning them by dragging.

Because the iPad and iPhone always show the first home screen upon being unlocked, you'll see a clear view of your wallpaper image at that moment.

Figure 55—Creating an empty home-screen "picture frame" on an iPhone

Tip 215

Rate songs

iTunes on your computer lets you rate tunes, and this can help when creating Genius playlists. You can rate songs from 0 to 5 stars.

To rate tunes on your iPad or iPhone, or adjust an existing rating, use the Music app. Just switch to the Now Playing screen when a song is playing (tap the link at the top right) and then tap the name of the song just above the playback controls on the iPhone, or at the top of the screen on an iPad. Then tap the star rating you want. Tapping in a blank spot to the left or right of the rating area will switch back to the song's title.

Tip 216

Quickly reject a call

To quickly reject a call so it goes to your voice mailbox, just press the Lock/Sleep button twice. Note that pressing it once will simply silence the ringer, as described in Tip 34, *Stop the phone's ringing, but still take the call*, on page 77.

Tip 217

View upcoming reminders

Anything you add to the Reminders app can be set to have an alarm, to remind you on a certain date and time. Just tap the (i) icon alongside a reminder and then tap the Remind Me on a Day switch before entering the details.

However, wouldn't it be useful to be able to view all your upcoming reminders before their alarms sound? Well, you can, and here's how:

- iPad: Open the Reminders app, then tap the Scheduled button at the left.

- iPhone: Open the Reminders app, then switch to list view (tap the cards at the bottom of the screen so each of your reminder list headings are shown). Then tap anywhere and drag down before tapping the alarm-clock icon at the top right of the screen.

Regardless of whether you're using an iPad or iPhone, you'll then be shown a special Scheduled list, showing the list of reminders. You'll even be able to select any of them in the list to mark them as completed so the alarm won't sound.

Tip 218

Scrub properly

Tapping and holding the playhead bar near a song or video title will let you "scrub" through the track—cue to a different position before or after the current playing point.

What's less well know is that if you tap and hold the playhead then drag your finger above the playhead all the way to the top of the screen, you can slow down the scrub rate, which is to say, how quickly the playhead will advance backward and forward through the track when you drag left and right. In fact, the higher you drag the your finger, the slower it will move, and there are four choices—high-speed scrubbing (which is default), half-speed scrubbing, quarter-speed scrubbing, and fine scrubbing. See the figure for an example on an iPhone, but it's best demonstrated by doing it, so give it a try!

If the playhead bar is at the top of the screen, drag down rather than up. This trick works on both audio and video tracks.

Figure 56—Fine scrubbing through a track on an iPhone

Tip 219

Copy items between iWork apps

Compared to a regular computer, iOS includes only primitive copying and pasting support. You can copy and paste photos and other such items but, generally speaking, any formatting will be lost in the process.

iWork is an exception. Any object added to a document in one iWork app can be copied and then pasted into another. For example, you might create a spreadsheet of numbers plus a bar chart in Numbers, then copy and paste them into a Keynote document, where it will appear perfectly.

Copying and pasting is done in the usual way—select the object until the pop-up menu appears, then tap Copy. Then tap in an empty space in the other app, and tap the paste button.

You can also try pasting items into non-iWork apps. As mentioned previously, though, any formatting likely will be lost.

Tip 220

Create your own ringtones

You can purchase ringtones, of course, but it's also possible to make your own from tracks within your iTunes library. For this to work, you'll need to use the Mac or Windows PC your iPad or iPhone syncs with.

Here are the steps:

1. Listen to the track in iTunes on your Mac or Windows PC and note the start time of the part you wish to use for the ringtone. It might be the chorus 1:04 into the song, for example (that is, one minute four seconds).

2. Select the tune in the list of tracks within iTunes, then press Ctrl-I (Cmd-I on a Mac) to open its Info dialog box. Click the Options tab.

3. Put a check mark in the Start Time and Stop Time boxes, then type into the Start Time field the time you noted earlier. Add 45 seconds and type that time in the Stop Time box. A rather useful feature here is that you can add the seconds together and enter something like 0:88. iTunes will convert this to 1:28 when you click OK.

4. Close the Info dialog box, then open the iTunes Options Preferences dialog box by clicking the menu icon at the top left and selecting the option (on a Mac press Cmd-, (comma) to open the Preferences dialog box in iTunes).

5. Ensure the General tab is selected, then click the Import Settings button alongside the When You Insert a CD heading. Look under the Import Using heading and make a note of the existing setting before ensuring AAC Encoder is selected.

6. Close the dialog box, then right-click the track you modified earlier and select either Create AAC Version or Create MP3 Version, depending on which option is visible.

7. Within seconds, a new track is created (with the length you entered earlier). Don't forget to revert the iTunes encoding settings to whatever they were previously, as described in step 5.

8. Copy the file to the desktop by dragging it there. Then give it an .m4r extension (*r* is for *ringtone*). For example, if the file was called Really Cool Song — Justin Bieber.m4a then you should rename it to Really Cool Song — Justin Bieber.m4r. In the iTunes song listing, delete the new short track you created earlier.

9. Double-click the ringtone file, and it will be imported into the Tones section in iTunes. Sync your iPhone, and it should be available as a ringtone choice within the Sounds section of the Settings app. If it's not, check that you've set iTunes to sync ringtones as well as music by selecting the device within the devices list, clicking the Tones heading, and putting a check mark in the Sync Tones box.

10. Repeat step 3, but this time remove the check from the Start Time and Stop Time boxes. This will ensure the track plays fully in the future.

Tip 221

Use Siri to maintain a grocery list

Here's a tip that's very simple in execution but is something few people think to do.

Although it makes sense to say to Siri something like, "Add milk to the grocery list," Siri includes no functionality for logging groceries. However, such a system is easily created.

Start by opening the Reminders app and, if using the iPhone, switch to the view showing all your reminder lists by tapping the card stack at the bottom of the screen. Then, on an iPad tap the Edit button then Add List, or on the iPhone tap the plus (+) icon. Either action will create a new list, which you should call Grocery.

From now on, giving Siri a command like, "Add milk to the grocery list" will work fine, and the item will appear on the "Grocery" list in Reminders. You can then consult the list within the Reminders app when visiting the super-market, and tap the radio button alongside each item to remove it from the list when you've added it to your cart. Additionally, you can call up Siri and say, "Read me the grocery list."

Tip 222

Listen to iTunes Radio worldwide

If iTunes Radio hasn't yet arrived where you live, you can still tune into it by creating a new Apple ID registered within the United States, as described in Tip 127, *Download from foreign App Stores or iTunes Stores*, on page 139.

Sign into the iTunes Store app on your iPad or iPhone using the new Apple ID, then quit the Music app using the multitasking bar in the usual way (no, that's not a typo—you must quit the Music app, even though you signed in using iTunes!). When you restart the Music app you'll find a new option at the bottom for iTunes Radio. Additionally, you'll be invited to set up the service by choosing an initial station.

Tip 223

Search on a web page

Imagine the scene: you're Googling a search term on your iPad or iPhone, and you find a page packed with text that may or may not contain the thing you're looking for. Reading through it is impractical. If you were searching on a regular computer you'd tap Ctrl-F or Cmd-F (or click Edit > Find) and type the search term so it's highlighted and you can jump straight to it. But how can you do this on an iPad or iPhone?

The solution is simple: just tap the URL/search bar, and type the search term again, but *don't tap the* Go *key to begin the search*. Instead scroll to the bottom of the suggested results and shortcuts that Safari provides. At the bottom you'll see an On This Page heading, and by tapping the Find entry beneath that you'll see that the search term is highlighted on the web page. Tap the left and right arrows on the toolbar at the bottom to jump to other instances on the page, and click Done to dismiss the search toolbar when you've finished searching.

Block calls and messages from certain people

Unwanted calls and messages are a fact of life, but your iPhone and iPad allow you to block certain contact details so that you don't receive calls (including FaceTime) or messages from them.

Once applied, a block will take effect immediately. Any calls from the blocked number will go straight through to voicemail, and FaceTime calls will show as unavailable. SMS and iMessages will appear to the caller to be delivered fine, although you won't see them. You will have no indication that number has attempted to contact you, although because the setting applies only to Apple hardware it won't stop the caller from leaving a voicemail message, for example. Additionally, some cellular carriers send you text messages whenever you miss a call, and these will not be blocked because they come from the carrier directly. You may be able to deactivate such messages by speaking to the carrier's technical-support helpline.

The blocked contact details are automatically synced among your devices (assuming you're using iCloud), so blocking a number on the iPhone will also block it on any iPads you own, for example.

Blocking After You Receive a Call or Message

Depending on the nature of the call, there are different ways of blocking contact details, as follows.

- Phone call: To block a number after you've received a call from it, open the Phone app, then tap the Recents icon at the bottom of the screen. Look for the number in the list (remember that the calls are arranged by time, so the most recent will be at the top), and them tap the (i) button alongside the number in the list. At the bottom of the screen that subsequently appears, tap the Block This Caller link. You'll be asked to confirm if that's what you really want to do, so click Block Contact to confirm.

- FaceTime: Open FaceTime, then tap to look at the Recents list, then tap the (i) alongside the entry for the caller before tapping Block This Caller, as with blocking a phone call.

- Messaging: To block somebody who's messaged you, open the Messages app, then tap on the message to view it. At the top right, tap Contact, then tap the (i) icon. At the bottom of the screen that subsequently appears on the iPhone, tap the Block This Caller link. On the iPad, you will need to scroll up the pop-out window to see the Block This Caller option.

Blocking a Number That Hasn't Yet Contacted You

It's also possible to block someone preemptively. To do so, you'll need to discover the individual's contact details, such as phone number, email address(es), or cell-phone number(s) the person uses for iMessage and/or FaceTime.

Following this you'll need to create an entry for the person in the Contacts app, if one doesn't already exist. Alternatively, you might choose to create a single new contact called Blocked (simply type that into the First Name field), to which you add the contact details of all individuals you want to block. (To add more than one phone number or email address to a contact card, tap the Add Phone or Add Email heading repeatedly to create new fields.) The figure here shows an example.

Figure 57—Creating a "Blocked" contact card on an iPhone

Once you've created the card, open the Settings app, then tap the Messages heading and then the Blocked entry in the list, which will be near the bottom.

Tap Add New and select either the contact card for the individual you want to block, or the Blocked contact card containing the details of many different individuals.

Unblocking a Number

To unblock a phone number, open the Settings app, then tap the Messages heading, and then the Blocked entry in the list, which will be near the bottom. Swipe your finger left on the entry for the individual you want to unblock, then tap the button when it appears. The change will take effect immediately.

To remove an entry from the Blocked contacts entry, repeat the steps in the section *Blocking a Number That Hasn't Yet Contacted You*, on page 199, to open the Blocked contact card, then tap the Edit button. Tap the red minus icon alongside the contact detail you wish to remove, then tap the Delete button to remove it.

Tip 225

View larger thumbnails in iPhoto

If you're viewing an album in iPhoto and want to view larger thumbnails of the photos—by viewing a group as a grid of four photos, for example—tap one photo to open it for viewing, then tap and hold others that you want to appear alongside it. All the selected photos will be thumbnailed in the editing area. To deselect an item from the group, just tap and hold its thumbnail again.

To cancel the selection, just tap another photo in the usual way to open it for viewing.

You can't edit photos while they're multiple-selected in this way, but you can tag them all, share them, favorite them, or hide them (see Tip 170, *Hide photos in iPhoto*, on page 166).

Tip 226

Fun things to ask Siri

Siri can answer quite a few questions and statements that are, essentially, unanswerable. A good suggestion is to activate Siri and recite movie quotes (for example, "Open the pod bay doors, HAL!" or "Show me the money!"), but the following also produce entertaining responses:

- What's the best computer? (Try asking about the best phone or tablet, too.)
- Make me a sandwich!
- I love you!
- I think you're beautiful!
- Do you love me?
- Do you believe in God?
- Are you a man or a woman?
- How old are you?
- You're cool!

- Sing to me!

- Take me to your leader!

- What's the answer to life, the universe, and everything?

- I need to hide a body!

- Tell me a joke!

- Tell me a dirty joke! (Don't worry—Siri won't do this.)

- Knock, knock!

- Testing: 1, 2, 3.

- I like your voice!

- Blah blah blah blah blah blah

- Beam me up, Scotty!

- What's your favorite movie? (Or song, team, color, and so on.)

- I'm tired!

- Who let the dogs out?

- How much wood would a wood chuck chuck if a wood chuck could chuck wood?

- What do you look like?

- What are you wearing?

- Do you have family?

- Will you be my friend?

- Would you go out with me?

- It's my birthday!

- Show me your butt!

- Guess what?

- Why did the chicken cross the road?

- What are you doing?

- Are you there?

- Thanks for being great!

- I'm drunk!

- What do you think about Descartes?

- Tell me a story.

- Who made you?

- Supercalifragilisticexpialidocious!

- Can you lend me money?

- How are you today?

- What are the lottery numbers?

- Who's your boss?

- Why did your voice change?

Tip 227

Check to see what Apple services are working

Sometimes you might find that iCloud or the App Store isn't working correctly and you may wonder if the problem lies with your connection or whether Apple is experiencing an outage. An easy way to check from any computer is to visit Apple's System Status page,[21] where the health of all Apple services is displayed. Alternatively, visiting the iCloud website on an iPad or iPhone will show a System Status link at the bottom of the page, which provides the same information.[22]

Tip 228

Make albums bigger in Cover Flow mode

If you're playing music and you turn your iPhone on its side (that is, landscape mode), the Now Playing information will be replaced with a mosaic of all the album covers in your music collection. You can use the pinch gesture to zoom in or out of the album covers to see more or fewer of them, just like you would zoom in or out of an image in the Photos app.

---

21. http://www.apple.com/support/systemstatus
22. https://icloud.com

Tip 229

View countdowns from the lock screen

The Clock app lets you set timers so you can count down from 30 minutes, for example. In fact, you can set timers for up to 23 hours and 59 minutes, and you don't have to have the Clock app open for the timer to keep counting down—it'll work in the background while you run other apps, or even if your iPad or iPhone is in sleep mode. Should you wake the phone, then under the main time display you'll see the remaining time for the countdown—offering a useful way to check the countdown without having to unlock the phone!

Tip 230

Let Siri take you to settings

Some apps add their own settings panel to the main Settings app, and in those apps you can ask Siri to take you straight to the settings. Simply start the app in question, then start Siri in the usual way (hold down the Home button) and say, "Settings."

This works with all built-in apps too, like Camera.

Alternatively, if you want to go straight to a particular Settings screen and aren't using that app, just say so: "Settings Pages" will take you to the Settings screen for Pages, for example. You can also specify subpages within settings—to view the Mail section of the Notifications component of Settings, you might say, "Settings Notification Mail."

Tip 231

Avoid explicit music or videos

If your iPad or iPhone is connected to a stereo system or you frequently let children use it, then you might want to limit what kind of music and movies it plays.

iTunes Radio Only

Tap the (i) button at the top of the screen when the station is playing, and then ensure the Allow Explicit Tracks switch is deactivated.

However, on some radio stations this switch defaults to Off, not allowing explicit tracks. If you don't want your listening to be so family-friendly, then you may choose to activate the switch!

System-Wide

Although iTunes Radio comes with its own ratings lock, you can also enable system-wide censoring of movies and music. To do so, open the Settings app, then tap the General heading. Scroll down to the Restrictions heading and tap the Enable Restrictions button at the top of the screen that appears. You'll be prompted to create a passcode specifically for use in the Restrictions setting, so don't forget it!

Scroll down to the Allowed Content section, and then select the various headings, tapping the subheadings within each section so a check mark appears alongside to allow only tracks of that age rating and below to be accessed. You might want to allow only movies of PG-13 and below to be viewed by anybody using the device, for example.

The changes take effect straight away.

Tip 232

Listen to the audio of videos—even after switching away from them

---

Apps like Videos and the third-party YouTube app will immediately pause the currently playing file when you switch away from them. This can be irritating if you simply need to do something quickly with another app. After all, we don't expect our televisions to suddenly stop working when we look away from them!

iOS has a solution to this problem. When you switch away from the app playing the video, immediately slide up Control Center from the bottom of the screen and tap the play button. You should hear the video start playing again, but only the audio. Should you switch back to the app, you'll find video playback carries on too.

However, to pause the video without switching back to the app, again use Control Center.

This trick works not only in apps dedicated to playing video, but also when playing videos on websites via Safari. It even works when the phone enters sleep mode, as explained in Tip 54, *Listen to just the audio of a music video*, on page 88.

Tip 233

Easily set start times in Calendar

When creating an event in the Calendar app and choosing a time, double-tapping the minute part of the date/time picker will switch the dial to show five-minute intervals (that is, 5, 10, 15, and so on) rather than single-minute intervals. This can be a real help when setting a time in a hurry. Double-tapping again will restore minute intervals. See the following figure for an example of the two settings.

This may work with the time and date pickers in other apps, too.

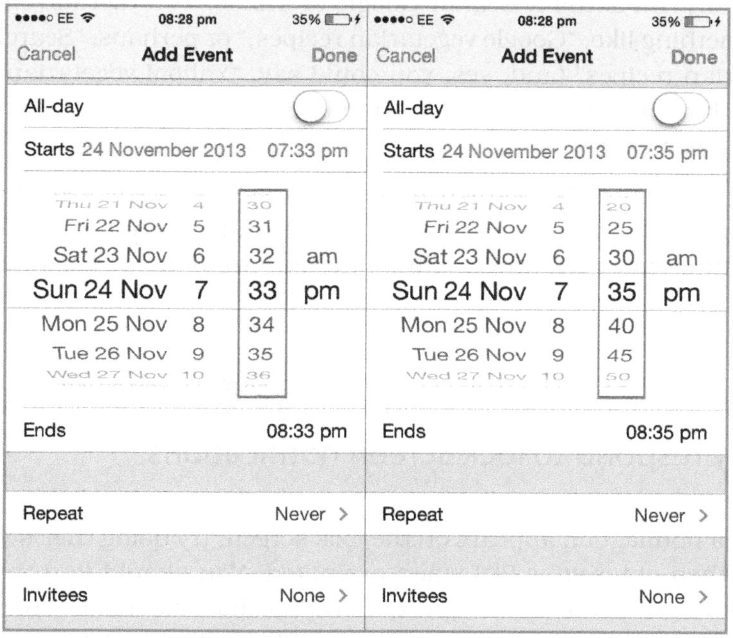

Figure 58—Setting the start time of an event with five-minute intervals on an iPhone

Tip 234

Have Siri read its results to you

Sometimes Siri will look things up for you, then show you them onscreen. Ask what your forthcoming appointments are, for example, and you'll see a list onscreen. Alternatively, ask Siri to look up Enid Blyton, and it'll show you a snippet from Wikipedia.

If you're driving or walking, however, reading from the screen isn't a safe option. In such a case, you can simply activate Siri again and say, "Read that back to me." Siri will then read out loud what it's just shown onscreen.

Tip 235

Search Google or Yahoo! with Siri, not Bing

For reasons best known to Apple, Siri's search engine of preference is Bing. However, Siri can actually search Google or Yahoo! You just have to ask it, saying something like, "Google vegetarian recipes," or perhaps, "Search Yahoo! for vegetarian recipes" (and, yes, you could say, "Yahoo! vegetarian recipes" too, even though *Yahoo-ing* hasn't quite entered the language in the same way that *Googling* has.

Searching this way isn't quite the same as using Siri's native search because it'll search and then open a standard Safari browser window showing the results, rather than showing them in the Siri window. But it's still pretty useful!

Tip 236

Quickly respond to lock-screen notifications

Whenever a notification appears on the lock screen, try doing this: swipe right across it, then enter your PIN when prompted. You should find that you're switched straight to the app in question, rather than the home screen, which you usually see when unlocking an iPad or iPhone. Swipe right on a missed-call notification, and you'll instantly return the call!

Tip 237

Select different language keyboards quickly

If you've set up more than one language keyboard (see Tip 146, *Be multilingual*, on page 151), you can quickly choose between them and get an overview of what keyboard languages are installed by bringing up the keyboard and tapping then holding the globe icon. See the following figure for an example. This can be especially useful if you're unsure which keyboard is currently activate—after all, several European languages use essentially the same QWERTY keyboard, and the differences can be subtle!

Figure 59—Choosing which keyboard to use on an iPhone

Tip 238

End calls and lock the screen in one movement

Tiny time-savers like this one can pay the biggest dividends: when you make a phone call on the iPhone, just click the Lock/Sleep button to end it and put the phone into sleep mode. No need to tap the onscreen End Call button!

Of course, this tip also serves as a warning—far from putting the display to sleep when on a call, the Lock/Sleep button will end it!

Tip 239

Instantly switch to the last-used app

The way the multitasking bar works in iOS 7 (see *Multitasking and Switching Apps*, on page 14) ensures that whenever it's activated, the app you used before the current one is always in the center of the screen. Therefore, to quickly switch back to that app, all you need do is double-click the Home button, then tap the screen roughly in the middle. You can do this in literally a couple of seconds once you get used to the gesture.

Tip 240

Lock the iPhone screen in landscape mode

Apple's engineers decreed that, while we can use the iPad's rotation-lock feature to lock the screen to portrait or landscape orientation, on the iPhone we can lock the screen to portrait orientation only (by tapping the button within Control Center—see *Control Center*, on page 34).

However, there is a way to lock an iPhone into landscape mode using a feature called AssistiveTouch. It's slightly more complicated than simply tapping a button in Control Center, however, and requires a little setup.

Setting Up

Before you can lock an iPhone screen in landscape mode, a little setup is necessary, as follows.

1. Open the Settings app, then tap the General heading, followed by the Accessibility heading.

2. Scroll down to Accessibility Shortcut, then tap to put a check mark alongside AssistiveTouch. Once this is done you can close the Settings app.

Locking the Screen to Landscape Orientation

Each time you wish to lock the screen to landscape orientation, follow these steps.

1. Open Control Center and tap the rotation-lock button.

2. Switch to the app where you want to lock rotation to landscape. This must be an app that supports landscape orientation, of course, such as Safari. Then triple-click the Home button (that is, click it three times in rapid succession).

3. A white dot will appear onscreen. When you tap it, the AssistiveTouch menu will appear.

4. Tap the Device icon on the menu, then tap Rotate Screen.

5. On the new menu that appears, tap the Left icon. The screen will immediately rotate to landscape.

6. Triple-click the Home button. This will deactivate the AssistiveTouch feature that allowed us to rotate the screen, yet leave the screen rotated and locked to landscape orientation.

The landscape lock will work for only as long as you remain within that particular app, although it will remain in place should you switch to the multitasking bar. However, when you return to the home screen or switch to any other app, the orientation will again be locked to portrait. At this point you can simply repeat the preceding steps to again lock the screen to landscape.

To deactivate the AssistiveTouch feature, repeat the preceding setup steps but this time remove the check alongside AssistiveTouch within the Settings app.

Tip 241

Attach files to calendar events

The good news is that calendar events can have files attached to them, and assuming you're using iCloud the attachment will automatically sync among all your devices. This is great for attaching a presentation document to an event you're attending, for example, or even a photo of a person you're supposed to be meeting to help with identification.

The bad news is that it's only possible to add attachments using the Calendar app on a Mac computer or via the iCloud website using the browser of any computer.[23] It's not possible to add attachments to events using an iPad or iPhone, although you can view them on those devices if the attachments are of a filetype understood by the device (that is, office documents, images, PDFs, and so on).

Here's how it's done:

- Mac: Open Calendar then create a new event by right-clicking on the day and time you want it to start and selecting New Event from the menu that appears. Give the event a name and then, if using Mavericks, click the Add Notes, Attachments, or URL heading and click the Add Attachment section. This will open a file-browsing window where you can select the attachment. On older versions of OS X, double-click the event you created,

23. https://icloud.com

then select the Edit button in the box that appears. Fill in the details of the event. Near the bottom of the pop-up window will be an Attachments field. Click it to add a file by selecting one from your computer's hard disk.

- iCloud: Visit the iCloud website and click the Calendar icon after logging in. Create the new event by clicking the plus (+) icon in the bottom-right corner, then fill in the details as usual. Click the Add File heading alongside the Attachment heading to choose from your hard disk a file you wish to upload.

Tip 242

Stream movies and music from your Mac or Windows PC

So you want your iPad or iPhone to play music and movies stored on your PC. The only way to do that is to copy them across using iTunes...right?

In fact, you can *stream* movies and music from a Mac or Windows PC using iTunes's Home Sharing feature. Streaming is where a file is played over the network from one device to another—a bit like a TV station broadcasting a program. It's not like syncing, in which the goal is to copy the full file across for future access. Instead, streaming allows one-off playback, and once playback has finished the file is no longer on the device.

Streaming a movie from a Mac or Windows PC to an iPad or iPhone is ideal if the device lacks the storage space to store large multigigabyte movie files. Additionally, it's an easier way to watch and listen to stuff if you don't want to sync with iTunes all the time.

The downside is the fact that Home Sharing works only over the local network, so you can use it only at home, for example. Additionally, you might find some movies purchased through iTunes can't be shared because of copyright restrictions. However, anything you rip yourself from CD or DVD, or download online, will be shared fine.

Here's how to set up Home Sharing and use it to watch a movie or listen to music.

1. On the Mac or Windows PC open iTunes, then click File > Home Sharing > Turn On Home Sharing. You'll be prompted to enter your Apple ID, so do so.

2. On the iPad or iPhone you want to stream the movies or music to, open the Settings app, then tap the Music heading. At the bottom will be a Home Sharing heading. You should already find that you're signed into home sharing, but if not tap the button and enter your Apple ID details when prompted.

3. To play back a movie, open the Videos app and then tap the Shared icon at the bottom if you're using an iPhone, or the Shared icon at the top if you're using an iPad. This will prompt you to choose a library that you'd like to access. Tap the one based on your username (for me, that's Keir Thomas's Library).

4. After a few seconds you'll see a list of items stored on the Mac or Windows PC, and tapping any will cue them up for playing, with a larger preview and the runtime listed, and tapping Play will start them playing as if they were stored on your device.

5. To listen to music or audio files, open the Music app then tap the Shared button on the toolbar at the bottom of the screen (on the iPhone you may need to tap the three dots to reveal the extra options) and again select the library of your Mac or Windows PC from the list. Following this, use the usual Artists or Songs icons at the bottom of the screen to select music—all items on the Mac or Windows PC will be integrated into your existing collection, as if they are stored on the device itself.

Tip 243

Turn off the iPhone flashlight quickly

The iPhone comes with a flashlight tool that's accessible only via Control Center. There's no other way of turning the flashlight on or off, and this can be annoying if—while using the flashlight—the phone enters sleep mode. Following this you may need to wake the phone, enter your passcode (or wait for Touch ID to work), and then open Control Center before turning off the flashlight.

However, a nifty trick lets you turn off the flashlight from a locked phone without opening Control Center. Just tap the camera icon at the bottom right of the screen. There's no need to actually activate the camera—tapping its icon is sufficient to turn off the flashlight.

For what it's worth, this trick also works when the phone is unlocked and the flashlight is active—rather than open Control Center to turn off the flashlight, you can just briefly start the Camera app. This will turn off the flashlight.

Tip 244

Quickly navigate through Pages

If you're editing a multipage document in Pages, you can quickly jump to another page by placing a finger at the right edge of the screen, holding for a split second, then dragging up or down. You'll see a thumbnail outline of each page as you drag, as well as its page number. The following figure shows an example.

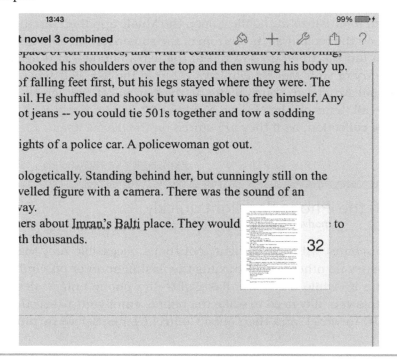

Figure 60—Navigating page-by-page through Pages on an iPad

As with all gestures, this takes some practice, but I find it works best if the finger is half on the screen and half on the surrounding border.

Tip 245

Delete a miskeyed Calculator entry

Have you ever miskeyed a number in the Calculator app on the iPhone? You meant to type 65535 but type 655335 instead. D'oh! On most calculators you have little choice but to tap the clear button and type the number all over again, but on the iPhone calculator app you can simply swipe left or right across the "LCD" number display. This is like tapping Backspace on a keyboard, and the most recent number you typed will be deleted. You can repeat the gesture to keep deleting as many of the numbers as you wish.

Tip 246

Ask Siri about driving directions

You can ask Siri to route you to a destination ("Route me to the nearest Starbucks") or to your own home ("Route home"), but that's not all that you can ask when driving a route planned by your iPhone or iPad. Try the following questions and command:

- What's my next turn?
- When's my next turn?
- How long until I get to my destination?
- How far is my destination?
- End navigation.

Tip 247

Look up callers online

Ever missed a call from an unknown number? If you're waiting for an important call, then it can be infuriating—was that the call? Or was it some telemarketer wanting to bend you ear? One way to find out is to look up the phone number online, and you can do this using a hidden feature of the recent-calls list.

Open the Phone app, then tap the Recents icon at the bottom. Find the unidentified number in the list, then carefully tap the (i) button at its right. On the screen that appears, tap and hold the phone number until the Copy pop-out menu appears. Tap it, then switch to Safari and paste the number into the URL/search field and tap Go.

Tip 248

Ultraquickly reply to emails and messages

Imagine this situation: you're looking through your emails and are about to reply to one, yet you're called away. There's no time even to tap away at the onscreen keyboard. The solution is to use Siri—as you're walking to your urgent appointment, just invoke it in the usual way, then say, "Reply...." Follow immediately with what you want your reply to be. You'll be shown a preview onscreen and can simply click Send to dispatch the message, as we see in the following figure.

This works in the Messages app in exactly the same way.

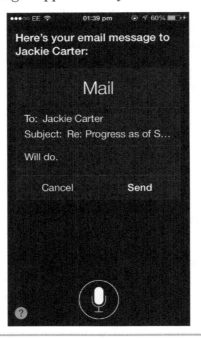

Figure 61—Using Siri to reply to an email you've read on an iPhone

Tip 249

Scroll and zoom when using brushes in iPhoto

When using the Brushes tool in iPhoto, tapping and then dragging on the screen applies the selected effect. So how do you zoom in and out or scroll around? After all, in most apps you accomplish this by tapping and dragging. To zoom in and out use the usual pinch gesture (that is, place a finger and thumb together on the screen and contract and expand them) or use two fingers bunched together—double-tap two fingers to zoom in, and double-tap again to zoom out. You can also tap and then drag with two fingers to scroll around.

Tip 250

Have Safari fill in credit-card details

Safari on the iPad and iPhone can be pretty helpful when it comes to remembering passwords for websites, but did you know that it can also remember credit-card details? This way you won't need to have your card on hand when shopping online, for example.

To set it up, follow these steps:

1. Open Settings, then tap the Safari heading and then Passwords & AutoFill.

2. Tap the Use Contact Info switch so it's activated, and then tap My Info and select your own details from the contacts list. Unless you want to enter your address each time, you'll need to ensure the contact card contains your details.

3. Once you've selected your contact card, scroll to the bottom of the screen and tap the switch alongside Credit Cards so it's activated, and then tap Saved Credit Cards.

4. Tap Add Credit Card, and provide your details. You'll note that you're not required to enter the security number on the back of the card. This is for security reasons, and will ensure anybody who steals or even uses your phone can't abuse your credit-card details! Therefore you'll need to enter the security number manually each time.

To use the details, tap inside the relevant address or credit-card fields when at the checkout of an online store and then tap the AutoFill button, which will appear above the onscreen keyboard.

To remove a credit card in the future, repeat the preceding steps as if entering a new credit card, then select the credit card in the list. You'll be prompted to enter your passcode for security purposes. Do so, then when you see the card details tap Edit > Delete Credit Card.

Tip 251

Create contact groups

If you open the Contacts app you'll see a button at the top-left corner called Groups. Tapping it will show an entry called All iCloud if your device is signed into iCloud, and All Facebook if your iPad or iPhone is signed into Facebook.

To see a particular contact group, put a check mark alongside it by tapping (remove checks alongside any others), and then tap Done at the top right.

You might notice a small problem, though. It's impossible to create new groups on an iPad or iPhone. Nor can you delete any groups. Why? Well, you'd better ask Apple! This is a shame because groups can be a good way of organizing contacts.

If you visit the iCloud website using a Mac or Windows PC,[24] however, you can use the Contacts functionality there to create and delete groups, as follows:

1. After you've logged into iCloud, click the Contacts icon.

2. Any groups you have will be listed at the left side. Clicking any then clicking the cog icon at the bottom left will show a menu offering an option to delete it.

3. To create a new group, click the plus (+) icon and select New Group from the menu that appears.

4. You'll be prompted to give the group a name, so do so.

5. Now switch back to your full contacts list by clicking All Contacts. Then drag and drop contacts from the main list into the new group. You can hold down Shift, or Ctrl on a Windows PC and Cmd on a Mac, to multiple-select files, and then drag them over en masse.

---

24. https://icloud.com

The group will then be synced with your iPad or iPhone.

Creating a group won't allow you to send group emails. However, that's possible using a different technique—see Tip 199, *Easily send emails to groups of people*, on page 183.

Tip 252

Cue back and forth in iMovie without hassle

To cue backward or forward in your iMovie project the usual method is to tap and then drag the timeline, but this can be problematic because you might accidentally select and move a clip or audio track. Instead, try dragging left and right on the playback preview window.

Tip 253

Allow only one person (or a select few people) to call you

Waiting for a phone call from one particular person (or organization), and want all other calls to go straight to voicemail? You can set this up on an iPhone by adapting the Do Not Disturb feature, as follows:

1. Follow Tip 251, *Create contact groups*, on page 216, to create a new contacts group at the iCloud website,[25] but add only one entry to it—the person or organization you want to be allowed to call you. In the Name field of the new contact, type something like "John only" or "Office only." To create the group, you need to have a contact card for the person or organization. If you don't, you can create one on your iPad or iPhone via the Contacts app, or at the iCloud site.

2. Open the Settings app on your phone, then tap the Do Not Disturb heading.

3. Tap the Allow Calls From heading, and then choose the new group you created in step 1.

4. Tap Back, then tap the Manual switch at the top to activate Do Not Disturb. Also ensure the switch alongside Repeated Calls is off and that Always under the Silence heading is checked.

---

25. https://icloud.com

From now on any calls not from the specified party will be sent straight to voicemail, although those will still show as missed calls in the Recents list of the Phone app. A side effect of using Do Not Disturb is that app notifications will also be turned off—new messages will arrive, for example, but you won't be notified about them. You can view them by pulling down Notification Center in the usual way.

You can adapt this tip easily to allow calls from a only small number of people by simply increasing the number of contact cards added to the group you created in step 1.

Tip 254

Edit iWork documents on a Windows PC

Need to edit or access your Pages, Numbers, or Keynote documents when you're away from your iPad or iPhone? Just visit the iCloud website on a Mac or Windows PC,[26] where you'll be able to edit documents within the web-browser window. Just select the Pages, Numbers, or Keynote option, then select the document from the list just as you would on your iPad or iPhone.

If you own a Mac, you might also consider downloading the desktop versions of Pages, Numbers, and Keynote from the Mac App Store—and they're free of charge if you bought your Mac after October 1, 2013![27]

Tip 255

Dial foreign numbers

Having trouble dialing a number preceded by a country code? Instead of dialing 00 at the beginning, just press and hold the zero button on the keypad. This will insert a plus symbol (+), at which point you should type the country code, followed by the number.

You might find it useful to edit within the Contacts app the numbers of your frequently dialed overseas contacts so that their numbers begin with a plus followed by their country codes.

---

26. https://icloud.com
27. https://www.apple.com/creativity-apps/mac/

Tip 256

Get transit directions

Although the Maps app can provide walking instructions (see Tip 61, *Default to walking directions in Maps*, on page 92), if you want a route that involves busses, trains, or trams, you're out of luck. Many third-party apps can fill in the gaps, however, and perhaps the best is Google Maps, which is free in the App Store.

To use the apps you can either launch them directly or open the built-in Maps app then choose your destination before tapping the right-facing arrow on the pin, tapping Directions To Here, then selecting the transit button (the icon looks like a train). When you subsequently tap the Route button you'll be switched to a list of any apps on your device or in the App Store that provide transit directions, as the following figure shows.

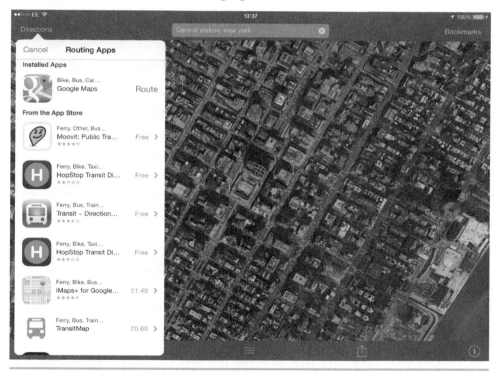

Figure 62—Getting transit directions in the Maps app on an iPad

Just tap the Route button alongside one to select it. In the case of some apps, like Google Maps, selecting the app will automatically switch to the app and fill in the destination field with what you specified, then select the transit/public transport option so all you need do is tap the route button.

Siri can invoke these third-party apps, too, although in a slightly indirect way. Just say something like, "Give me transit directions to…," and state your destination. Siri will say it's getting directions, then show the same list of third-party apps as mentioned a moment ago. Selecting one will open it with the destination automatically filled-in.

Tip 257

Remove "Recents" suggestions when emailing

When you start to type an address in a new email on your iPad or iPhone, a list of autocompleted suggestions will appear. The list comes from two sources—your contacts list and a list iOS 7 creates based on addresses you've emailed recently.

Problems can arise when the list gets too long and if you type the wrong address and then send an email—iOS 7 isn't clever enough to realize when the email is bounced back, and will continue to suggest the incorrect address in the list of suggestions.

The answer is to remove the errant entries from the list of suggestions by tapping the (i) button alongside any of them and then tapping Remove from Recents. This will work only for those that have the word Recent above them in the list that appears when you start typing. All others entries in the list are from your list of contacts, and must be manually looked up and edited using the Contacts app.

Tip 258

Create a cut-out around images in iWork apps

A cut-out around an image is where the background is removed, usually to remove annoying details or just to allow the text to flow freely around the subject of the image.

The iWork apps can do this automatically for most images, although the results aren't as perfect as manually cutting out an image in an application like Photoshop.

Insert the image in the usual way (tap the plus icon—+—at the top of the screen, then select from your camera roll/photo stream). Ensure the photo is selected by tapping it once, then tap the format inspector (the paintbrush icon), then tap the Image tab in the pop-out window and tap Instant Alpha.

Use your finger to paint over the background part of the image. The app will instantly realize the area you mean and highlight it, and dragging more will increase the area. Repeat this step for all the background areas. Should you make a mistake, tap Undo at the top left. When you've finished, tap Done on the floating toolbar beneath the image.

To alter the word wrap around the image in Pages, again select the image and tap the format inspector. Then tap the Arrange tab in the pop-out window, then the Wrap heading, and select what kind of word wrap you'd like. Generally speaking, the Around option is the best one for a word wrap like that seen in magazines and some books.

Tip 259

Create "vibrate only" notifications

Your iPhone has a number of ways of notifying you when something's happened, like an email or new message being received. It can show a dialog box or flash a brief message at the top of the screen. It can also make a noise or even play an tune. You can choose these options by selecting the Notification Center heading in the Settings app, as explained in *Notifications*, on page 46.

One thing you don't appear to be able to do, however, is have the iPhone simply vibrate without doing anything else. You can achieve this by turning off the ringer using the switch on the side of the iPhone, but then you won't hear *any* alert sounds—including the phone ringing.

However, there is a way of creating a vibration-only notification for individual apps that doesn't involve turning off all alerts. It's just a little counter-intuitive. Open the Settings app, then tap the Notification Center heading. Select the app or service for which you'd like vibration notifications (this works with Phone, Messages, Reminders, Calendar, FaceTime, and Mail), then tap the Alert Sound or Reminder/Calendar Alerts heading. On the page that opens, tap the Vibration heading, then select any of the entries you'd like; the default is Staccato. (You can also create your own vibration pattern, as explained in Tip 172, *Use custom ringtones and vibrations for individual callers*, on page 167.) Return to the previous screen, then under the Alert Tones heading, select None.

Tip 260

Open a web page in a non-Safari web browser

One of the rules of using an iPad or iPhone is that, although you can install alternatives to the built-in apps, you can't make the new app the system default. In other words, if you tap a web link in any apps it will open in Safari —even if you prefer to use an alternative browser like Google Chrome day-to-day. To get around this you can use a bookmarklet (Tip 299, *Boost Safari with bookmarklets*, on page 252), as discovered by developer Jon Abrams.[28] Set it up as follows:

1. Open Safari on your iPad or iPhone, then browse to http://applekungfu.com/shortcut.html.

2. Tap the share button (the box with the upward-facing arrow) on the browser toolbar, then tap the Bookmark icon (it looks like an open book). Tap the Save button.

3. Tap the Bookmark button on the browser toolbar, then open the Favorites list by tapping it. Then tap the Edit button. Locate your new bookmarklet, which will probably be called Favorites, then tap it.

4. Tap the address component, then remove the first part of the address —everything up to and including the pound (#) sign before the word javascript. To do this you'll need to scroll left in the small text field—perhaps the best way of doing so is to tap and hold until the magnifying glass appears, then drag left beyond the pop-out window/text field for a few seconds. (See Figure 63, *Erasing the URL component of a bookmarklet on an iPad*, on page 223.)

5. Type a new name in the field above the URL—something like Open in Google Chrome should be OK, then tap Done on the keyboard.

6. Tap Done within the list of bookmarks.

---

28. http://blog.jonabrams.com/post/26099585134/open-in-chrome

From now on, when viewing a page that you want to open in Chrome, just open the Favorites bookmarks list and tap the Open in Google Chrome entry.

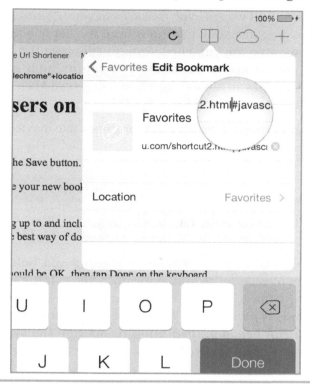

Figure 63—Erasing the URL component of a bookmarklet on an iPad

Tip 261

Manually sync music to your iPad or iPhone

There are two standard ways to sync music from iTunes to your iPad or iPhone. The first is simply to sync everything in your iTunes collection. This is the default setup—all music gets synced with your iPad or iPhone.

Alternatively, you can choose to sync only certain items by attaching the device (or ensuring it's within Wi-Fi range if you have Wi-Fi syncing enabled), then selecting it in the iTunes interface, clicking the Music tab at the top, and then clicking the Selected Playlists, Artists, Albums, and Genres heading.

Then you can make your selection from the check boxes beneath that show your entire collection.

However, there is a third way to sync music from your iTunes library. Simply click and start to drag any song in iTunes from the list of songs, and a side panel will open showing any attached devices. Dropping the item on any of the devices will copy it across instantly. You can multiple-select items by holding down `Shift`, or `Ctrl` on a Windows PC and `Cmd` on a Mac, and drag them across in this way too.

This works for more than music; it'll work for things like movies, books, apps, and so on, as well.

Tip 262

Raise the iPhone to your ear to dictate

We usually activate Siri on the iPhone by clicking and holding the Home button, but it can also be set to automatically activate if the phone is raised to somebody's ear. This is achieved via the built-in accelerometer, which can detect certain kinds of movements. To activate the feature, open the Settings app, tap the General heading, then tap Siri. Activate the switch alongside Raise to Speak. Note that Raise to Speak works only while the phone isn't in sleep mode.

Raise to Speak has an undocumented secondary feature, too. When the onscreen keyboard is visible and you're typing within an app such as Notes, you can raise the phone to your ear and begin dictating. Once you hear a single beep, whatever you say will be converted into text (the same as tapping the microphone button on the onscreen keyboard).

Using the iPhone in this way can be very useful when traveling or if you don't have time to type, because nobody will suspect that you're dictating and will assume that you're simply taking a call.

Tip 263

Rearrange reminder lists on the iPhone

When viewing all your reminder lists on the iPhone (to view the lists tap the card stack at the bottom of the screen), you can rearrange them by tapping and then dragging any of them. This is more important than it might seem because the list at the bottom of the "heap" will show some reminders even though the list view is active. You might have to tap and drag to see them, but the reminders will be there.

Tip 264

Stop "sampling" alert sounds when setting an alarm

When you set an alarm in the Clock app you can choose which alert tone you want by tapping the Sound heading. The problem is that selecting any in the list will cause that sound to play, which you might not want to happen if you're in a quiet environment. Turning down the alarm volume using either the side buttons or the option in Settings helps, but the alarm volume can't be muted. It can only be turned down to one bar, which is quiet but still audible.

A solution of sorts is to very quickly double-tap the alert sound to select it. If you do it right, you'll hear nothing. If you're a little slow in your double-tap you might hear a brief snatch of the alarm sound; practice makes perfect!

Tip 265

Put a call on hold

If you need to do something or speak to somebody else during a call you can tap the Mute button to deactivate the microphone and ensure the caller can't hear you (if the numeric keypad is visible, tap the Hide button to see the Mute button). Unfortunately, this won't silence the other individual, which can be very distracting if they're in a noisy environment or are also talking to another person.

The solution is to tap and hold the Mute button until it changes to read Hold. Then the call will be muted for both sides of the call, so neither party will hear the other.

To deactivate hold (or mute), just tap the button again.

Tip 266

Interview people using your phone

The Voice Memos app on the iPhone implies that it's there to record spoken notes to yourself, but it's actually a very useful voice recorder for interviewing people, and the iPhone microphone is sensitive enough to pick up somebody talking on the other side of a table it's placed on provided the room is quiet.

The iPhone's main microphone is on the bottom, so you should ensure that's pointing at the individual you want to record. You'll notice an unusual but useful thing when you turn the phone upside down to point it at the individual—the display rotates to show you the controls. The Voice Memos app is the only app where this happens!

Once you've recorded the interview, you can get it off the phone by tapping the share button and emailing or messaging the file to yourself, or you can sync with iTunes on a Mac or Windows PC, where it'll be stored as a regular audio track among your music files.

Tip 267

Create events years in advance in Calendar

Although you can simply ask Siri to create an event using any date you specify, including in the next millennium if you wish, creating an event taking place years ahead in the Calendar app is a little more time consuming.

The usual way to create an event in Calendar is to tap the plus (+) button at the top right, then fill in the details in the Add Event pop-up window. Tapping the Starts field will show the date-picker tool, which lets you scroll through days one at a time. While you can scroll this listing quickly, it still takes a long time to advance to a date a year or two ahead, and it can also get confusing.

The solution is to tap the All Day switch above this in the Add Event window. This switches the date picker to a different view whereby you can scroll the day, month, and year separately, making it easy to choose a date any number of years ahead. Once you've picked the date, simply deactivate the All Day switch, and set the time using the ordinary date picker.

Tip 268

Make and change tab stops in Pages

This tip requires the ruler to be visible in the Pages app; the ruler is shown by default on an iPad although on an iPhone you may need to tap the wrench icon at the top right and then the Ruler heading.

Creating a new tab stop is easy, and you might already know how to do so—just tap and hold in a blank spot on the ruler, and a left tab stop appears along with a line within the document giving an idea how the tab stop will affect the text. (Remember that the ruler is visible only when you're editing text and the keyboard is visible.)

How to get rid of a tab stop is less well-known, but is equally easy—just drag it down onto the document area for a few seconds, and it'll vanish.

You can alter the function of a tab stop by double-tapping it, which will cycle through the available types of tab (see the following figure).

Figure 64—The various kind of tab stops available in Pages

The tab types are are as follows:

- Center stop (diamond icon): Text will center at the tab position.

- Right stop (right-facing wedge icon): Text will right-justify at the tab position.

- Decimal stop (small circle icon): The tab applies to the decimal point of any number you type—integers will appear at the left of the tab stop, and fractions at the right.

Tip 269

Fix annoyances and make iOS easier to use

iOS is nearly perfect, but a few small quirks can make it less than 100 percent pleasurable to use. The following are a few issues that are frequently mentioned, along with solutions (see also Tip 9, *Stop being told twice about new messages*, on page 59).

- Increase background contrast: If you find it hard to discern icon text against the wallpaper on your home screens, you can increase background contrast. To do so, open the Settings app, then tap the General heading. Tap the Accessibility entry in the list, and then the Increase Contrast entry. Tap the switch so that it's activated. (Note that this also has the effect of removing blurred backgrounds behind things like Control Center or Spotlight search results, which can also make the text there easier to read.)

- Make text boldface: In addition to using the preceding tip, you can make text throughout the user interface easier to read. To do so, open the Settings app, tap the General heading, and then tap the Accessibility heading within that. Tap the switch alongside Bold Text to activate it. You'll be prompted to reboot your device.

- Enlarge text: You can increase the font size in certain apps. To do so, open the Settings app, tap the General heading, then tap the Text Size entry in the list. Drag the slider to the right step by step, monitoring the changes on the example text preceding the slider. You might also choose to switch to an app like Mail to see what effect the changes have. Note that changing the font size won't work in all applications.

- Turn off keyboard clicks: Whenever you type iOS makes a clicking sound, which can certainly help when you're learning to use the onscreen keyboard but can quickly become redundant. To turn off the sound, open the Settings app, then tap the Sounds heading and deactivate the switch alongside the Keyboard Clicks heading.

- Turn off effects: Some people find that zooming in and out of apps can induce motion sickness. Additionally, the moving wallpaper (something known as *parallax*) can also cause problems for certain people. You can deactivate both by opening the Settings app, tapping the General heading, then tapping Accessibility. There, tap the Reduce Motion heading and tap the switch alongside it so that it's deactivated.

- Stop Control Center from appearing during games: During frantic game playing it's not difficult to accidentally touch the bottom of the screen and thereby activate Control Center. Tip 80, *Lock out notifications while using an app*, on page 104, explains how to lock your iPad or iPhone to one app, without anything able to intrude, and is perhaps the best solution for this problem. However, you can also remove Control Center's ability to be activated when apps are running—although you'll still be able to activate it elsewhere. To set this up, open the Settings app then tap Control Center heading and deactivate the switch alongside the Access within Apps text.

Tip 270

Create shortcuts to autotype text

iOS lets you create keyboard shortcuts. These are words or abbreviations that, when typed, are replaced with other words, sentences, or even entire paragraphs. The default example built into iOS 7 is "omw." When typed within any app, this is replaced with "On my way!" This is very useful in the Messages app.

The shortcut word is replaced only when followed with a space, punctuation symbol, or `Return`. If a shortcut word is followed immediately by a letter or number, then replacement won't occur. This means you can use shortcut words like "sinc" for "Sincerely yours" without any fear that typing the word "since" will prompt the replacement.

Once a shortcut has been created it will automatically sync via iCloud with any other iOS devices or Mac computers you might own.

On an iPad or iPhone there are four instances when shortcuts are particularly useful:

1. To avoid having to manually type your email address into web forms, something that can be time consuming using an onscreen keyboard

2. When entering commonly used phrases or words if you frequently write in a second language (this saves the confusion of switching to an international keyboard each time)

3. To insert popular emoji or kaomoji (see Tip 7, *Use emoji—full-color emoticons*, on page 57, and Tip 107, *Use kaomoji emoticons*, on page 125) without having to switch keyboards

4. To correct common typos or misspellings, and stop iOS from autocorrecting certain things you frequently type

Creating a Keyboard Shortcut

To create a keyboard shortcut, open the Settings app, then tap the General heading before following these steps, which vary depending on the kind of device you own:

- iPhone: Tap the Keyboard section, then scroll to the bottom and tap Shortcuts. You'll then see any existing shortcuts, and should tap the plus (+) button to create a new shortcut.

- iPad: Tap the Keyboard section, then tap Add New Shortcut at the bottom.

Regardless of which device you use, on the screen that follows, on the Phrase line type the word, sentence, or paragraph that you wish to be expanded upon demand, and in the Shortcut field type the shortcut word that will be replaced. Then tap the Save button.

Email Shortcut

Many websites request that you type your email address. An iPad or iPhone's onscreen keyboard can make this difficult—to access the @ symbol you must switch to the numbers/symbols keyboard, for example.

Therefore, a useful trick is to create a shortcut for your email address, perhaps using "zz" as the shortcut. Whichever shortcut you choose, remember that it must be something entirely unlikely to arise during everyday typing—using "email" as the shortcut wouldn't be satisfactory, for example, because there's a chance you might type that in everyday correspondence.

Foreign-Language Words or Phrases

If you regularly type foreign-language words or phrases, then switching to an international keyboard (see Tip 146, *Be multilingual*, on page 151) can be confusing.

The solution is to create a shortcut for certain foreign words or phrases you use frequently. Obviously, when typing the word or phrase you should use the international keyboard, but use the default English keyboard to type the shortcut word or abbreviation. The shortcut should be something short yet memorable, and something that won't come up in everyday typing. For example, for the German phrase "Bitte schön," you might type simply "bitte."

Kaomoji or Emoji

Switching to the emoji or kaomoji keyboard and finding what you want can be time consuming. Creating a shortcut for commonly used emoji or kaomoji symbols therefore makes sense—you might choose to type the famous kaomoji table-flip symbols in the Phrase field, for example, with "tf" as the shortcut.

Commonly Mistyped or Misspelled Words

Although iOS is good at correcting common typos—it will replace "teh" with "the," for example—you may well use more obscure words of which it has no knowledge but that are still easy to get wrong when typing.

Additionally, you might choose to create shortcuts for words that iOS auto-corrects wrongly—if writing about the book *Supernature*, by Lyall Watson, you might want to stop iOS from automatically considering "Supernature" a typo (it splits it into two separate words). Creating a shortcut for the word will stop iOS from doing this (although you might also consider Tip 98, *Add words to the spelling dictionary*, on page 119).

Tip 271

Mass-delete photos

It's not hard to build up a substantial photo collection on your iPad or iPhone. Deleting one or two of them is easy, but deleting all of them is extremely time consuming. The solution is to attach the iPad or iPhone to your computer, as described in Tip 198, *Get pictures off your device without iCloud*, on page 182, and then delete them using the file browser in Windows or the Preview app in Mac OS X.

Tip 272

Change iMovie's theme without re-editing

It might seem counterintuitive, but if you're creating a project in iMovie, you can change the theme at any time by simply selecting a new one—click the cog icon at the bottom right, then tap a different theme. It will be applied immediately.

Tip 273

Be reminded at a place via your iPhone

The Reminders app in iOS 7 on the iPhone includes *geofencing* capabilities, which is a technological way of saying that the app can remind you of something via a notification when you arrive at or leave a particular place. That place can be a home or office, a town or city, or potentially an entire country or continent. Here's how to set it up:

1. Create a new reminder in the usual way by opening the Reminders app, choosing a list, then tapping on an empty line and typing the details of the reminder (that is, something like "Pick up dry cleaning").

2. Tap the (i) icon alongside the entry, and activate the switch alongside Remind Me at a Location. Then tap the Location heading beneath that.

3. In the search field type a zip/postal code, address, or business name. This will search for the place and show a list of results.

4. Select the correct location, then tap either When I Arrive or When I Leave to choose at which point during your visit you want the reminder to appear.

5. The location will be shown on a map at the bottom of the screen, and it'll be surrounded by a blue circle. This is the geofence area you'll have to enter or exit for the reminder to appear. By default it's set at a diameter of 100 meters, which is the smallest geofence area it's possible to set, but by dragging the black dot at the border of the geofence you can enlarge the area.

6. By dragging the geofence border to the screen edge and then lifting your finger, you'll zoom out from the map, as the figure here shows. You can then drag the fence border again to increase the area. By repeatedly doing this, you can enlarge the geofence to cover an entire town, city, state, or even country. In fact, the geofence can be as large as 1,500 miles (approximately 2,414 kilometers)—more than enough to cover a significant proportion of the continental United States, or most of western Europe!

7. Once you've set the area, tap Details to return to the previous screen, and then Done to save the Reminder. Note that the Location field of the reminder will still read the business or zip code you searched for, and won't reflect the size of the geofence.

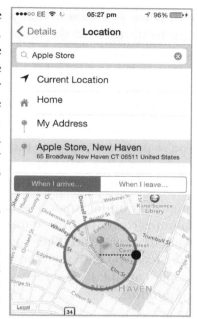

Figure 65—Creating a geofence notification on the Reminders app using an iPhone

8. Note that for geofenced reminders to work correctly, you'll need to ensure Background App Refresh is activated under the General heading of the Settings app and that Location Services are activated (which you'll find under the Privacy heading of the Settings app). Additionally, no alert set within the Reminders app will work if you quit the app via the multitasking bar.

Tip 274

Use your iPhone when parking

Your iPhone or even your iPad can be very useful when parking.

To find a parking lot, just ask Siri where the nearest one is. Tap the map display you see, and you'll open Maps, where you can set the location as a destination in order to plan a route so you can drive straight there.

However you chance upon your parking space, to remember where you've parked open the Maps app then tap and hold the current location to drop a pin. When you want to find your way back to the car, you can use the Maps app to navigate to the dropped pin (and Tip 55, *Make maps orient to the direction you're facing*, on page 89, can be particularly useful in this situation). GPS usually is accurate to only a few feet of your location, but in a large parking lot or a busy town, you'll still be able to get back to a location close enough to your vehicle to spot it.

You can also send the pin to other Apple users so they can find you once you've parked. Simply tap the right arrow on the pin's pop-out then tap Share, and select Message or Mail. (The Find My Friends app can also be used for this, and you can install it for free via the App Store.[29])

Just paid up for a parking meter? Tell Siri to "count down" however many minutes you've paid for, minus five or ten minutes to make sure you can walk back to your car in time. You can view or cancel the countdown by opening the Clock app, although the time remaining will also appear beneath the time display on the lock screen. Alternatively, you can simply tell Siri, "Cancel countdown."

Tip 275

FaceTime on TV

If you have an Apple TV connected to your TV (or are using software on a Mac or Windows PC that lets people connect via AirPlay) you can use iOS's AirPlay mirroring feature to display video and audio of the person you're chatting to on a FaceTime call on a bigger screen. Usefully this doesn't make the iPad or iPhone screen go blank, so you can show the call on a TV for the benefit of others while still using the iPad or iPhone to take the call. Here are the necessary steps:

1. Start the FaceTime call in the usual way.

2. Drag up Control Center from the bottom of the screen, and tap the AirPlay button (if there's no AirPlay button, then ensure the Apple TV is switched on).

3. Select the Apple TV entry in the list, and ensure the switch alongside Mirroring is activated.

---

29. https://www.apple.com/apps/find-my-friends/

Remember during the call that although the audio and video have been transferred to the big screen, the microphone on the iPad or iPhone is still responsible for picking up the audio.

When you've finished the call, again open Control Center, tap the AirPlay button, and tap to switch back to the iPad or iPhone (or select the headphones option if you have headphones attached).

Tip 276

Get Siri to request bank-account details

Some banks offer SMS services whereby you text a particular word outlining what you want (such as BAL or HIST), plus some digits from your account. By return SMS message you'll receive the details.

While there's no built-in integration of Siri with these services, it's easy to set up.

Setup

Here are the steps to set up your iPhone so Siri can make bank requests.

1. Visit your bank website and set up SMS banking service. Once you've done that, make a note of the protocol required to make an SMS request. For example, Bank of America requires you to text 692632 with a four-letter query word, such as BILL or HIST, followed by the last four digits of your account number.[30]

2. Add a new contact on your iPhone (open the Contacts app and click the plus icon—+) and in the First Name field type Bank.

3. In the Add Phone field, type the number for SMS banking. Click Done when you've finished.

Asking Siri

To use your new setup, start Siri and say, "Text bank inquiry," then spell out the four-letter query term, followed by the required digits from your account number (the last four in the case of Bank of America). For example, you might say something like, "Text bank B I L L 4 5 6 7." When the return text is received, you can ask Siri to read it to you by saying, "Read text."

---

30. https://www.bankofamerica.com/online-banking/sms-text-banking.go

Tip 277

Create folders in iCloud storage

Some apps, such as those in iWork, store their documents in iCloud and present a list of them whenever you tap the Documents link. You can arrange these documents into folders, just like on a desktop computer's file system. Tap and hold any document until it begins to wiggle, then drop it on top of another document. As when rearranging home-screen icons, a folder will be created automatically. Tap Done when you've finished.

As with app folders on the home screen, it's not possible to put a folder inside another folder. Folders can contain only documents.

To delete folders, simply empty them of their contents by dragging documents out of them or deleting the documents they contain.

Tip 278

Stop being told about spam messages

iMessage spam is rare, although SMS spam can be a problem if your number happens to end up on a direct-marketing list.

If the spam is sent consistently from a particular number, you can follow tip Tip 224, *Block calls and messages from certain people*, on page 198, to block that number, but SMS spammers are wise to this and often use a variety of different numbers or disguise their number.

While blocking them in this case is impossible, you can at least make sure you don't get notified of their messages by activating a hidden setting that will mean notification of messages will appear only if the sender is in your address book. You'll still receive all messages sent to you, regardless of who they're from. You just won't be notified of them in Notification Center or via onscreen alerts.

To set this up, open the Settings app then tap the Notification Center heading. Tap Messages within the list, then scroll to the bottom and put a check mark alongside Show Alerts from My Contacts. To deactivate the feature in the future, repeat the steps to open the Messages notifications and this time tap Show Alerts from Everyone.

Tip 279

Add a "Phone me," "Message me," or "FaceTime me" link to email signatures

Tip 71, *Create fancy email signatures*, on page 98, explains how to create email signatures, but wouldn't it be useful to add a link that—when tapped on the recipient's iPhone—would let the person instantly call you, instantly start an SMS/iMessage conversation, or instantly initiate a FaceTime call?

To do so, you'll briefly need to use the email program on a desktop computer, as follows:

1. In your desktop email client or on the web page for your webmail service, create a new email and address it to yourself.

2. Create a new link in the body of the email. This is usually done by clicking a button on the toolbar or by tapping Ctrl-K on a Windows PC or Cmd-K on a Mac.

3. To create a "Call me" link, in the URL field type tel://, followed by your number with no spaces or symbols (for example, tel://6365550113). Then click to create the link.

4. For a link to start an iMessage or SMS, type sms:// into the URL field followed by the cell number or email addresses you have registered for your iMessage account (that is, something like sms://keir@example.com. You can discover your iMessage address(es) by opening the Settings app and tapping Messages > Send & Receive.

5. For a FaceTime link, in the URL field type facetime://, followed by the address or cell-phone number you have registered for FaceTime calls (that is, something like facetime://john@example.com). You can discover your FaceTime address by opening the Settings app, tapping FaceTime entry, and looking under the heading that reads You Can Be Reached by FaceTime At.

6. Click to create the link, then click Send on the email to send it to yourself.

7. Copy the link(s) in the email in the usual way—by tapping and selecting Copy—then switch to the Settings app and tap the Mail, Contacts & Calendars link, then the Signature entry in the list, and paste the text into your signature in the usual way—by double-tapping a blank spot and selecting Paste.

iPad and iPhone recipients of your emails containing the signature will be able to tap the link(s) to start a phone, iMessage, or FaceTime conversation with you, although they'll have to confirm they want to do so when a pop-up dialog box appears—a security precaution Apple put in place. Mac users can use the FaceTime link(s) to start a FaceTime conversation.

Note that some email clients automatically add http:// to any link you create, which means this trick won't work. The solution is to switch to another client or temporarily use your email service's webmail interface.

For what it's worth, by using skype:// with the preceding instructions, followed by your Skype username, you can make happen a Skype call whenever the link is tapped or clicked.

Tip 280

View Coordinated Universal Time/Greenwich Mean Time

If your job requires a knowledge of UTC/GMT then all you need do is open the Clock app, select the World Clock icon, and then tap the plus (+) icon. Then type UTC into the search field. You'll find it as an option, despite the fact it's not a place. Selecting it will add it to the list of world clocks.

Tip 281

Instantly close all browser tabs

Sometimes you might find that you have a great many browser tabs open. Closing them all one by one can be difficult, but there's no way to close them all at once. Even if you quit Safari the tabs will still be there. However, there is a solution. (It involves a few seconds of work, but it can be quicker than individually quitting all the tabs.)

The solution is to activate private browsing mode, then answer yes to closing all the current tabs, as in the following figure. To do so on an iPhone, open Bookmarks by clicking the icon at the bottom, then tap Private at the bottom left. Tap Close All in the dialog box, then return to the bookmarks list and tap Private again to deactivate private browsing mode.

On an iPad, open a new tab so your bookmark thumbnails are visible, then tap Private at the bottom left. Tap the Close All button in the dialog box, then tap Private again to deactivate private browsing mode.

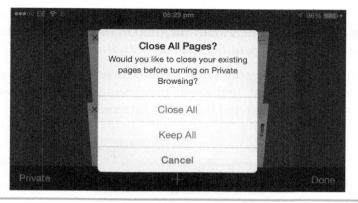

Figure 66—Closing all the browser tabs on an iPhone

Tip 282

Listen to music while playing games

Most games have their own music and sound effects, so any music playing when you start the game will be stopped. If you want to continue listening to your own music, however, the solution is surprisingly simple—swipe up from the bottom to reveal Control Center and then start the music again by tapping the play button (you'll probably need to swipe up twice because when a game is being played, Control Center doesn't appear as easily to avoid accidental activation). Of course, you might first want to go into the game's settings and turn off its own music first.

A minority of games are wise to this trick, unfortunately, but in our tests most worked just fine while music was playing.

Tip 283

Move the cursor using gestures in Pages

Pages features a handful of one-, two-, and three-finger gestures that help you navigate through sentences and paragraphs of text. Each gesture can only be done when the onscreen keyboard is visible, and must be done in the document-editing area. They don't work in other apps.

To move the cursor left or right, swipe horizontally left or right with one finger. To jump to the next word or back to the previous word, swipe left or right horizontally with two fingers. Finally, to jump to the end or beginning of the current line, swipe left or right horizontally with three fingers.

These gestures take some trial and error because it's easy to accidentally scroll the document instead. In my tests they seemed to work best with small swipes. However, once mastered they work extremely well.

Tip 284

Turn voice recordings into ringtones or alert tones

Tip 220, *Create your own ringtones*, on page 195, explains how to create your own ringtones from music files, but what if you want to create a ringtone of your own voice, or perhaps something else you might want to record using your iPhone, such as the sound of a child laughing or the revving engine of a favorite car?

It's very simple to do so, although in addition to your iPhone you'll need a Mac or Windows PC that you've previously synced with via iTunes. Note that it isn't possible to record using the iPad because it doesn't include the Voice Memos app, which is used in these instructions, although any recordings made on an iPhone and converted into ringtone format using the following steps can subsequently be used on an iPad.

1. Open the Voice Memos app, then tap the red record button to make your recording. Click the Done button when finished, and enter a name for your recording.

2. Select the recording, then click the Edit button if you want to trim the recording to remove unnecessary material at the start or end—just click the crop icon (the square with extended lines), then drag to define the area you want to keep, and tap Trim. When finished, tap Done.

3. Select the recording, then tap the share button and choose to create a Mail message. Send the email to yourself.

4. Switch to the desktop computer and open the email message. Extract the file to a folder or the desktop, and rename its extension from .m4a to .m4r.

In other words, if the filename was James laughing.m4a, then you'd rename it to read James laughing.m4r.

5. Open iTunes, then drag and drop the file on top of the program window.

6. In iTunes, select Tones from the drop-down in the top-left corner. Locate the new recording you created and then drag and drop it onto the iPhone or iPad icon that appears in the Devices pop-out (note that the pop-out won't appear until you start to drag the icon!). The file will instantly be copied across to your device.

7. On the iPad or iPhone, open Settings, then tap the Sounds heading. Choose what you'd like to use the sound for (that is, as a ringtone or text tone), then tap that heading and select your sound. It should be at the top of the list.

Tip 285

Monitor currency exchange rates in the Stocks app

The Stocks app on the iPhone is theoretically limited to showing data about stocks and indexes, but it can also show currency exchange rates. Information from the Stocks app is also reflected in Notification Center, providing an easy way to track the current exchange rate when abroad, for example.

To set this up, open the Stocks app with the iPhone held in portrait mode, then tap the menu icon (three lines) at the bottom right. Then tap the plus (+) icon at the top left and, in the Type a Company Name or Stock Symbol field, enter one of the country codes that are listed on the Yahoo! Currency Converter page.[31] For example, for a US dollar–to–British sterling exchange rate, you'd type USDGBP. For Canadian dollars to euros, you'd type CADEUR. Then select the symbol underneath in the search results.

To show nothing but the currency exchange rate in the Stocks app, essentially changing its function, simply delete the existing stocks and indices by tapping the menu button at the bottom right, tapping the red "no entry" signs to the left of the entries you'd like to delete, then tapping the Delete button that appears.

---

31. http://finance.yahoo.com/currency-converter

Tip 286

Search only a single email account

The Mail app's search feature is very powerful but has a limitation: by default it searches all your mailboxes. If you have only one email account set up on your iPad or iPhone then this isn't an issue, but if you access multiple email accounts then you might want Mail to search only your Hotmail account, for example, and not your Yahoo! account.

The solution is simple, although a little convoluted. Start the search in the usual way—by viewing your messages for the account you want to search, then dragging down until the Search field appears. Type the search and then, in the list of results, drag down again. Two hidden headings will appear: All Mailboxes and Current Mailbox. Tap the latter to search just the current mailbox.

Tip 287

Dictate like a pro

Whenever the onscreen keyboard appears on your iPad or iPhone you can tap the small microphone icon to dictate rather than type. Although dictation is mostly intuitive, here are a few tips to let you get the most out of it.

Specifying Capital Letters, Spacing, and Line Breaks

Here's how to take control of capitalization, spacing, and line breaks when dictating:

- Capitalizing a word: Say, "cap" before the word you want to capitalize. For example, to enter the phrase "We should all read the good Book," you would say, "We should all read the good *cap* Book."

- Using title case (capitalizing the first letter of the major words in a sentence): Say, "caps on" before the words you want in title case and then say, "caps off" after. For example, for the phrase "The Town of Bath Is Lovely in Spring," you'd say, "*caps on* the town of bath is lovely in spring *caps off.*"

- All caps: To capitalize an entire word (the equivalent of using the `Caps Lock` key when typing), say, "all caps." For the phrase "I need the report RIGHT NOW," you'd dictate, "I need the report *all caps on* right now *all caps off*." You can put an individual word in all capital letters by just saying "all caps" before it: "I need the report *all caps* now and not later" produces "I need the report NOW and not later."

- All lowercase: To dictate words without any capitalization whatsoever, use "no caps" in the same way as described for "all caps." Dictating "I want to live in *no caps on* new york *no caps off*" produces "I want to live in new york."

- Prevent hyphenation: iOS's dictation feature is clever enough to hyphenate words that need it, but you can stop it from doing so by saying "spacebar": "This is a low *spacebar* budget enterprise" will produce "This is a low budget enterprise."

- Force hyphenation: If you say something that you think should be hyphenated but iOS's dictation doesn't realize it should, you can simply say, "hyphen"—"He was a no *hyphen* good man" will type "He was a no-good man."

- Remove spaces altogether: To create a sentence or series of words without spaces (*compounding* words), use "no space." As with the dictation terms already covered, you can use it singularly to indicate two words should be joined, or you can turn it on and off before and after a series of words: "We are super *no space* bad" will type "We are superbad"; saying "We are *no space on* super bad and groovy *no space off*" will type "We are superbadandgroovy."

- Inserting line breaks: To insert a line break, say, "new line." To insert a paragraph break (that is, an empty line before the following sentence), say, "new para."

Specifying Punctuation, Symbols, and Numerals

In most cases, inserting punctuation is intuitive and obvious. Saying, "full stop" or "period" will insert that symbol, for example. Saying, "copyright sign" will insert a copyright symbol, and saying "at sign" will insert @. (Note that the word "symbol" can't be spoken instead of "sign.") Saying "inverted question mark" will produce the ¿ symbol. See Table 2, *Symbols and how to request them via dictation*, on page 244, for how to ask for lesser-used symbols.

Symbol	What to ask for
&	"Ampersand"
[ ]	"Open bracket" and "close bracket"
{ }	"Open brace" and "close brace"
®	"Registered sign"
§	"Section sign"
^	"Caret"
£	"Pound-sterling sign"
#	"Pound sign" (British users should say, "hash sign")
< >	"Less-than sign" and "Greater-than sign"
|	"Vertical bar"
°	"Degree sign"

Table 2—Symbols and how to request them via dictation

Saying something like, "She was no *quote* good *end quote* at her job," will produce the following:

She was no "good" at her job.

Currency symbols, including the dollar, must be followed by "sign" if not used with numbers: to produce "$31" you can simply say, "thirty-one dollars" but to type "We need more $" you would have to say, "We need more *dollar sign.*"

You can also insert a long dash by saying "em dash." To insert an ellipsis (…), say either "dot dot dot" or "ellipsis."

Should you want to use Roman numerals, just say them as you would normally, preceded by numeral: "The year of my birth was *numeral* MCMLXXII." Similarly, to insert a numeral rather than the word for the number (that is, "5" rather than "five"), say, "numeral" beforehand: "There were *numeral* five of them" will type "There were 5 of them."

Inserting Emoticons

What if you want to indicate your general emotional state via clever use of punctuation? Apple has thought of that. Simply saying, "smiley face," "winky face," and "frowny face" will insert :-), ;-), and :-(, respectively.

Tip 288

Apply a watermark to documents in Pages

Adding a watermark to documents in Pages is easy, although the technique isn't obvious.

1. Create the watermark within the document itself, perhaps in some space at the end of the body of the document. The watermark can be text, a picture, a shape, or a combination of any of these. If it's to apply to the whole page, any text you type will have to be made big—for a US Letter or A4 page, select a font size of at least 72 point.

2. Because the watermark is applied under the text, you'll also need to ensure the text is in a light color to avoid making it hard to read the body of the document (although you can alter the watermark's transparency later). To change the color of text, highlight it and then tap the format inspector (the paintbrush icon). On an iPhone tap the Color heading; on an iPad tap the font name at the top of the pop-out dialog box, then tap Color. Light gray is a good choice.

3. Once you've created the watermark, highlight it, then cut it to the clipboard.

4. Switch to Doc Setup view by tapping the wrench icon, then Document Setup. Double-tap anywhere on the page (except in the header or footer area), and then tap Paste when it appears.

5. The watermark will be inserted as a text box that you can reshape by dragging the handles surrounding it. You can also rotate it using the pinch gesture, just like you might rotate an image in the Photos app. If you need to make an emergency edit of the text, double-tap the text box (see Figure 67, *Adding a watermark in Pages on an iPad*, on page 246).

6. To alter the transparency of the watermark, select the text box then tap the format inspector. In the pop-out window, tap the Style tab, then the Style Options heading beneath. Then select the Effects tab and drag the opacity slider.

7. Once you've finished, tap the Done button to return to editing the main document, where you'll see the watermark in action.

To remove the watermark, repeat the preceding steps to enter Doc Setup view, then tap the text box and select Delete on the menu that appears.

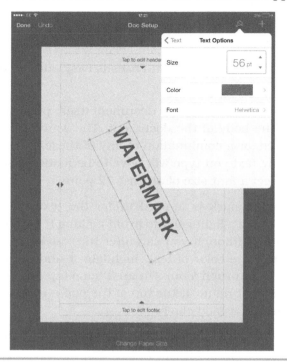

Figure 67—Adding a watermark in Pages on an iPad

Tip 289

Control Keynote remotely from another iPad or iPhone

Keynote Remote is a free app available in the App Store that lets you remotely control a Keynote presentation that's being given on an iPad, an iPhone, or a Mac computer. Keynote Remote needs be installed only on the device you wish to use as the remote control, which can be an iPhone or iPad.

Once you've installed it on the device you wish to use as the remote control, tap the Link to Keynote button, then tap the New Keynote Link heading. This will show a passcode. What you do next depends on whether you want to control an iPad, an iPhone, or a Mac computer running Keynote:

- iPad/iPhone: On the iPad or iPhone that's going to give the presentation, tap the settings button (the wrench icon), then the Presentation Tools option, and finally Remote. Tap the Enable Remotes switch and tap the iPad or iPhone's entry in the list beneath it. Enter the passcode from the remote-control device when prompted, and the two will be linked.

- Mac: Open the Preferences dialog box (`Cmd-,`), then click the Remote icon and put a check mark next to Enable iPhone and iPod Touch Remotes. Then click the Link button alongside the entry for the device running the Remote software, and enter the passcode when prompted.

You need to do this setup only once. Both apps will remember each other for future use.

To play a presentation via remote control, open the presentation on the iPad, iPhone, or Mac you wish to use for presenting, then open the Keynote Remote app. Tap the Play Slideshow button within the Keynote Remote app's window. Swiping left on the remote-control device will advance to the next slide, while swiping right will advance to the previous one. Tapping the Options button will let you quickly jump to the beginning or end of the slideshow or cancel it. Any presenter notes you added will appear on the remote-control device but not on the device being used to give the presentation.

Tip 290

Rotate and crop photos in iPhoto

iPhoto offers a handful of ways of rotating and cropping images, all of which you can use by tapping the crop tool.

For example, iPhoto will attempt to detect if the photo has a horizon in it. If it does, you'll see a small arrow at the right of the horizon, which—when clicked—will automatically rotate the image so that the horizon is straight. This might not always work out for the best, of course, so you can easily tap Undo to return the photo to the way it was.

You can also use the pinch gesture, and rotate the image by rotating one finger around another or tapping and then dragging the dial at the bottom of the screen. (If nothing happens when you rotate the dial, tap the padlock icon at the bottom right to ensure it's unlocked.)

However, none of these techniques are as much fun as rotating the entire iPad or iPhone to straighten an image. To do this, tap the dial underneath the image once, then raise and lower each side of the iPhone or iPad, as if playing a driving game. The image will rotate to match. Once you're happy with the changes, tap the dial again to lock the rotation.

Tip 291

Temporarily stop the screen from rotating when viewing photos

Turn your iPhone or iPad on its side, and its screen will rotate to match, assuming rotation lock isn't activated (see *Control Center*, on page 34). Return it upright, and again the screen will rotate to match. However, sometimes rotating isn't desirable—you might want to see how a photo shot in portrait mode looks when viewed horizontally, for example. To temporarily stop the screen from rotating when using the Photos app, hold a finger or thumb on the screen before rotating the device. Beware that the screen will quickly rotate once you lift your finger.

Tip 292

Upload GarageBand songs to iCloud

If you have one or more iPads or iPhones, you can share your GarageBand creations between them using iCloud. However, unlike with the iWork apps, whatever files you create are not automatically saved to iCloud. Instead you must select to share them with iCloud, although subsequently any edits or additions you make to the song on any device will sync automatically with iCloud.

To share a file with iCloud, return to the My Songs screen, then either tap and hold the song until it starts wobbling, or tap the Select button at the top right of the screen then tap the song. Then tap the cloud icon at the top left and tap Upload Song to iCloud. Finally, tap Done.

To subsequently remove a song from iCloud so it exists only on your iPad or iPhone, again tap and hold the song you want to remove until it starts wobbling, or tap the Select button at the top right of the screen, tap the song you want to remove, then tap the cloud icon and select Remove Song from iCloud.

Note that this will mean the song is removed from any other iPads or iPhones it was synced with.

Tip 293

Quickly search the Web or Wikipedia

If you're on the home screen and swipe down, you'll see the Spotlight search bar. However, the text that appears in the search box (Search iPhone or Search iPad) isn't entirely accurate. If you type something, at the bottom of the list of results will be two entries: Search Web and Search Wikipedia (see the figure here). Tapping either provides a convenient way of searching either online resource without having to fire up Safari (although the search results will still be shown in Safari).

If you use this technique frequently, and otherwise do not use Spotlight Search to locate things like emails or contacts, you can make your device show only the Search Web and Search Wikipedia entries in its results. To do so, open the Settings app, then tap the General heading. Tap the Spotlight Search heading and tap the check mark alongside every one of the entries until they've all been deactivated.

Figure 68—Using Spotlight to search the Web or Wikipedia on an iPhone

Tip 294

Apply multiple effects in iPhoto

When editing images in iPhoto, you might notice a limitation: you can apply only one effect to an image. It's not possible to turn an image black and white, for example, and then apply a vignette. As soon as you switch to the Artistic effects group to apply the vignette, the black-and-white effect will be canceled.

The solution is to apply the black-and-white effect, then use the share button to save a copy of the edited image to the camera roll (see Tip 196, *Export high-res edited images in iPhoto*, on page 181), then open the edited version and apply the vignette effect. You can repeat this as many times as necessary if you wish to apply multiple effects. While it's somewhat time consuming, it has the advantage of saving "versions" of your image, so you can switch back to an earlier version should your newer edits be less successful than you might've wished.

Tip 295

Recover an iPhone that's been disabled

After a certain number of incorrect passcode attempts have been entered at the lock screen, an iPhone will disable itself, initially for a minute, then for five minutes if more incorrect password attempts are tried. (This assumes that you haven't set the device to automatically wipe after 10 password attempts—see *Lock-Screen Passcode*, on page 30.)

Rather than wait for the phone's disable lock to time out, you can simply attach the device via a USB cable to the computer it usually syncs with, then start iTunes on the Mac or Windows PC and click the Sync button (even if you don't have anything new to sync to the device). This will return the device to the usual lock screen, where you can type your passcode like normal.

Tip 296

Switch from one call to another while wearing headphones

Sometimes when on a call you might find somebody else is calling, in which case you'll hear beeping and a message on the screen offering to let you switch to the other call. However, if you're wearing Apple headphones you can switch to the incoming call by clicking the center button on the in-line remote control. To switch back to the original call, again click the center button. Indeed, assuming either caller doesn't hang up, you can switch between the two calls in this way as many times as you like!

Tip 297

View a list of songs you've heard on iTunes Radio

Heard a tune playing on iTunes Radio that you really liked and want to buy? Tap the back button at the top right, then tap the history link. This will show the tracks that've been played recently. Tapping any will play a short preview so you can make sure it's the song you were thinking of. Then you can tap the price at the right to reveal a Buy Song button that will open the iTunes app with an option to purchase the song or the album it's on.

Tip 298

Access iOS files via iTunes

Many apps let you generate files, and while they also usually let you share them via services like iCloud or Dropbox, if you save the files to the iPad or iPhone's storage an interesting question arises: can you transfer the files to your Mac or Windows PC? Additionally, can you import files created on your Mac or Windows PC into the app's file-storage area?

Sometimes iTunes provides the answer, assuming that you've chosen to sync your iPad or iPhone with your Mac or Windows PC. Attach the device by a USB cable, or ensure you're within range if you've activated Wi-Fi syncing, then select the device from the list at the top right of the iTunes window.

Select the Apps tab, then scroll down to the File Sharing heading and select the app in the list (if it's there—some apps don't sync with iTunes in this way). Depending on the app, you might then see the list of files stored on the device. Additionally, you might be able to drag and drop any from your computer, then click Sync for them to be transferred to the app's file-storage area.

This can be an excellent way of importing lots of documents from your Mac or Windows PC into the iWork apps, for example, although iWork operates a little differently—after adding the file(s) within iTunes, as we see in Figure 69, *Adding files to the Pages app via iTunes*, on page 252, open the app concerned then switch to its document listing. Then tap the plus (+) icon and select Copy from iTunes. Tap a file to import it, then repeat the step to import any others. As you do so, they'll disappear from the list within iTunes.

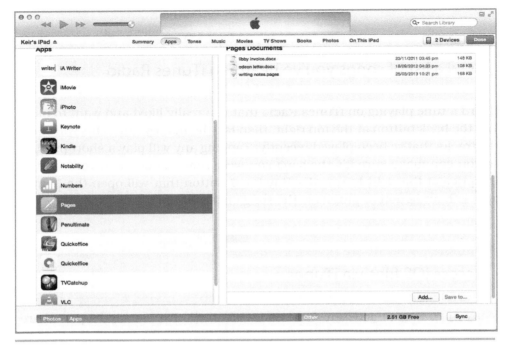

Figure 69—Adding files to the Pages app via iTunes

Tip 299

Boost Safari with bookmarklets

Unlike its desktop cousins, the Safari browser on the iPad and iPhone doesn't support browser extensions (at least not yet!). Although many useful functions are built in, what you see is what you get.

Unless you use bookmarklets, that is. These are small snippets of JavaScript code that perform certain tasks, such as redirecting the current page to an online translation service so you can read it in English, or adding the current site to social-media sites not officially supported by iOS, such as Pinterest or Tumblr.[32,33]

The trick is to add these snippets of bookmarklet code as bookmarks so that they're always accessible on either the bookmarks menu or the Favorites bar.

---

32. https://www.pinterest.com
33. https://www.tumblr.com

Although there are several sites containing lists of bookmarklets, those known to be compatible with Safari on an iPad or iPhone are contained in a list maintained by Amit Agarwal at the Digital Inspiration blog.[34] Follow these steps to add any bookmarklets to Safari:

1. Visit the Digital Inspiration website in Safari, then tap the link for the bookmarklet you wish to add to your bookmarks list. This will open a page with a movie or animation showing the bookmark in action.

2. Tap the share button on the browser toolbar, then select the Bookmark icon. Then tap the Save button.

3. Tap the Bookmark button on the browser toolbar, then tap the Edit button. Locate your new bookmarklet, then tap it.

4. Tap the address component, then remove the first part of the address —everything up to and including the pound (#) sign. To do this you'll need to scroll left in the small text field—perhaps the best way of doing so is to tap and hold until the magnifying glass appears, then drag left beyond the pop-out window for a few seconds.

5. Click Done when you've finished, then tap Done in the parent window.

Your bookmarklet will now be ready for use. Should you wish to remove it in the future you can do so just like with any other bookmark—open the bookmarks list, then swipe left on the bookmarklet entry and tap the red delete button.

Tip 300

Create shared calendars and Reminder lists

You can share both calendars and lists with other iCloud users from the Reminder app. You might share a calendar of household events with your spouse and children, for example, or create a shared shopping list that everybody can add to.

Sharing Calendars

Here are the steps required to create and then share a new calendar on an iPad or iPhone—read step 1 then skip straight to step 4 if you want to share an existing calendar:

---

34. http://www.labnol.org/software/iphone-ipad-bookmarklets/18969/

1. Open the Calendar app and then tap the Calendars link at the bottom (the iPhone will need to be held in portrait mode for this button to be visible).

2. On the menu that appears, tap the Edit button, then tap the Add Calendar entry beneath the list of existing calendars.

3. Create and type a name for the Calendar as prompted and, if you wish, choose a color for it beneath. Tap Done when you've finished.

4. You'll be returned to the pop-out list of calendars. Tap the (i) icon at the right of the entry for the calendar you want to share, then tap the Add Person entry under the Shared With heading.

5. Enter the individual's email address, but ensure you use the one that the individual used to register with iCloud. Alternatively, enter the @icloud.com or @me.com email address, as provided as part of the person's iCloud account. If the individual is one of your contacts, you can also type her name and have it autocompleted based on your contacts list.

6. You can invite several people here, or just one person. Once done, click the Add button.

7. The other person will now be sent an invitation by email. Once she's responded to it and gained access to the shared calendar, you'll be told via a notification message.

To view which calendars are shared in the future, again tap the Calendars button at the bottom of the Calendar app window. Any calendars that are shared will be indicated, along with the names of the people you're sharing them with.

To unshare the calendar, open the Calendars listing as described previously, then tap the (i) symbol alongside the calendar and tap the View & Edit entry in the list. Then tap the Stop Sharing button.

Sharing Reminder lists

Although it's possible to share Reminder lists, it's not possible to do so via the Reminders app in iOS. Instead, you must use the iCloud website. Here are the steps required to create a new Reminders list then share access to it with others—skip straight to step 3 if you wish to share an existing Reminder list:

1. Open the Reminders app on your iPad or iPhone. If using an iPad tap Add List at the bottom left; if using an iPhone tap the card display at the bottom

of the screen so all the reminder lists are visible, then tap the plus (+) button at the top left of the screen.

2. Type a name for the new list and, if you wish, assign it a custom color by making a choice from the list beneath. Tap Done when you've finished.

3. Move to a Mac or Windows PC and then visit the iCloud website.[35] Log in using your iCloud/Apple ID and click the Reminders icon.

4. Ensure your new list is selected at the left, then tap the icon to the right of it in the list—the icon looks like the Wi-Fi-signal symbol within iOS, but actually refers to sharing settings.

5. A pop-out window will appear inviting you to type the Apple ID/iCloud name of the individual you want to share the list with. Alternatively, if the individual is one of your contacts you can type her name.

6. You can add as many people as you wish. Once done, click the Done button. The individual(s) will be sent an email containing the invitation. You'll see a notification message when the invitation has been accepted.

In the future, to view who the reminder list is shared with, again open the list at the iCloud website and click the sharing icon. The individuals will be listed in the pop-out window.

To stop sharing the list, view the list at the iCloud website as described previously, then view the sharing settings and click the person's name in the list before clicking Remove Person.

Tip 301

Create an ultrastrong passcode

As explained in *Security*, on page 30, the default four-digit passcode you use to protect an iPad or iPhone can be expanded into longer passwords or passphrases, involving numbers and letters. And as explained in Tip 20, *Lock your iPad or iPhone with a long PIN*, on page 66, you can also simply create longer PINs. However, there's yet another way to make passcodes harder to guess, and that's to involve non-English characters and/or unusual punctuation. This increases the number of possible combinations for hackers to try, which makes their task significantly more difficult.

---

35. https://icloud.com

Open the Settings app, then tap the General heading and then the Passcode Lock entry within the list. You'll be prompted to enter your existing passcode to proceed.

Deactivate the switch alongside Simple Passcode if you haven't already, or tap Change Passcode if you have. Then type your new passcode but involve foreign letters within it by tapping and holding keys like E, O, or even Z and selecting an entry from the pop-up menu. Additionally, you might choose to include lesser-used punctuation such as worldwide currency symbols, which will appear on a pop-out menu when you tap and hold the dollar-sign key on the numbers/symbols keyboard. See the next figure for an example.

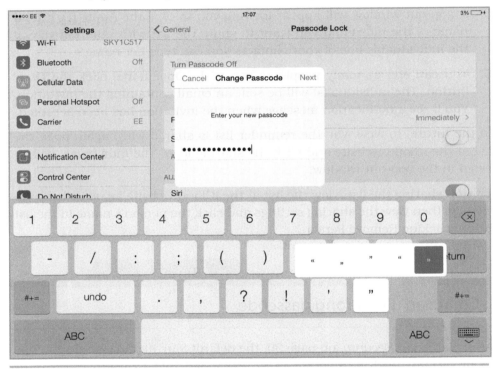

Figure 70—Creating an ultrastrong password on an iPad

Remember that you'll have to remember the passcode, so you shouldn't make it too elaborate. You also should create something that isn't too time consuming to type each time you want to wake your iPad or iPhone from sleep—you need to strike the best balance between security and convenience.

Tip 302

Stop apps from using cellular data

A sad fact of life is that data used as part of a cellular plan is a very different proposition from data used via a Wi-Fi connection at a home or office. Because of this, the iPhone and iPad let you control which apps can use cellular data—you might choose to let a game you play while on a train use cellular data, for example, but deactivate cellular data for a photo-sharing app that is better synced over Wi-Fi.

Deactivating All Cellular Data

One option is to simply stop all apps or iOS services from using data when Wi-Fi isn't available. You can do this by opening the Settings app, tapping the Cellular heading, and deactivating the switch alongside the Cellular Data heading.

Turning Off Cellular Data on an App-by-App Basis

You can designate which individual apps are able to access cellular data. Open the Settings app, tap the Cellular heading, then scroll down to the bottom of the page that follows. Deactivate the switches alongside any app for which you wish to deny cellular data.

Tip 303

Save battery life

Like all battery-operated devices, your iPad or iPhone eventually runs out of juice, and that's usually when you need it most. If you're out and about for a long period without a power source in sight, try the following tricks, which deactivate some notorious electricity-eating features. Some involve deactivating features via Control Center—see *Control Center*, on page 34.

- Turn of LTE/4G: One of the reasons for purchasing an iPhone is its broad 4G support, but turning it off may save some juice. Your phone will fall back to 3G connections, which are often very speedy (depending on the strength of the cellular signal, of course). To deactivate 4G, open Settings, tap the Cellular heading, then deactivate the switch alongside Enable 4G.

Needless to say, if your cellular contract doesn't provide 4G data connections then you should disable this in any case.

- Turn off Wi-Fi and/or Bluetooth: When out of range of Wi-Fi, an iPad or iPhone will constantly search for nearby base stations and may even attempt to connect to some public Wi-Fi services if you've connected in the past. If you're going to use only cellular data outside of your home or office, it makes sense to deactivate Wi-Fi when you're out. You can do so from Control Center. Similarly, enabling Bluetooth when you're not going to use a Bluetooth device will burn through battery power. You can disable Bluetooth via Control Center. Try to avoid using Bluetooth devices, too—rather than using a Bluetooth headset, for example, you might choose to use standard wired headphones.

- Disable Location Services: Some apps need to use Location Services (see *Location Services*, on page 5). The Maps app simply can't work without it, for example. For other apps the need is less pressing, and deactivating Location Services can help save juice when they're running. To try it out, open the Settings app, tap the Privacy heading, and then open the Location Services section. You'll see a list of apps that request to use Location Services. Simply deactivate the switch alongside those that don't absolutely need it.

- Turn off AirDrop: AirDrop uses both Bluetooth and Wi-Fi to determine if devices nearby are attempting to share files with you. Therefore it makes sense to activate AirDrop only when you need it, and to keep it turned off otherwise. You can turn it on or off using Control Center.

- Turn off parallax: iOS 7 offers 3D special effects, such as the way the home-screen icons appear to float above their background (an effect known as *parallax wallpaper*). These effects can burn through battery power, though, so turning them off is wise if you want to avoid recharging frequently (turning them off also helps some people avoid motion sickness). You can do so by opening the Settings app, tapping the General heading, and then tapping Accessibility. Tap the Reduce Motion entry in the list, and deactivate the switch.

- Turn off background app refresh: Some apps will continue to work when you switch away from them. They may continue to periodically grab new data, for example, or use Location Services. For some apps this makes sense—it's useful for mapping apps to keep working if we temporarily switch away. For other apps, however, it's not strictly necessary. To control which apps refresh data when in the background, open the Settings app, tap the General heading, then select Background App Refresh. Deactivate the switches alongside any app you don't want to consume resources in the background, which may be most of them.

- Turn off automatic app updates: Automatic app updates are a neat idea, but they chew up battery life. You can choose to disable them over cellular connections (which can help save battery life while you're away from your home or office) or turn them off completely. To choose which, open the Settings app, then tap the iTunes & App Store heading. Deactivate the switch alongside the Use Cellular Data option at the bottom to turn off updates while away your the home or office, or uncheck Updates to disable automatic app updates entirely, regardless of whether you're using Wi-Fi or cellular data.

- Turn off notification updates: Notification Center provides a weather update, along with stocks information and possibly a mention of how long it would take you to get home/drive to work. All of this requires a quick Internet look-up each time you activate Notification Center (and a GPS look-up for driving details), and this eats battery power. You can deactivate them by opening the Settings app, tapping the Notification Center heading, and deactivating the switches alongside Today View, Stocks, and Next Destination.

- Turn down the screen brightness as much as possible: I've saved the best for last: screen brightness has the biggest effect on battery life. Set the screen brightness as low as possible without affecting the usability of your iPad or iPhone. You can do this via Control Center, but it's also a good idea to deactivate auto-brightness by opening Settings, tapping the Wallpapers & Brightness heading, and deactivating the switch alongside it. This will stop iOS from raising the brightness level to what it believes is the best setting based on ambient lighting conditions.

Tip 304

Add more detail to iMovie's timeline

The timeline at the bottom of the iMovie screen shows a series of thumbnails representing each clip, but this can make it hard to find the exact spot where you want to insert something or make a cut—especially with a large clip.

One solution is to add more detail to the timeline by using the pinch gesture (that is, a thumb and finger placed together then expanded). However, it'll only work if you limit the gesture to the space the timeline takes up, and don't move beyond its boundaries—you can't simply place a finger and thumb on the timeline and expand as if expanding a photo. Instead of using a finger and thumb, you might choose to use one finger from each hand together, and then draw them apart horizontally. This gesture has the same effect when used on the main video-playback preview within the iMovie interface, which provides more space.

Tip 305

Create an apps wish list

Ever seen an app that you find interesting but don't want to purchase right now? The App Store app features a way to create a list of apps you'd like to buy. It's called the Wish List, and you can add any app to it by viewing the app's details, then tapping the share button at the top of the screen and tapping the Add to Wish List button.

You can later view the Wish list by tapping the menu icon at the top right of the screen (the icon looks like three lines). Apps can then be bought in the usual way by tapping to view them, then tapping the price button. To remove an item from the Wish List, just swipe left on the line in the usual way then tap the red delete button.

A limitation of the Wish List is that it can't contain free apps. Only apps sold for a fee can be added. The logic behind this decision is that there's no reason not to immediately "buy" an app that's free. (If you're thinking you don't want to get a free app because your device might not have enough storage space, see Tip 212, *Get free apps even if your device doesn't have the space*, on page 191.)

Tip 306

View forgotten passwords

Have you ever forgotten the password for a site? Most of us have, but if you've ever entered it within Safari on your iPad or iPhone and asked it to remember the password, then there's a chance you'll be able to view it. Follow these steps:

1. Open the Settings app, then tap the Safari heading.

2. Tap the Passwords & AutoFill entry within the list, then tap the Saved Passwords entry.

3. This will show a list of sites for which you've asked Safari to save login details. Look for the site within the list and then tap it.

4. You'll be prompted to enter your passcode, so do so.

5. You should now see the website address, your username, and the password.

Tip 307

Limit Safari to a selection of websites

If you loan your iPad or iPhone to your children, you might not want them browsing just any old websites. iOS includes the ability to limit Safari to just a list of sites that you can specify (usually referred to as a *whitelist*), or to let users access any and all sites with the exception of those that are pornographic or that you ban by adding them to a list (a *blacklist*).

Whitelisting Sites

To allow users to access only certain sites that you specify, follow these steps:

1. Open the Settings app, then tap the General heading.

2. Tap the Restrictions entry in the list. If this is the first time you've used the Restrictions function of iOS, tap the Enable Restrictions heading and then follow the steps when prompted to create a four-digit PIN. This will protect your settings so they can't be changed without authorization, so you should remember whatever PIN you create and make it different from that used to unlock the device.

3. Tap the Websites entry in the list, then put a check mark alongside the Specific Websites Only heading.

4. In the list below that, add the sites you'd like users to be able to access. A default list of suggestions is supplied, but you can delete these in the

usual way, by swiping left on each entry in the list. To add a new site, tap the Add a Website entry beneath.

5. You'll need to type a title for the site, and the site's URL. The title can be anything you want, but you should note that it will appear at the top of the screen in the thumbnail listing of sites that appears whenever a new tab is opened in Safari.

The changes will take effect immediately. Anyone who tries to access sites not on the list will be told the page is restricted. To make an exception, tap the Allow Website button to authorize visiting the site, in which case you'll need to enter the PIN you created earlier. This exception is permanent, which is to say the site URL is added to the list of whitelisted sites within the Settings app (so if you visit a page like http://www.example.com/data/page.html, http://example.com will be added to the whitelist, so any part of http://example.com will now be accessible). Any sites added to the whitelist in this way can be deleted as described previously by opening Settings, switching to the Websites section under the Restricted heading, and swiping to the left before selecting Delete.

Blacklisting Sites

To allow users to access all sites except pornographic sites and those you specify, follow these steps:

1. Open the Settings app, then tap the General heading.

2. Tap the Restrictions entry in the list. If this is the first time you've used the Restrictions function of iOS, tap Enable Restrictions and follow the wizard when prompted to create a four-digit PIN. This will protect your settings so they can't be changed without authorization, so you should remember whatever PIN you create and make it different from that used to unlock the device.

3. Tap the websites entry in the list, then put a check mark alongside the Limit Adult Content heading.

4. Under the Never Allow heading, tap the Add a Website heading, then, when prompted on the next page, enter the URL of the site to which you want to prohibit access.

Repeat the steps as many times as you wish to create a list of sites. To deactivate either whitelist or blacklist mode, open the Settings app, then tap the General heading, then the Restrictions heading in the list. Then tap Disable Restrictions.

Tip 308

Switch Siri's voice to male

Tired of Siri sounding like a woman? Just open Settings, tap the General heading, then tap Siri > Voice Gender > Male. Note that only certain languages, including US English, have both female and male voices.

Tip 309

Quickly view all images received from somebody via iMessage

If someone has sent you a load of images via iMessage, you can quickly view all of them in a list. To do so, open the conversation with the individual in the Messages app, then scroll to the top. If you see a link that reads Load Earlier Messages, tap it. Again scroll to the top, and if the link appears again, tap it again. Repeat until all the messages are loaded, then tap any picture to open it for viewing full-screen. Look to the bottom right of the screen, where you'll see a menu button (its icon is three lines)—the following figure shows an example from an iPhone.

Figure 71—Viewing all messages from a particular sender on an iPhone

Clicking this will then show a list of images, and you can tap any to view it full screen. To return to the list again, just tap the menu icon once more.

You can also swipe left or right to view the images in sequence.

Tip 310

Stop Facebook from posting to the wrong audience

Whenever you opt to share something via Facebook (that is, you tap the share button, then the Facebook option) you'll be prompted to not only type a note to go with the posting, but also to choose what audience you wish to see it. You can choose to share it with just your friends, for example, or to make the posting public.

Should you change this setting, be aware that it's remembered for the next time you post. In other words, if you decide to make one post public, all subsequent postings will also be public unless you specifically choose to change the setting the next time you share something.

Note that sharing via Twitter using iOS doesn't feature the ability to mark postings as private.

Tip 311

Easily email the text of a web page

Although the share button can email the link for the web page you're currently viewing in Safari, it seemingly can't send the text of the web page. But this trick changes that, and it works with most web pages.

Safari features a Reader tool, which removes all unnecessary detail from compatible web pages, showing only the body text. What are compatible web pages? They're usually articles, blog posts, or pages that generally involve a lot of words, and you'll know if the page you're looking at is compatible because the Reader icon will appear at the left of the website address on the URL bar. The icon looks like a paragraph of text.

To send the content of a web page via email, simply tap the Reader icon within Safari to activate reader view, then tap the Sharing button and then the Mail icon. See the following figure for an example. A new message will be created containing the web page's text.

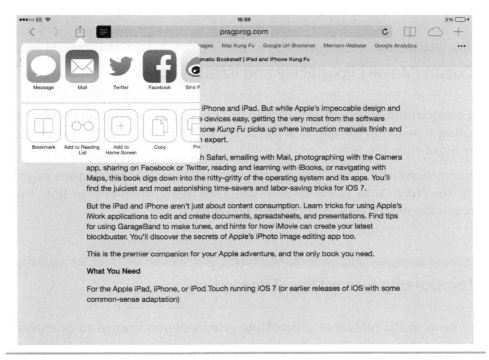

Figure 72—Emailing just the text of a web page using the Reader feature of Safari on an iPad

Tip 312

Tell iOS where you work

A handful of features in iOS 7 depend in iOS knowing the address of your place of work. For example, Siri understands the concept of work, and on an iPhone you can ask it to remind you of something when you get there (see Tip 273, *Be reminded at a place via your iPhone*, on page 232). Additionally, Notification Center on the iPhone can display how long it will take you to get to work in the morning.

To add a work address to iOS, open the Contacts app, then find your own contact card by searching for it. Tap the Edit button, and scroll down to the Add Address button. This will then show fields for your work address, which you should fill in.

Tip 313

Cut an iMovie clip quickly and easily

Got a clip within an iMovie project and want to split it into two bits? One way of doing so is to tap the clip to select it, tap the (i) button, tap the menu icon (two dots), then tap Split.

A much easier and more accurate way is to position the playhead where you want the cut to take place, then swipe down along the playhead line, just beneath the clip. Presto—the clip will be sliced in two.

Tip 314

Temporarily turn off FaceTime video

Ever been in the middle of a FaceTime video call and wanted to deactivate the video temporarily? There's a really simple solution—just click the Home button. This will return you to your home-screen icons, as usual, and the call will continue in the background. The other person will still be able to hear you (and vice versa) but all the other person will see onscreen is the word "Paused." To restore video to the call, tap the green flashing text at the top of the screen that reads "Touch to Resume FaceTime," or tap the FaceTime icon in the usual way.

Tip 315

View non-local weather on an iPad

Although the iPhone comes with a neat little Weather app, the folks at Apple decided the iPad didn't need such a thing. While it's possible to get a weather overview for the current location by bringing down Notification Center and switching to the Today tab, it's apparently impossible to get the weather for another town or city.

However, weather details for other places are available on the iPad—without the need to install a third-party app! Just open the Clock app, then tap the World Clock icon at the bottom. Places for which you've added a clock will appear on the small map at the bottom of the screen, and a weather icon will appear alongside them indicating current conditions. The temperature will also be shown.

Just tap the Add button to add a new clock for any place you want to know about (don't forget that you can swipe the clock display left to reveal more clocks). The downside is that you can only view the weather in this way for cities that the Clock app has in its database, and that's limited to major cities worldwide.

Tip 316

Create a security camera

AirPlay is Apple's technology that lets you broadcast movie and audio playback to a TV with an Apple TV box attached to it, or to a Mac or Windows PC running AirPlay receiver software like AirServer.[36] However, you can also opt to mirror whatever appears in the iPad or iPhone display to a receiving device or software, and if you then switch to the Camera app, you'll see onscreen whatever the camera points at. This allows you to create a makeshift security-camera setup—just leave the iPad or iPhone camera pointed at a door, for example, and then watch what it sees via AirPlay on a television or Mac/Windows PC.

Tip 317

Record more-fluid HD video

iMovie offers the ability to record video clips directly within the application—just tap the camera icon at the bottom right while editing a project. On older models of iPhones and all iPads, this doesn't offer any advantages over using the built-in Camera app, but on the iPhone 5 and later recording directly in iMovie has a unique feature: you can switch the recording definition to 720p HD rather than 1080p HD by tapping the button at the bottom right.

At first glance this might seem undesirable—who would want to record at less than maximal resolution? However, recording video at 720p using iMovie boosts the frame rate to 60 frames per second (FPS), rather than 30, which is the default with 1080p.

36. http://www.airserver.com

Higher frame rate (HFR) recordings are much more fluid and lifelike. HFR was recently used for the first time in mainstream cinema for *The Hobbit* and *Avatar 2*. Additionally, clips recorded in HFR can be converted to slow motion without significant blurring.

The best proof is to experiment—try recording a scene at 1080p and 30 FPS, then recording the same scene at 720p and 60 FPS. Watch them consecutively to see the difference.

Tip 318

FaceTime from your iPad to your iPhone (or vice versa)

It might seem as if it's impossible to FaceTime-call your iPhone from your iPad, or vice versa, because they share the same Apple ID login. It would be like phoning your own number! However, by following the steps in Tip 3, *Let people FaceTime-call a specific iPad, iPhone, or Mac*, on page 54, and registering different email addresses or cell-phone numbers for each device, it is possible to place video or audio-only FaceTime calls between the two devices—useful if you loan somebody your iPad, for example, and want to call that person from your iPhone.

After setting up each device with a different FaceTime contact email or cell-phone number, you'll need to create a contact card within Contacts for the other device, specifying the email address or cell-phone number as the only field within the card. Then use this new contact card within FaceTime to call the desired device.

Index

S

Learn iOS and Mac OS X

Get a solid grounding on development for iOS, or discover the the coolest, most helpful tricks and tips in Mac OS X.

iOS SDK Development

Since the iPhone's launch in 2008, the iOS platform has added two new device families, thousands of new APIs, new tools and programming practices, and hundreds of thousands of new apps. Yours can be one of them. This book guides you through the state of the art of iOS development, including the radically overhauled Xcode 4 toolchain, the iOS 6 SDK, and the new iPhone 5. You'll accelerate your development with new tools like Storyboards, practice on new APIs like the Twitter framework, and learn the latest features of the Objective-C programming language.

Chris Adamson and Bill Dudney
(296 pages) ISBN: 9781934356944. $35
http://pragprog.com/book/adios

Mac Kung Fu (2nd edition)

Squeeze every drop of juice from OS X with over 400 quick and easy tips, tricks, hints and hacks in *Mac Kung Fu: Second Edition*. Exploit secret settings and hidden apps, push built-in tools to the limit, radically personalize your Mac experience, and make "it just works" even better. In addition to core OS X technologies, this significantly revised and expanded update to the best-selling first edition dissects new OS X Mountain Lion tools such as iCloud, Notifications, Reminders, and Calendar.

Keir Thomas
(424 pages) ISBN: 9781937785079. $39
http://pragprog.com/book/ktmack2

More for iOS

Learn how to do full-stack testing of your iOS apps and get up to speed with the latest version of Core Data.

Test iOS Apps with UI Automation

If you're an iOS developer or QA professional tapping through an app to reproduce bugs or performance issues you thought were solved two releases ago, then this is your book. Learn how to script the user interface, assert correct behavior, stub external dependencies, reproduce performance problems, organize test code for the long haul, and automate the whole process so the machine does the work. You'll walk through a comprehensive strategy with techniques using Apple's tools that you can apply to your own apps.

Jonathan Penn
(226 pages) ISBN: 9781937785529. $36
http://pragprog.com/book/jptios

Core Data (2nd edition)

Core Data is Apple's recommended way to persist data: it's easy to use, built-in, and integrated with iCloud. It's intricate, powerful, and necessary—and this book is your guide to harnessing its power.

Learn fundamental Core Data principles such as thread and memory management, discover how to use Core Data in your iPhone, iPad, and OS X projects by using NSPredicate to filter data, and see how to add iCloud to your applications.

Marcus S. Zarra
(256 pages) ISBN: 9781937785086. $33
http://pragprog.com/book/mzcd2

The Joy of Math and Healthy Programming

Rediscover the joy and fascinating weirdness of pure mathematics, and learn how to take a healthier approach to programming.

Good Math

Mathematics is beautiful—and it can be fun and exciting as well as practical. *Good Math* is your guide to some of the most intriguing topics from two thousand years of mathematics: from Egyptian fractions to Turing machines; from the real meaning of numbers to proof trees, group symmetry, and mechanical computation. If you've ever wondered what lay beyond the proofs you struggled to complete in high school geometry, or what limits the capabilities of the computer on your desk, this is the book for you.

Mark C. Chu-Carroll
(282 pages) ISBN: 9781937785338. $34
http://pragprog.com/book/mcmath

The Healthy Programmer

To keep doing what you love, you need to maintain your own systems, not just the ones you write code for. Regular exercise and proper nutrition help you learn, remember, concentrate, and be creative—skills critical to doing your job well. Learn how to change your work habits, master exercises that make working at a computer more comfortable, and develop a plan to keep fit, healthy, and sharp for years to come.

This book is intended only as an informative guide for those wishing to know more about health issues. In no way is this book intended to replace, countermand, or conflict with the advice given to you by your own healthcare provider including Physician, Nurse Practitioner, Physician Assistant, Registered Dietician, and other licensed professionals.

Joe Kutner
(254 pages) ISBN: 9781937785314. $36
http://pragprog.com/book/jkthp

Sound and Games

Add live sound to your apps, and explore a faster way of building mobile games for Android and iOS.

Programming Sound with Pure Data

Sound gives your native, web, or mobile apps that extra dimension, and it's essential for games. Rather than using canned samples from a sample library, learn how to build sounds from the ground up and produce them for web projects using the Pure Data programming language. Even better, you'll be able to integrate dynamic sound environments into your native apps or games—sound that reacts to the app, instead of sounding the same every time. Start your journey as a sound designer, and get the power to craft the sound you put into your digital experiences.

Tony Hillerson
(196 pages) ISBN: 9781937785666. $36
http://pragprog.com/book/thsound

Create Mobile Games with Corona

Develop cross-platform mobile games with Corona using the Lua programming language! Corona is experiencing explosive growth among mobile game developers, and this book gets you up to speed on how to use this versatile platform. You'll use the Corona SDK to simplify game programming and take a fun, no-nonsense approach to write and add must-have gameplay features. You'll find out how to create all the gaming necessities: menus, sprites, movement, perspective and sound effects, levels, loading and saving, and game physics. Along the way, you'll learn about Corona's API functions and build three common kinds of mobile games from scratch that can run on the iPhone, iPad, Kindle Fire, Nook Color, and all other Android smartphones and tablets.

Printed in full color.

Silvia Domenech
(220 pages) ISBN: 9781937785574. $36
http://pragprog.com/book/sdcorona

The Pragmatic Bookshelf

The Pragmatic Bookshelf features books written by developers for developers. The titles continue the well-known Pragmatic Programmer style and continue to garner awards and rave reviews. As development gets more and more difficult, the Pragmatic Programmers will be there with more titles and products to help you stay on top of your game.

Visit Us Online

This Book's Home Page
http://pragprog.com/book/ktios
Source code from this book, errata, and other resources. Come give us feedback, too!

Register for Updates
http://pragprog.com/updates
Be notified when updates and new books become available.

Join the Community
http://pragprog.com/community
Read our weblogs, join our online discussions, participate in our mailing list, interact with our wiki, and benefit from the experience of other Pragmatic Programmers.

New and Noteworthy
http://pragprog.com/news
Check out the latest pragmatic developments, new titles and other offerings.

Save on the eBook

Save on the eBook versions of this title. Owning the paper version of this book entitles you to purchase the electronic versions at a terrific discount.

PDFs are great for carrying around on your laptop—they are hyperlinked, have color, and are fully searchable. Most titles are also available for the iPhone and iPod touch, Amazon Kindle, and other popular e-book readers.

Buy now at *http://pragprog.com/coupon*

Contact Us

Online Orders:	*http://pragprog.com/catalog*
Customer Service:	*support@pragprog.com*
International Rights:	*translations@pragprog.com*
Academic Use:	*academic@pragprog.com*
Write for Us:	*http://pragprog.com/write-for-us*
Or Call:	+1 800-699-7764